Re-imagining Democracy

This interdisciplinary book draws on leading scholarship on one of the most influential and consequential social movements of the past decades: Spain's 15-M movement. The volume explores the legacy, impact and outcomes of the movement, and the lessons it offers for understanding mobilization in times of crisis

The book opens with a theoretical reconsideration of the positive ways social movements can impact democracy, moving the field forward significantly. It also offers rich case studies to explore a range of areas of interest to social movement scholars. Chapters explore the biographical consequences of participation in social movements; how memories of the movement inspired new mobilizations; the reciprocal influence between the 15-M movement and feminist economics; how urban democracy was transformed by municipalism arising from the movement; how the movement generated a "Caring democracy" in the face of the Covid pandemic; and how it gave rise to a new radical democratic media ecosystem. The book explores the movement's political economy as well as reflects on one of its unintended consequences: the rise of the penalization of counter-hegemonic protest in contemporary Spain. Although focused on a single emblematic movement, it offers significant insights and lessons for scholarship on contemporary politics and movements.

Re-imagining Democracy provides a valuable resource for scholars and students interested in the challenges faced by contemporary democracies, the dynamics of social movements in times of crisis and the profound impact of social movements on contemporary democracy. The chapters in this book were originally published as a peer-reviewed special issue of *Social Movement Studies*.

Cristina Flesher Fominaya is Editor-in-Chief of *Social Movement Studies*, a Founding Editor of *Interface* Journal and author of *Social Movements in a Globalized World* (2020) and *Democracy Reloaded* (2020). She is Professor of Global Studies at Aarhus University, Denmark. She publishes widely on European and global social movements, hybrid parties, digital politics and media, collective identity, democracy, autonomy and political participation.

Ramón A. Feenstra is Associate Professor at the Universitat Jaume I of Castellón, Spain. He has published the books *Kidnapped Democracy* (2019) and *Refiguring Democracy. The Spanish Political Laboratory* (co-authored with Simon Tormey, Andreu Casero and John Keane, Routledge, 2017). He is a former editor of *Recerca. Revista de Pensament I Anàlisi*.

Re-imagining Democracy

Legacy, Impact and Lessons of Spain's 15-M Movement

**Edited by
Cristina Flesher Fominaya
and Ramón A. Feenstra**

LONDON AND NEW YORK

First published 2024
by Routledge
4 Park Square, Milton Park, Abingdon, Oxon OX14 4RN

and by Routledge
605 Third Avenue, New York, NY 10158

Routledge is an imprint of the Taylor & Francis Group, an informa business

Introduction © 2024 Cristina Flesher Fominaya
Chapters 1–9 © 2024 Taylor & Francis

All rights reserved. No part of this book may be reprinted or reproduced or utilised in any form or by any electronic, mechanical, or other means, now known or hereafter invented, including photocopying and recording, or in any information storage or retrieval system, without permission in writing from the publishers.

Trademark notice: Product or corporate names may be trademarks or registered trademarks, and are used only for identification and explanation without intent to infringe.

British Library Cataloguing in Publication Data
A catalogue record for this book is available from the British Library

ISBN13: 978-1-032-59011-0 (hbk)
ISBN13: 978-1-032-59012-7 (pbk)
ISBN13: 978-1-003-45255-3 (ebk)

DOI: 10.4324/9781003452553

Typeset in Minion Pro
by Newgen Publishing UK

Publisher's Note
The publisher accepts responsibility for any inconsistencies that may have arisen during the conversion of this book from journal articles to book chapters, namely the inclusion of journal terminology.

Disclaimer
Every effort has been made to contact copyright holders for their permission to reprint material in this book. The publishers would be grateful to hear from any copyright holder who is not here acknowledged and will undertake to rectify any errors or omissions in future editions of this book.

Contents

Citation Information vii
Notes on Contributors ix

Introduction—re-imagining democracy: legacy, impact and lessons of Spain's 15-M movement 1
Cristina Flesher Fominaya

1 Reconsidering social movement impact on democracy: the case of Spain's 15-M movement 6
Cristina Flesher Fominaya and Ramón A. Feenstra

2 What has become of the Indignados? The biographical consequences of participation in the 15M movement in Madrid (2011–19) 37
Héloïse Nez

3 15-M movement and feminist economics: an insight into the dialogues between social movements and academia in Spain 57
Astrid Agenjo-Calderón, Lucía Del Moral-Espín and Raquel Clemente-Pereiro

4 Transforming urban democracy through social movements: the experience of Ahora Madrid 76
Fabiola Mota Consejero and Michael Janoschka

5 Caring democracy now: neighborhood support networks in the wake of the 15-M 94
Carlos Diz, Brais Estévez and Raquel Martínez-Buján

6 The rise of a new media ecosystem: exploring 15M's educommunicative legacy for radical democracy 114
Ángel Barbas and Emiliano Treré

7 The mobilising memory of the 15-M movement: recollections and sediments in Spanish protest culture 135
Manuel Jiménez-Sánchez and Patricia García-Espín

8   15-M Mobilizations and the penalization of counter-hegemonic protest in contemporary Spain   154
Kerman Calvo and Aitor Romeo Echeverría

9   The political economy of the Spanish *Indignados*: political opportunities, social conflicts, and democratizing impacts   171
Eduardo Romanos, Jorge Sola and César Rendueles

Index   191

Citation Information

The following chapters were originally published in the journal *Social Movement Studies*, volume 22, issue 3 (2023). When citing this material, please use the original page numbering for each article, as follows:

Chapter 1
Reconsidering social movement impact on democracy: the case of Spain's 15-M movement
Cristina Flesher Fominaya and Ramón A. Feenstra
Social Movement Studies, volume 22, issue 3 (2023), pp. 273–303

Chapter 2
What has become of the Indignados? The biographical consequences of participation in the 15M movement in Madrid (2011–19)
Héloïse Nez
Social Movement Studies, volume 22, issue 3 (2023), pp. 304–323

Chapter 3
15-M movement and feminist economics: an insight into the dialogues between social movements and academia in Spain
Astrid Agenjo-Calderón, Lucía Del Moral-Espín and Raquel Clemente-Pereiro
Social Movement Studies, volume 22, issue 3 (2023), pp. 324–342

Chapter 4
Transforming urban democracy through social movements: the experience of Ahora Madrid
Fabiola Mota Consejero and Michael Janoschka
Social Movement Studies, volume 22, issue 3 (2023), pp. 343–360

Chapter 5
Caring Democracy Now: Neighborhood Support Networks in the Wake of the 15-M
Carlos Diz, Brais Estévez and Raquel Martínez-Buján
Social Movement Studies, volume 22, issue 3 (2023), pp. 361–380

Chapter 6
The rise of a new media ecosystem: exploring 15M's educommunicative legacy for radical democracy
Ángel Barbas and Emiliano Treré
Social Movement Studies, volume 22, issue 3 (2023), pp. 381–401

Chapter 7
The mobilising memory of the 15-M movement: recollections and sediments in Spanish protest culture
Manuel Jiménez-Sánchez and Patricia García-Espín
Social Movement Studies, volume 22, issue 3 (2023), pp. 402–420

Chapter 8
15-M Mobilizations and the penalization of counter-hegemonic protest in contemporary Spain
Kerman Calvo and Aitor Romeo Echeverría
Social Movement Studies, volume 22, issue 3 (2023), pp. 421–437

Chapter 9
The political economy of the Spanish Indignados: *political opportunities, social conflicts, and democratizing impacts*
Eduardo Romanos, Jorge Sola and César Rendueles
Social Movement Studies, volume 22, issue 3 (2023), pp. 438–457

For any permission-related enquiries please visit:
www.tandfonline.com/page/help/permissions

Notes on Contributors

Astrid Agenjo-Calderón is Lecturer at the Department of Economics, Quantitative Methods and Economic History, Pablo de Olavide University, Seville (Spain). Agenjo-Calderón research focuses on feminist political economy.

Ángel Barbas is Lecturer at the Dpto. de Teoría de la Educación y Pedagogía Social of the Universidad Nacional de Educación a Distancia (UNED) of Madrid, Spain. His research interests include educational dimension of social movements, activist media practices and media as socioeducational agents.

Kerman Calvo is Associate Professor in Sociology at the Department of Sociology and Communication, Universidad de Salamanca, Spain. His areas of interest include social movements and LGTBI studies.

Raquel Clemente-Pereiro is Consultant in Germinando Cooperative, an entity that is part of the Social and Solidarity Economy and that develops its activity in the fields of agroecology, environmental education and entrepreneurship of women in rural areas from an ecofeminist perspective.

Carlos Diz is a social anthropologist and Lecturer at the Department of Sociology and Communication Sciences at the University of A Coruña (Spain). His most recent work focuses on the intersectional analysis of collective action, precarity, mobilities and migration studies.

Aitor Romeo Echeverría is a PhD candidate at the Department of Sociology and Communication, Universidad de Salamanca, Spain.

Brais Estévez is an urban geographer who currently works as an independent researcher. He has done research in Barcelona, where he studied on urban controversies and the politics of public spaces in the context of a strong crisis of representation.

Ramón A. Feenstra is Associate Professor at the Universitat Jaume I of Castellón, Spain. He has published the books *Kidnapped Democracy* (2019) and *Refiguring Democracy. The Spanish Political Laboratory* (co-authored with Simon Tormey, Andreu Casero and John Keane, Routledge, 2017). He is a former editor of *Recerca. Revista de Pensament I Anàlisi*.

Cristina Flesher Fominaya is Editor-in-Chief of *Social Movement Studies*, a Founding Editor of *Interface* Journal and author of *Social Movements in a Globalized World* (2020) and *Democracy Reloaded* (2020). She is Professor of Global Studies at Aarhus University, Denmark. She publishes widely on European and global social movements, hybrid parties, digital politics and media, collective identity, democracy, autonomy and political participation.

Patricia García-Espín is Lecturer in the University of Granada. Her research focuses on political participation and the effects, problems and the public opinion about participatory democracy and active political engagement.

Michael Janoschka has been teaching and researching at the Institute of Geography, Universität Leipzig (Germany) since autumn 2019. His research focuses on: Processes of gentrification, displacement and dispossession in the neoliberal city; Mechanisms and effects of the financialization of housing markets; Urban conflicts, collective action and the establishment of new urban governance approaches.

Manuel Jiménez-Sánchez is Associate Professor in the Department of Sociology at Universidad Pablo de Olavide de Sevilla, Spain. His research interests focus on political participation, social movements and environmental politics.

Raquel Martínez-Buján is Senior Lecturer at the Department of Sociology and Communication Sciences at the University of A Coruña (Spain). Her research has been oriented to the study of international migration, sociology of care, sociology of family and social policies.

Lucía del Moral-Espín is Lecturer at the University of Cadiz (Department of General Economics, Area of Sociology) where she teaches Social Policy and Research Methods at the Faculty of Industrial Relations. Her research is characterized by interdisciplinarity and is focused on Feminist Studies, Well-being, Childhood and the Commons.

Fabiola Mota Consejero is Associate Professor of Political Science at the Universidad Autónoma de Madrid (Spain). Her research interests include social capital, political participation and civil society, territorial politics and devolution.

Héloïse Nez is Senior Lecturer in Sociology at the Université de Tours (France) and a researcher at the UMR Citeres (cities, territories, environment and societies). Her research focuses on citizen knowledge, participatory democracy and social movements in France and Spain.

César Rendueles is Tenured Scientist at the Spanish National Research Council (CSIC). His research interests include Political Sociology, Spanish politics and Podemos.

Eduardo Romanos is Associate Professor in the Department of Applied Sociology at the Universidad Complutense de Madrid, Spain. His main research interests are in the areas of political sociology and historical sociology, with a particular focus on social movements and protest.

Jorge Sola is Assistant Professor in the Department of Sociology: Methods and Theory at the Universidad Complutense de Madrid and researcher at TRANSOC Institute. His areas of interest include economic sociology, political sociology and social theory. His research has focused in the precarization of labour markets and the class dimension of political change.

Emiliano Treré is Reader in Data Agency and Media Ecologies in the School of Journalism, Media and Culture (JOMEC) at Cardiff University, UK. His research interests include digital activism, algorithmic agency and disconnection studies.

Introduction—re-imagining democracy: legacy, impact and lessons of Spain's 15-M movement

Cristina Flesher Fominaya

Pro-democracy movements emerging after the global crash of 2008 have transformed contemporary democracies, and contemporary scholarship on democracy, in significant ways. This book, which is a republication of a peer-reviewed special issue in *Social Movement Studies Journal*, offers a deep reflection on some of these transformations through the perspective of arguably the most influential of these movements, Spain's 15-M movement, known internationally as the "Indignados" or indignant or outraged movement. The articles presented here build on a previous attempt to capture the roots, dynamics and impact of contemporary European social movements in times of crisis (Flesher Fominaya and Feenstra 2020). Although focused on a single emblematic case study, the analysis here offers much broader insights for our understanding of how social movements can impact democracy. Reflecting on these impacts over a decade later allows us to see how some of the immediate effects of the movement have played out over time, what its legacy has been and what, if any, lessons can be learned from it.

Tracing and measuring social movement outcomes is a notoriously challenging area of research (Giugni 1998), but one that can offer fruitful insights with which to reflect on contemporary democratic challenges. In the first contribution presented here, *Reconsidering social movement impact on democracy: the case of Spain's 15-M movement*, Cristina Flesher Fominaya and Ramón Feenstra offer an in-depth and sustained consideration of how social movements can impact democracy through the case of 15-M. Two common approaches in the literature focus on either how movements innovate in governing institutions (primarily through a process of institutionalization), or on norm diffusion in society (e.g. changing the ideas and expectations about democracy). Both of these outcomes were clearly evident in 15-M's aftermath. 15-M transformed public opinion on democracy and raised public expectations for transparency and participation (which in turn transformed the ways established political parties presented and organized their relations with citizens). The movement also led to the emergence of new movement-parties and municipalist movements, each of which attempted democratic innovations from within the institutional sphere. However, as a laboratory of democratic experimentation, in addition to leading to many conscious initiatives for democratic innovation, 15-M also inadvertently led to many unintended and unforeseeable outcomes. What we argue in this article is that to fully understand social movement impact on democracy, we need to look carefully at institutionalization and norm diffusion, but also *beyond* them to capture a wider range of impacts. We also need to consider the important role of imaginaries and not just practices in these transformative processes.

One of the often-overlooked impacts of social movements is that they affect themselves and other movements through building social capital and networks, thereby strengthening these networks and increasing citizen participation in democracy through protest, mobilization and a range of other forms of democratic engagement. 15-M transformed Spain's electoral landscape, but also the younger generation's understanding of Spain's recent history and transition to democracy (Revilla-Blanco and Molina-Sánchez 2021). 15-M also transformed Spain's political culture within and beyond social movements by spreading new feminist and technopolitical imaginaries about reclaiming democracy and its institutions for the people, and prioritizing citizen and environmental care over a neoliberal capitalist agenda. The *acampadas* (camps in public squares) and subsequent mobilization enabled hybridity and synergy across previously more separate logics and arenas of collective action. This fuelled a transformation in which bridges between more vertical and horizontal logics blended with synergies between *inter alia* technopolitics, hacker ethics, feminism and critical political economy, forming a potent critique of austerity politics and above all the logics and imaginaries that animate these policies. All of this underlay the outpouring of democratic experimentation that was 15-M, which continued to develop over time (Flesher Fominaya 2020).

One key social movement impact on democracy comes from the influence of the movement on future generations of activists, future mobilizations and the future of 15-M participants. In her contribution, *What has become of the Indignados? The biographical consequences of participation in the 15M movement in Madrid (2011–19)*, Héloïse Nez traces the biographical legacy of 15-M, showing how the movement had profound impacts on the political and life trajectories of activists in the movement, even on those who had a shorter or less intense implication in the movement.

More surprising still, the impact and legacy of social movements on future generations or future mobilizations of activists doesn't only work directly through participants in the movement but also *indirectly*. In their article, *The mobilising memory of the 15-M movement: recollections and sediments in Spanish protest culture*, Manuel Jiménez Sánchez and Patricia García Espín show how 15-M managed to mobilize and profoundly influence activists who had never directly participated in the movement. They offer the concept of "mobilizing memory" to show that participants in later mobilization who had not participated in 15-M nevertheless traced subjective changes in their understanding of protest to the movement. Their interviews revealed four main legacies and impacts for these activists, who changed their understanding of themselves and protest as a result of exposure to the movement: The first was that 15-M showed them that protest could be effective, and it legitimized protest as a positive (rather than a negative or sanctioned) social activity. The second was the learning of protest repertoires such as sit in and campouts in public spaces. The third impact was their increased awareness of key social issues such as the housing crisis in the Spanish context. Finally, they became self-reflexive about themselves as new political subjects committed to active citizenship.

Movement-produced knowledge has long been recognized as a core contribution of social movements to democracy and society (see e.g. Cox and Flesher Fominaya 2009, Eyerman and Jamison 1991), but the ways movement imaginaries and practices are transferred into new arenas is still understudied. In their contribution, *The rise of a new media ecosystem: exploring 15M's educommunicative legacy for radical democracy*, Emiliano Treré and Ángel Barbas show how 15-M contributed to the rise of a new media eco-system of independent media (see also Flesher Fominaya and Gillan 2017) with a clear educommunicative orientation rooted in 15-M. The new media ecosystem is also characterized by other elements derived from 15-M: synergies and mutual support and a rich community of subscribers and users. The recognition of the value of information for a radical democratic regeneration stimulated the revitalization of civic journalism, a potent legacy of the movement that continues to influence the political landscape.

In their contribution, *15-M movement and feminist economics: an insight into the dialogues between social movements and academia in Spain*, Astrid Agenjo-Calderón, Lucia del Moral-Espín and Raquel Clemente-Pereiro look at another understudied area of research which is the interplay between movements and academia in the dialogic production of knowledge and critique. For the authors, *feminist economics* refers to both a heterodox body of economic thought and also to a political roadmap proposal for action. Their analysis not only documents the dialogic interplay between the arenas of activism and academia but also shows how feminist committees within 15-M had to engage in active pedagogy, and serve as counter hegemonic groups within 15-M, transforming movement culture actively from within. This perspective disrupts comfortable narratives about seamless emergences and diffusions of movement culture and norms, and points to the processes of confrontation, dialogue and reciprocal exchange within heterogeneous movements. The analysis also shows how movements can have an activating effect on academia, stimulating practitioners to adopt more critical and political perspectives.

Fabiola Mota Consejero and Michael Janoschka's contribution, *Transforming urban democracy through social movements: the experience of Ahora Madrid*, continues with the examination of internal divergences and pluralism within 15-M by tracing the impact of 15-M's democratizing practices and expectations for democratic change on concrete policy initiatives within Madrid's Ahora Madrid, the municipalist platform that won the mayorship of Madrid in 2015. They demonstrate the close flow of exchange between movement and Ahora Madrid policy makers but also argue that mutually exclusive and contradictory positions and expectation hampered the attempt by Ahora Madrid to institutionalize itself and to develop a coherent participatory innovation from the institutions. As such the analysis offers valuable lessons and reflections for similar or new "transferable innovations" (McAdam and Tarrow 2010) stemming from heterogeneous pro-democracy movements, and points to the need for understanding these internal movement differences when evaluating movements' political and institutional consequences.

Another crucial way movements impact democracy is on their ability to transfer their knowledge, networks, resources, ethos and imaginaries to new challenges and threats (Flesher Fominaya 2022). In their contribution, *Caring democracy now: neighborhood support networks in the wake of the 15-M*, Carlos Diz, Brais Estévez and Raquel Martínez-Buján adopt an ethics of care standpoint to analyze the lasting power of a "caring democracy", one which is committed to democratic renewal that focuses on sustaining life. They show how the 15-M democratic legacy was renewed in the face of the Covid-19 pandemic, specifically through the creation of network groups of caring neighbors who adopted and adapted 15-M ethos and practices to care for the most vulnerable in Mutual Aid Groups (GAMs). The GAMs drew on the feminist ethics of care that was promulgated in 15-M (and flourished thereafter) to center vulnerability and interdependence in the context of the coronavirus crisis. They also focused on socio-material practices (mask making, resource mapping, counselling, etc.) as forms of direct provision of care. These forms of direct collective self-empowerment and provision are connected to a radical vision of democracy that places caring at the center, and which are a legacy of the ecosystem of democratic innovation that 15-M generated.

Finally, movements can fall short in their short and medium-term impacts, despite their best efforts, or can lead to unwelcome consequences through no fault of their own. An example of the former is the movement's inability to profoundly challenge the neoliberal political economic agenda, as Eduardo Romanos, Javier Sola and César Rendueles argue in their contribution, *The political economy of the Spanish Indignados: political opportunities, social conflicts, and democratizing impacts*. They argue that an inability to closely work with labor movements and to overcome neoliberal institutional inertia led to a limited impact in the arena of political economic democratization, despite strong challenges to housing policies and other material anti-austerity demands. Their analysis calls attention to the need to place an analysis of class relations and capitalist dynamics in evaluating pro-democracy movements genuine impact.

Upsweeps in mass mobilization often offer opportunities for increased repression under the guise of restoring social order, but far more pernicious are the less visible legal changes that can have long term impacts in the form of delayed and retroactive fines and penalties as well as more immediate impacts on risk and cost assessments designed to dissuade dissent (Flesher Fominaya 2017). Recent research on digital repression has expanded our understanding of how new technologies are mobilized to raise the costs of protest and mobilization (Earl, Maher and Pan 2022). But technologies of repression can also have their roots in the past. In their contribution, *15-M Mobilizations and the penalization of counter-hegemonic protest in contemporary Spain*, Kerman Calvo and Aitor Romeo Echeverría offer an in-depth analysis of one the most profound and unwelcome impacts of 15-M, which is the increase in the penalization of protest in Spain (a trend that this wave of mobilizations also spurred in other European contexts). In their contribution, they show us how the movement stimulated new technologies of repression including invasive policing, securitization and criminalization. These technologies built on a culture of fear and anxiety about insecurities that characterized the Spanish penal system prior to 15-M, but which was mobilized and intensified in the wake of the social unrest the movement expressed.

Taken together, these contributions offer much more than a look backward to the dynamics and impacts of the 15-M movement. They stimulate us to rethink the relationship between social movements and democracy more broadly; to reconsider the ways we think about and analyze movement consequences and legacies; and they offer us sometimes surprising new understandings of movement impacts. The insights provided here will hopefully stimulate new lines of research into social movement outcomes and their impacts on democracy. As we slip further into democratic backsliding in so many places, this is something we need now more than ever.

Aarhus, May 1, 2023

References

Cox, L. and Flesher Fominaya, C. (2009) Movement knowledge: what do we know, how do we create knowledge and what do we do with it?. *Interface: A Journal for and about Social Movements*, 1(1), 1–20.

Earl, J., Maher, T. and Pan, J. (2022) The digital repression of social movements, protest, and activism: A synthetic review, *Science Advances*, 8(10), DOI: 10.1126/sciadv.abl8198

Eyerman, R. and Jamison, A. (1991) *Social Movements: A Cognitive Approach*. Cambridge: Polity.

Flesher Fominaya, C. (2017) European anti-austerity and pro-democracy protests in the wake of the global financial crisis, *Social Movement Studies*, 16(1), 1–20, DOI: 10.1080/14742837.2016.1256193

Flesher Fominaya, C. (2020) *Democracy Reloaded*. Oxford: Oxford University Press.

Flesher Fominaya, C (2022) Mobilizing during the COVID-19 pandemic: From democratic innovation to the political weaponization of disinformation, *American Behavioral Scientist*, DOI: 10.1177/00027642221132178

Flesher Fominaya, C. and Feenstra, R. (2020) *Routledge Handbook of Contemporary European Social Movements: Protest in Turbulent Times*. London: Routledge.

Flesher Fominaya, C. and Gillan, K. (2017) Navigating the technology-media-movements complex, *Social Movement Studies*, 16(4), 383–402, DOI: 10.1080/14742837.2017.1338943

Giugni, M. (1998) Was it worth the effort? The outcomes and consequences of social movements. *Annual Review of Sociology*, 24(1), 371–393.

McAdam, D., and Tarrow, S. (2010) Ballots and barricades: On the reciprocal relationship between elections and social movements. *Perspectives on Politics*, 8(2), 529–542. https://doi-org.ez.statsbiblioteket.dk/10.1017/S1537592710001234

Revilla-Blanco, M., and Molina-Sánchez, C. (2021) Ciclo de protesta y cambios en el sistema de partidos español: 15M, Mareas y nuevos partidos. *Forum Revista Departamento de Ciencia Política*, 20(20), 206–232. https://doi-org.ez.statsbiblioteket.dk/10.15446/frdcp.n20.88762

Reconsidering social movement impact on democracy: the case of Spain's 15-M movement

Cristina Flesher Fominaya and Ramón A. Feenstra

ABSTRACT
Social movement impact on democracy has primarily been treated in two ways in the literature: the role of social movements in promoting democratization in the form of regime change; and a more recent literature on the ways social movements initiate democratic innovation in governing institutions and norm diffusion in already existing democracy. In this article, we argue that to fully understand social movement impact on democracy, we need to look beyond these two main approaches, as important as they are. Using the emblematic case of Spain's 15-M pro-democracy movement to illustrate our conceptual proposal, we draw on existing literature to argue that social movements can impact democracy in several key arenas currently not sufficiently considered in the literature. We provide examples of democratic impact emerging from the experimentation around the central problematic of 'real democracy' in the 'occupied squares' to highlight several ways social movements' democratic impact might be explored. We develop the concepts of hybridity and democratic laboratory to analyze these impacts and discuss their relation to contemporary theorizing about democracy and movement outcomes. We argue that adopting this broader approach to the democratic impact of social movements leads to a more nuanced understanding of movement outcomes and 'success'.

Introduction

The decade that has passed since the intense mobilizations of the 'occupy movements' or 'movements of the squares' following the global crash of 2008 allows us to evaluate some of the major consequences of these movements and to gauge some of their longer-term effects. Understanding the consequences and legacies of social movements requires the passage of a certain amount of time between critical protest events or intense periods of mobilization and the evaluation of outcomes. This is especially true of impacts that take longer to percolate through society, such as shifts in cultural values or biographical consequences. Time also enables us to re-evaluate the impact of shorter-term changes that might be reversed or quickly fade once the intensity of mobilization has passed.

Movement outcomes have long been of interest to scholars, yet scholarship to date has been conditioned by dominant trends and methodological challenges related to measuring the complex, contradictory, and often unexpected or unintended outcomes of movements across time and space (Flesher Fominaya, 2020b; Giugni, 2004, 2008; Bosi, Giugni & Uba, 2016;). These challenges have meant that most scholarship in the area has focused on short term and more easily measured effects of movements on policy and institutions (Amenta & Caren, 2004; Giugni, 2008) rather than on more diffuse and harder to trace cultural impacts. Despite these limitations, the field has addressed several areas of impact, including biographical (Whittier, 2004; Nez, 2021), cultural (Gelb & Hart, 1999; Meyer, 1999; Rucht, 1999), institutional (Raeburn, 2004; Staggenborg, 1988, 2013) electoral/political (Gamson, 1990), and social capital (Diani, 1997; Tindall et al., 2012) effects. Genealogical approaches have also allowed scholars to look at how movements shape subsequent movements, despite periods of demobilization or abeyance (Flesher Fominaya, 2015a; Whittier, 1995, 1997).

One key area of analysis of movement outcomes has been the analysis of movement impact on democratization and democratic innovation, which has been treated in two ways in the literature. The first explores the role of social movements in producing democratization, usually through regime change from a dictatorial or authoritarian regime towards a democratic system (Giugni, 1994; Giugni et al., 1998; Tarrow, 1989; Tilly & Wood, 2015). Many of these works tend to adopt a regional focus such as Eastern Europe (Chilton, 1994; Tarrow, 1995; Oberschall, 2000; Keane, 1998), Latin America (Hipsher, 1998; Sandoval, 1998, Johnston and Almeida, 2006), Southern European countries (Groves et al., 2017; León, 2010; Tarrow, 1995), or Africa (McCorley, 2013).

Tilly's work (Tilly, 2004) on the historical relationship between social movements and democracy development has been particularly influential. For Tilly, 'Democratization [...] includes any significant move from a polity's present configuration toward broad, equal citizenship with binding consultation and extensive protection' (1993/1994, p. 21). Tilly argues that correlation does not imply causation, but writes 'obviously, though not necessarily, movements that explicitly demand more of the four facets of democracy, if successful, promote democracy' (1993/1994, p. 21). Tilly offers a second conjecture, which is that the greater the presence of a broad variety of movements and claims, the more likely 'an increase in the breadth of citizenship and the extent of consultation' (1993/1994, p. 21). Yet he concludes that 'at best the proliferation of social movements only promotes democracy under limited conditions. It only occurs when movements organize around a wide variety of claims including explicit demands for democracy and the state gains capacity to realize such claims at least as fast as the claims increase.' (1993/1994, p. 22).

Describing the precise relationship between social movements and democratization is a complex matter because movements can cause very varied impacts depending on, for instance, the context, the historical era, or their claims and objectives (Giugni, 1998). While much literature focused on the role of state-centred 'old' movements, such as the labour movement, in democratization processes, the 1980s and 1990s saw a proliferation of works arguing for the role of so-called 'new social movements' in developing 'prescriptions' for democratization due to their internal concern for democracy.[1] In all cases, the focus lies primarily on the democratic impact of social movements on the state.

The second line of inquiry has been more recent literature on the impact of social movements on governing institutions and on the dissemination of democratic values and ideals (Clemens, 1998; Schneiberg & Lounsbury, 2008) or the generation of democratic innovations (Della Porta & Felicetti, 2017; Flesher Fominaya, 2022). This literature examines, for example, the influence of movements in promoting democratic consolidation within representative systems in processes that are bottom-up, and in which repertoires like referenda or deliberative processes are encouraged (Della Porta, 2015; Della Porta & Felicetti, 2019; Della Porta, Fernández, et al., 2017; Feenstra, 2015). In this endeavor, Della Porta (2020) has provided one of the most ambitious explorations on how social movements can 'save democracy' through her analysis of how several movements following the global crash have produced democratic innovations from below. Her analysis points to 'the importance of social movements as incubators of emerging ideas about democracy' and 'the spreading of emergent norms' (Della Porta, 2020, p. 159). She argues that, 'Even when the results do not match the original goals of their promoters, they have positive spillover effects on democratic life affecting both the political game itself [...] and the relationship between representative institutions and the citizenry' (Della Porta, 2020, p. 145). This literature has also built on previous work on the relations between movements and parties and on so called movement parties or hybrid parties, defined as 'coalitions of political activists who emanate from social movements and try to apply the organizational and strategic practices of social movements in the arena of party competition' (Kitschelt, 2006, p. 280). Often characterized as populist, these movement parties are widely recognized to be a result of increasing dissatisfaction with really existing democracy as well as an (unintended) outcome of mass mobilizations against austerity and for greater democracy across Europe (Kaldor & Selchow 2013; Flesher Fominaya, 2017).

In this article, we argue that although these approaches are extremely valuable, they are still quite limited in the scope of impact on democracy they allow for social movements, in particular in the state centric focus they adopt. In this article, we draw on extensive existing literature to use the emblematic case of a single pro-democracy movement, Spain's '15-M movement', to trace some of the effects of the movement on Spanish democracy, focusing on experimentation around the central problematic of 'real democracy' in the 'occupied squares'. In doing so, we tie the existing literature on democracy within movements (e.g. Blee, 2012; Breines, 1989; Flesher Fominaya, 2020a; Maeckelbergh, 2009; Polletta, 2012) to emerging literature on the effect of social movements on democracy within and beyond social movements (Della Porta, 2020; Flesher Fominaya, 2020a). We argue that although 15-M did not produce regime change (or the 'Spanish revolution' some activists hoped for) it had at least seven forms of impact on democracy in different arenas: 1) Increasing citizen participation through mass mobilization and building social capital in movement networks, 2) influencing public opinion and raising demands for 'greater' democracy, 3) transforming the electoral landscape, 4) democratic innovation in movement groups and civil society organizations, 5) experimenting with party forms, 6) democratic innovation in the institutions, and 7) reclaiming and revalorizing representative democracy through regeneration. While arenas 3, 5 and 6 do focus on impacts in institutional arenas, we understand institutional impacts in a way that goes beyond institutional procedural reforms (e.g. changes to increase citizen participation) to also understand how certain movement democratic imaginaries influence innovation within institutions. Our discussion of the remaining arenas encourages scholars to look beyond state institutions for democratic innovation stemming from pro-democracy social movements.

While we separate these impacts and arenas analytically, one of our purposes is to show the interactions between arenas resulting from the initial experience of participation in 15-M, their often hybrid nature and their synergistic effects. In addition, we will use the concept of democratic laboratory to unpack some of the defining characteristics of this concept.

Work on the influence of past participation of political action inside institutions has tended to focus on institutions as a means of effecting change in particular policy areas or issues (e.g. environment, womens' rights) (Bosi et al., 2016). Here we are looking at democracy itself (including, but not limited to, democratic institutions), as an object of change. The reclaiming of democratic institutions for the citizens was a key feature of 15-M political framing from its inception in what has been called the 'democratic turn' (Flesher Fominaya, 2015a). As we will show, the outcomes of the initial 15-M protest camps on democratic innovation initiatives encompass both institutional and non-institutional arenas as well as 'hybrid' ones. Hybridity between autonomous and loosely organized forms of collective action and more institutional forms has also been a noted feature of the movement (Flesher Fominaya, 2020a; Martínez, 2016), and we will further develop its importance below.

Despite their importance, in this article we are leaving aside questions of biographical consequences on individuals (Nez, 2021) to focus primarily on organizations, including formal institutions (governing structures at municipal and state level, formally and legally constituted NGOs), as well as loosely and informally organized movement initiatives. Despite 15-M's well documented influence on other movements and innovations beyond Spain (e.g. Flesher Fominaya, 2019; Kroll, 2011; Romanos, 2016), we are also limiting our analysis to Spain.

This is a conceptual paper that draws both on our extensive experience in the field and the most significant literature on impacts and outcomes of the 15 M over the last decade. Although we draw extensively on empirical studies to support our argument, this article is not intended as a self-contained empirical case study. An exhaustive analysis of democratic impacts would be far beyond the scope of this article and is not our purpose here. Therefore, we have purposively selected core examples in key arenas of democratic action to illustrate our conceptual argument that social movements can impact democracy not only within but also beyond the state and institutional arenas. Because our focus here is on the impact of democratic innovation developed through experimentation of the 'democratic laboratories' in the occupied squares, we are also leaving aside the important unintended and unwelcome impacts of the movement on democracy, such as increasing criminalization and penalization of protest and critique (see Calvo & Romeo, 2022; Flesher Fominaya, 2017). We are also not evaluating the success or merit of specific democracy innovation initiatives nor implying they are necessarily successful or without flaws or problems.

The great democracy debate

In recent years, several social movements have made the slogan 'real democracy' popular by demanding more in-depth participatory practices in representative political systems. Although citizen satisfaction with representative democracy has declined, the democratic ideal enjoys almost undisputed legitimacy as the best available political system (Flesher Fominaya, 2020a; Norris, 2014). Another slogan that has become popular in the last few years is 'They don't represent us', reflecting citizen dissatisfaction with representative structures, and emphasizing the distance that lies between those governed and those governing. However, there are many different ways of interpreting and implementing the democracy ideal based on the 'power of the demos'. For centuries, this has attracted debate in political theory and philosophy, much of which concerns just how much power or decision-making ability should be redistributed across the political community, and how this redistribution should occur (Sartori, 1999). Democratic theory proposals on the amount of political responsibility to allocate to the *demos* cover a wide spectrum of options, ranging from the most elitist to the most demanding and most participatory (with plenty of options in between).

Despite problems defining and measuring democracy, the most common form of democracy today is some form of representative-electoral democracy (which can be combined with other forms such as constitutional democracies, or some forms of direct democracy such as national referendums). At the end of 2015, Freedom House classified 125 out of 195 states 'electoral democracies' (Freedom House, 2016, p. 9, Economist Intelligence Unit 2022). This format is based on the idea that citizens's participatory capacity is primarily defined through voting (while the responsibility of the rulers is to represent the people's preferences). Despite its dominance, this model is today contested by many other visions of the democratic, that understand citizens' political capabilities differently and that propose alternative political repertoires, including the integration of meaningful deliberation into democratic processes, direct participation, monitoring of democratic institutions and rights, or using random selection processes (Della Porta, 2009).

Some proposals and models of democracy argue for the need to strengthen the processes of deliberation in the formation of public opinion and its influence on the political structure (Habermas, 1996). These models defend the importance of reinforcing deliberation processes not only in the configuration of the political agenda, but also in the influencing of decision-making (Fishkin, 1997). Here, participation is understood as having to be defined in communicative terms so that citizens can embark on rational deliberative processes in relation to matters of public interest. Deliberative conceptions of democracy insist on the importance of high-quality public opinion formation resulting from inclusive, plural and non-coercive processes.

Other proposals insist on the need to implement numerous mechanisms of direct participation in which citizens can collectively decide their future. This vision of democracy encompasses a variety of approaches, such as the 'radical democracy' of Pateman (1979), the 'strong democracy' of Barber (2003), or the 'participatory democracy' of Santos and Avritzer (2004), which share a resolute defense of the need to create effective mechanisms of participation (and not merely symbolic ones) in decision-making. The idea is that both participation and decision-making should not exclusively lie in representatives' hands. In relation to this proposal, other models are also put forward that look to the possibilities offered by digital technology and technopolitical logics of collective action to promote forms of digitally enabled democracy (Coleman, 2012; Flesher Fominaya, 2020a, 2020b; Toret, 2013; Romanos & Sádaba, 2015;). At their heart, these technopolitical imaginaries are fuelled by the belief that new technologies can facilitate collective participation repertoires at scale and the effective harnessing of collective intelligence to regenerate democracy for the contemporary age.

Other proposals place their hopes on the regenerative potential that civil society may exercise by proliferating monitoring mechanisms that sound the alarm when an abuse of power occurs (Keane, 2009). Therefore, these proposals trust in the transformative capacity that comes with oversight of the processes of centers of power (Keane, 2009, 2022; Rosanvallon, 2008; Schudson, 1998). In this way, monitory democracy can improve democratic quality and transparency without relying on direct participation in public matters. Proponents also consider that the technological potential of digital media can potentially drive this political repertoire (Keane, 2013).

Finally, there are proposals that consider the random selection of representatives as an innovative tool capable of democratizing specific democratic processes or institutions (Moreno Pestaña, 2017). Introducing this mechanism is understood as a means to creating the possibility for citizens to be both governed and governing. As such, it is a means to diversify the profiles of representative bodies (Burnheim, 2006; Manin, 1997; Sintomer, 2012, 2017). The objective focuses on narrowing the distance between governing parties and citizens, and promoting principles such as inclusion and the rotation of posts. The ultimate idea is to go beyond a representative-electoral model based on selecting 'the best' (Van Reybrouck, 2016; Burnheim, 1985). Although hailed as a participatory alternative by some, Talpin (2015) has noted that the use of random selection has been strategically used as a means of diluting the participation of social movements and politicized actors in institutional participatory reforms, thereby deradicalizing and shifting the balance of power away from movements. This fact has not been lost on movement actors, who can resist random selection systems that threaten their input into the process. Each of the proposals above have been critiqued and hotly debated by proponents and opponents.

Although we have clearly distinguished between ideal typical models of democracy in this section, what we hope to show below is that, as in any laboratory, these different models find new synergies and cross-contaminations as they are mixed together in the context of specific experiments and innovations. Crucially, we need to distinguish between theoretical models and activist imaginaries. Activists rarely hold pure ideal typical conceptions of democracy. Debate on what democracy means and how it should be implemented has been, and continues to be, broad in the area of theory, philosophy and political science, and is also a matter that has been thoroughly debated in the heart of social movements. Pro-democracy movements have claimed 'real democracy' as a central part of their mobilisations in the last decade, and feel the need to place participative dynamics at the heart of their initiatives and structures. In Spain's 15-M movement, all of the alternatives discussed above have found a place for expression in some form. In this article, we will consider some of the key manifestations of these visions of democratic regeneration aimed at moving society closer to 'real democracy'. The expression 'democratic laboratory' has frequently been applied to the case of Spain's 15-M movement yet rarely defined or expanded upon. In this article, we will develop the concept through the exploration of emblematic case studies and their relation to contemporary theorizing about democracy.

Democracy in Spain's 15-M: A democratic laboratory

From 1939–1975, the Spanish political system went through 36 years of Franco's dictatorship and a subsequent period of transition to a representative-democratic system (1975–1978) in a process guided mainly by the elites of the country (Gunther et al., 1988; Günther & Montero, 2009). The advent of democracy brought with it a progressive consolidation of civil society. The 1980s saw the emergence of what are known as 'new social movements'. Thus, anti-war, feminist, ecologist and anti-globalisation movements appeared in the last decades of the 20th century (Tejerina & Perugorría, 2012), with the anti-NATO protests in 1986 (Alberich-Nistal, 2012) being notable for their strength and impact on social movements, despite failing in their primary goal. However, the consolidation of social movements in Spain was not without some organizational weakness and moments of inaction (Romanos & Aguilar, 2016). Despite these limitations, the entry of the new century witnessed significant demonstrations in relation to the ecological crisis of the Prestige ship oil spill (2002– 2003); against the Iraq War in 2003, and the protests after the Atocha bombings in Madrid on 11 March 2004 (Flesher Fominaya, 2011; Romanos & Sádaba, 2022; Sampedro, 2005). In 2011, the emergence of 15-M stood out for the novelties it presented in terms of the breadth and survival of diverse political repertoires, the creativity of its actions and the eruption of newly visible autonomous actors (outside the trade unions and parties) (Flesher Fominaya, 2015a). The literature on social movements in Spain has been growing (especially since the 1990s) in relation to this historical evolution (see Betancur Nuez & Santos, 2023). For this article, the literature linked to the period 2011 and onwards will obviously be key.

In 2011, Spain's 15-M movement took democracy itself as its central problematic (Feenstra et al., 2017; Flesher Fominaya, 2015a, 2017; Flesher Fominaya, 2020a; Tormey, 2015) arguably to a greater degree than any other anti-austerity movement following the global financial crash of 2008. The original banner of the 15-May 2011 protest march read 'Real Democracy Now! We are not commodities in the hands of politicians and bankers!'. The centrality of democracy as a problematic and imaginary not only set the movement apart from other anti-austerity movements in the European wave but also from the previous wave of mobilization in the global justice movement (Flesher Fominaya, 2017, 2020a). Following the initial protest march, Madrid's Puerta del Sol was 'occupied' by a small group of activists whose numbers exploded in the following days after police repression and movement networks mobilized. The original 'Acampada Sol' was embedded in Madrid's wider network of autonomous social movements and squatted social centers, which nourished it with multiple resources, including experienced activists with a strong concern for and practice with alternative and prefigurative forms of internal democracy. Soon camps were sprouting up all across Spain's central squares.

Occupied camps in public squares were sites of democratic experimentation, cross-contamination and synergy. Open assemblies or 'agoras in the plazas' sought to bridge divides and include people of all political persuasions and walks of life, to model a public sphere characterized by mutual respect and tolerance, and decision-making based on a combination of deliberation and consensus and non-hierarchical relations between participants (Candón Mena, Montero Sánchez & Calle Collado, 2018). The camps were sites where multiple democratic imaginaries combined and sometimes collided, and during the almost month-long occupation in Madrid, thousands of proposals to regenerate democracy were collected (Flesher Fominaya, 2020a; Gerbaudo, 2016; Simsa & Totter, 2017). The camps also manifested a form of hybridity between autonomous and institutional spaces (Flesher Fominaya, 2020a; Martínez, 2016). Autonomous movement culture dominated in the forms of practice in the camps (non-hierarchical deliberative and participatory assemblies, as well as myriad collective organizing practices, see Flesher Fominaya, 2020a; Gómez Nicolau, 2023) but was tied to demands for institutional reform and an openness to dialogue and alliance building with more institutional actors (as long as it was on the movement's own terms, as seen in the refusal to accept any flags, acronyms or symbols from institutional left organizations) (Flesher Fominaya, 2020a; Martínez, 2016). Despite its strong anti-representative and non-partisan orientation, from the very beginning there were people in the square longing for a more institutionalized and electoral expression of the movement. Hybridity was also seen in autonomous activists' concern with reclaiming existing democratic institutions for the good of the citizens, which was a notable feature of the camps, and a distinguishing characteristic with respect to previous mobilizations in the global justice movement where the focus often centered on the creation of alternatives (e.g. 'another world is possible') in autonomous 'submerged' spaces (Flesher Fominaya, 2015a, 2017, 2020b). There were also calls for a '*proceso constituyente*', a participatory process to develop a new constitution (such as that undertaken in Iceland after the Saucepan Revolution in 2008). This desire to reclaim institutions 'for the people' later influenced the transition of many 15-M activists and assemblies to participate in hybrid-party and municipalist electoral processes and lists beginning in 2014–2015 (Flesher Fominaya, 2020a; Font & García-Espín, 2020; Ibarra Güell et al., 2018; Lobera, 2015; Roth et al., 2019), and renewed engagement and collaboration between unions and autonomous 15-M assemblies and activists in the 'mareas' (see below).

Democratic experimentation in the squares encompassed deliberative and participatory forms, integrating the tradition of autonomous 'assembly style' organizing for debate and decision-making, but also practices of collective self-empowerment in areas such as organizing food, childcare and upkeep of the physical space. Autonomous assemblies within the camp took control over diverse aspects of camp life, including the information point, assemblies for art production, kitchen, library, media and communication, and legal support. The camp was also internally structured along thematic or operational lines, with different assemblies treating areas such as feminism, political economy, or media and communication (see Figure 1). Diverse movement traditions combined in the squares to create a new political subject and actor, not only as a form

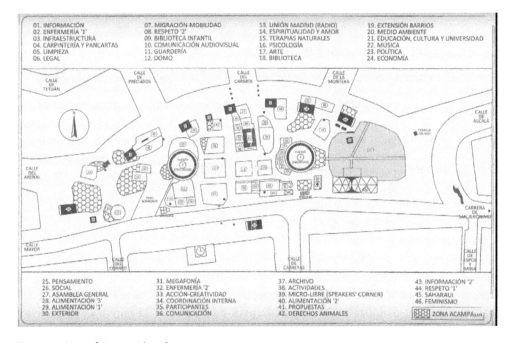

Figure 1. Map of Acampada sol.

of spontaneous combustion but as the result of deliberate strategies at cross contamination, such as the attempts to queer and feminize (or feminist-ize) the camps (Galdón Corbella, 2018; Gámez Fuentes, 2015; Trujillo, 2018, Cruells and Ezquerra, 2015). The result was the consolidation of a collective political subject and political culture that became known simply as 15-M (Flesher Fominaya, 2020a), and whose imaginaries and specific forms of praxis carried over into a multitude of spaces beyond the squares, and whose mobilization and experimentation around the central problematic of democracy continued to impact Spanish democracy in several key ways long after the camps were gone. While scholars such as Talpin (2015) have juxtaposed deliberative forms of participation with collective action repertoires (with the latter being contentious and conflictual e.g. stopping evictions or *protests*, and the former being characterized by dialogue e.g. assemblies), in pro-democracy movements like 15-M, deliberation and participation is not just a form of prefiguration, but is a form of protest and critique against deficient 'really existing democracy' that fails to live up to the democratic ideal of 'real democracy' (a concept encompassing a wide range of imaginaries and practices in the movement). In modelling a different way of enacting 'democracy' activists were also highlighting the participatory shortcomings of a democracy in which citizen participation was limited primarily to voting every few years. But how did 15-M really impact Spanish democracy once the camps were lifted?[2]

Drawing on our own extensive research on 15-M and a wealth of research conducted by other scholars we have analyzed the existing literature to arrive at seven arenas in which we feel there is compelling evidence for the impact of 15-M on democracy in Spain. As we will show, these purposively selected arenas of impact support our broader argument that social movements can impact democracy within and beyond institutional arenas, and that widening our gaze in this way can lead to a richer understanding of the relation between social movements and democracy.

15-M's impact on democracy in 7 arenas

Increase in citizen participation: building social capital in movement networks

One of the often-overlooked impacts of social movements is how movements affect themselves, and other movements (Whittier, 2004). Diani (1997) recognized the impact of social movements on social capital, and also developed an analysis that measured the impact of social movements by the range of social ties emerging from sustained mobilization. He defined social capital in terms of mutual trust and recognition among actors but without necessarily implying the presence of a shared collective identity. In Spain's 15-M, the result of the acampadas was a broad range of movement initiatives and a period of intense and sustained mobilization that involved millions of Spanish citizens (see Figures 2 and 3).

In this way, not only did 15-M's *acampadas* contribute to social capital in movement networks, but this process also impacted democracy by mobilizing the participation of citizens in the political life of the country around myriad issues, while at the same time shaping forms of mobilization in the trademark participatory *15-mayista* (15-M style) mold. In this way, movement actors took forms of praxis and ways of thinking about 'real democracy' beyond the squares and into myriad new and pre-existing spaces.

Figure 2. Initiatives emerging from Acampada sol–Source. autoconsulta.Org. April 2014. BY-NC-SA.

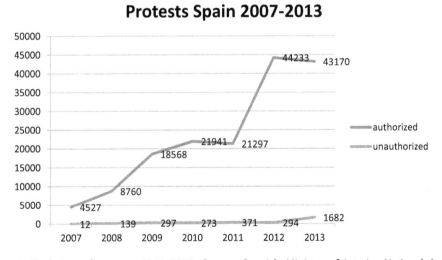

Figure 3. Evolution of protests 2007–2013. Source: Spanish Ministry of Interior National Annual Statistics.

These were not all necessarily pure 15-M spaces, but the expectation that participatory principles be followed in organizing spaces became *de riguer*, even in many spaces that had previously been organized along more hierarchical and representational lines. One important example of hybridity in this regard was the emergence of the *mareas* (or color tides) which were organized sectorally (health workers, education workers, scientists, etc.) but infused those spaces with participatory but also conflictual repertoires of action. One of the most visible and active was *Marea Blanca*, whose health professionals marched through the city weekly to protest against privatization and health cuts, and to demand health care for all (Martínez & San Juan, 2020; Sánchez, 2013). In Madrid, the small group of die-hard 15-M 'campers' who attempted to keep the general assembly going in the Puerta del Sol for several years after the camp ended would be drowned out by a massive wave of Marea Blanca participants sweeping through the square (Flesher Fominaya, fieldnotes), showing how the movement had evolved and transformed into other arenas of collective action. One Marea Blanca activist, Mónica García Gómez, who is currently the coordinator and spokesperson of the political party Más Madrid[3] in the Assembly of Madrid (The Autonomous Community of Madrid's Parliament), explained the influence of 15-M on Marea Blanca in an interview, noting that '15-M was where people made important contacts and got their first taste of organizing', as well as giving them 'the experience and hope that change can be made in the streets' (The People's Health Movement, n.d.).

Another important example of post-acampada 15-M mobilization were the 2014 Marches of Dignity, which saw tens of thousands of protesters walking from all corners of Spain to converge in Madrid. The manifesto combined demands for housing, employment, and economic justice with an end to austerity and patriarchy, and a refusal of the public assumption of the debt burden for bank bailouts and rescue packages, weaving together key 15-M demands at the height of corruption scandals in the governing Partido Popular (Flesher Fominaya, 2014). As Martinez (2016) points out, at that point not only were some institutional left symbols and markers tolerated, they were in some cases explicitly agreed to by 15-M actors.

Although mobilization had been increasing following the global financial crash, 15-M marked a clear 'before and after' tipping point. Mobilization across Spain increased over the next few years, more than *doubling* post 15-M to 44,233 mobilizations in 2012. In 2013, the number of authorized protests dipped very slightly to 43, 170, but the number of *unauthorized* (by authorities) protests rose from 294 in 2012 to 1682 in 2013[4] (see Figure 3).

Influencing public opinion on democracy

In addition to social capital and increase in mobilization, impact on democracy can also be measured by citizen discussion and awareness of the movements demands and ideas about democracy. Survey data showed that 15-M demands also had an important influence on public opinion and awareness beyond those who participated in 15-M related demonstrations. As Sampedro and Lobera (2014) show, between 7 and 8 of every 10 Spaniards agreed with protester demands, an overwhelming degree of consensus ranging 'from 81% at the outset, to 68% a few days before the first anniversary (Sampedro & Lobera, 2014, p. 65).'

The influence of 15-M was also defined by its capacity to influence the media agenda. The movement generated a broad debate around democracy in Spain, both in the camps and online networks, achieving notable success in getting the issues onto the media agenda. Thus, this case is characterized as an exceptional example where online networks manage to 'challenge the competitive advantage of traditional players' (González-Bailón et al., 2013, p. 961). Despite the breadth of issues debated in the camps and on the networks, the 15-M showed the capacity to transfer to the media and public opinion as a whole the debates around issues such as the electoral and party system, privileges of the political class, separation of powers, rights to housing and the regulation of the banking sector (Casas-Salleras et al., 2016; Casero-Ripollés & Feenstra, 2012).

Transforming the electoral landscape

The intense mobilization following 15-M's also impacted Spain's political and electoral landscape, leading to the breakdown of the two-party system and the emergence of new political parties with parliamentary representation (Revilla-Blanco & Molina-Sánchez, 2021). But Revilla-Blanco et al. 2015 argue that even before Podemos[5] emerged, and parties such as Ciudadanos[6] experienced a huge upswing in votes, 15-M represented not just the end of political bi-partisanship but also social bi-partisanship. They see 15-M as reflecting a generational change in which young people no longer share a consensual understanding about Spain's 'successful' transition to democracy. The 15-M cycle of mobilization brought forth an ideological reconfiguration that transformed the political landscape in Spain, and the 2011 general election provided clear evidence of this, with the major parties (PP and PSOE) losing millions of votes, whereas votes for the smaller parties (IU, UP y D) and abstention and null votes increased significantly (Revilla et al., 2015; Revilla-Blanco & Molina-Sánchez, 2021). As Hughes (2011) captured when he quoted a 15-M activist's remark that 'Young people took to the streets and all of a sudden all of the political parties got old', the electoral results show a subsequent impact on the two-party system. Revilla-Blanco and Molina-Sánchez detail this when they state that PP and PSOE 'have lost 8.2 million votes and 101 seats in Congress—comparing vote results in the 2008 and 2016 elections-, whilst two new electoral options, Unidos Podemos -the result of the coalition between Podemos and Izquierda Unida- and Ciudadanos, gathered eight million votes and 93 seats' (2021, p. 226). A trend that was accentuated in the November 2019 elections, when compared 'to 2008 results, PP and PSOE obtained nearly 10 million votes less and 114 less seats' (Revilla-Blanco & Molina-Sánchez, 2021, p. 226). Evidently, other factors (political disaffection, economic difficulties after the Great Recession, etc.) also explain part of this impact in the electoral cycle (Rama et al., 2021) but the mobilisation of 15-M had a clear effect on the Spanish electoral space (Casanueva, 2021) and on the 'exhaustion' of the 'two-party dominance' (Garrido, 2017).

Democratic innovations in movement groups, and civil society organizations: reclaiming democracy for "the people" through hybridity and technopolitics

Research on the Global Justice Movement showed that the greater the concern with internal democracy in social movement groups, the less ready these organizations were to cooperate with the state, including cooperation in democratic innovations (Della Porta, 2009; Talpin, 2015). This reluctance reflects tensions between different orientations to collective action, often characterized as horizontal versus vertical or autonomous versus institutional (see Flesher Fominaya, 2007). This would lead us to expect an inverse relation between increased internal democracy in the movement and democratic innovation and institutions via movement engagement. This inverse relationship did not hold for 15-M. The hybridity we have noted in relation to the 15-M movement shows that there is no longer such a clear opposition between a willingness to engage the state and a lack of institutionalization in more autonomous, loosely organized and 'horizontally' oriented groups. One reason for this is the rise of technopolitical or digitally enabled democratic imaginaries which believe that the rise of user generated content and input via digital tools has enabled a genuine means to decrease the gap between citizens and representatives. Tecno-political frameworks actively pursue democratic innovation through the harnessing of digital tools and are influenced by hacker ethics and 'radical geek' and open software traditions and milieus (see e.g. Coleman, 2012; Levy, 1984; Postill, 2018). Hacker ethics combine a commitment to transparency and information sharing, with an orientation toward innovation and problem solving through the development of technical solutions and self-organized labour. As such it has important synergies with autonomous orientations to collective action. Romanos and Sádaba (2016), for example, show that techno-political frameworks facilitated the transition of 15-M participants from activist to electoral spheres of collective action (see also Flesher Fominaya, 2020a). The belief that digital tools would enable democratic innovation in institutional settings and processes helped more autonomous 'horizontal' activists overcome their reluctance to engage in more vertical institutional initiatives.

The 15-M related group 15MPaRato is a great example of how technopolitical and digitally enabled democratic imaginaries shaped hybrid collective action that sought to reclaim democratic institutions for citizens while also spreading the movement's belief in 'people power'.[7] 'The citizens did it' was a key slogan they used to claim credit for their successful actions-thereby spreading a belief in the power of the people to reclaim and transform democracy. Other ambitions for digitally enabled democratic regeneration include improving citizens access to high quality information online, modeling transparency, and exercising monitory functions through their whistle blowing activities (i.e. their use of the X mailbox and collaboration with journalists to expose corruption) (Feenstra & Keane, 2014; Flesher Fominaya, 2020a; Jeppesen, 2021; Postill, 2018; Siapera, 2016, 2017).

15MpaRato is organized as a catalyst group of small-committed activists embedded in a larger movement network that supports them with resources when needed. Hacker ethics form a key part of their operating logic. The group not only managed to bring charges against former IMF director Rodrigo Rato but also exposed one of the largest corruption scandals in recent Spanish history uncovering fraud and collusion between financial and political elites including members of all the major establishment political parties and unions (Flesher Fominaya, 2020a; Mattoni, 2018). In this way 15MpaRato managed to harness citizen collaboration in aid of public scrutiny of issues of public concern, increasing transparency through monitory and whistleblowing activities. They define themselves as 'an activist project working and proposing advanced solutions in fields related to digital rights and democracy mechanisms for transparency, participation and citizen control of power and institutions; the defense of citizen journalism for the right to know, inform and be informed; the technical, communications and legal fight against corruption' (15MpaRato n.d).

15MpaRato is one example of a wider range of initiatives that attempt to harness digital tools to regenerate democracy and which were nourished in the *acampadas*. One example of this was the open-source platform '*Propongo*' or 'I propose' that was developed by hackers in *Acampada Sol* and which enabled anyone to make political proposals.

There are many other initiatives that centre on experimentation and innovation based on monitoring by civil society (monitory democracy). One example is Civio, the not-for-profit organisation whose task focuses on overseeing and encouraging Spanish administrations to use transparent accounting reports (Casero Ripollés & López-Meri, 2015; Feenstra & Keane, 2014). Similarly in the mass media field, different initiatives have emerged, such as Eldiario.es, Infolibre, La Marea, all with clear links to 15-M, and which seek to promote journalism models whose driving motive are understood as exercising strict control of political and economic power (Barbas & Treré, 2022; Casero-Ripollés, 2020). In a similar vein, other initiatives include Maldita.es, which monitors and oversees the mass media and journalists' practices and the spreading of fake news. Maldita.es actively works to counter disinformation and improve the quality of information and media literacy in the public sphere. Experimentation in the monitoring area offers the opportunity for civil society and social movements to fight for transparency. However, this political repertoire arguably continues to maintain a clear separation between those governing from those governed, raising the question of whether monitory mechanisms necessarily bring us closer to the 'real democracy' ideal and its demand for greater citizen participation in decision-making and deliberation.

While many of these initiatives were autonomous from institutional politics, other spaces occupied a *hybrid space* that enabled more experimentation, yet still worked in collaboration with municipal institutions. One example was Madrid's Laboratory of Collective Intelligence for Participatory Democracy (2016–2019), a project that emerged from a collaboration between Medialab Prado and the Government Area of Citizen Participation, Transparency and Open Government of the city of Madrid (directed by 15-M veterans). The laboratory held a series of workshops and conferences on participatory democracy with participants from around the world, seeking to develop democratic innovations, often facilitated by digital tools (see Bermejo, 2017). This formed part of a wider ecosystem of initiatives designed to experiment with and apply initiatives to build an urban commons characterized by greater citizen participation (for a review of initiatives in Madrid, see Gutierrez, 2017).

Experimenting with party forms

The search for more open and participatory parties as a means of innovating in forms of political expression and representation predates 15-M (e.g. the Greens across Europe, Pirate Parties, etc.) In the Spanish context, however, 15-M led to a gradual shift towards an electoral strategy that included close attention to democratic innovation in form and content. The leap "from 'occupying squares' to 'occupying institutions'" (Thompson, 2021, p. 321) in 2014 came with an alternative understanding of what representation must mean. Indeed, the success of the transition from streets to squares owed much to the extensive discursive work of new party formations, such as Podemos and Barcelona en Comú that spoke directly to a 15-M constituency, integrating key frames and demands with promises to transform the nature and form of the parties, and were themselves made up of actors who had participated in the movement (Flesher Fominaya, 2020a).

Different electoral initiatives have attempted to experiment to promote more horizontal types of parties that move away from the dynamics of the conventional parties, which they protested against in 2011 (Portos, 2021). These political parties aim to generate new leaderships, as well as new types of political parties that are open to citizens, and seek to encourage an ongoing consultation and deliberation process of consultation and deliberation (Alabao, 2016; Flesher Fominaya, 2020a; Rubio-Pueyo, 2017; Tormey and Feenstra, 2015).

In the 2014 European Elections initiatives like Partido X and Podemos emerged that sought to transfer 15-M concerns to new forms of internal democracy by resorting to the potential offered by technologies. Their attempt to collaboratively develop and launch open selection processes from their electoral lists was one aspect of innovation (Chironi & Fittipaldi, 2017; Subirats, 2015a, 2015b). Partido X was a much purer form of technopolitical party (or internet party as they are sometimes known) with a core of activists strongly influenced by hacker ethics and by other digital parties. Podemos made use and fanfare of digital tools such as Agora Voting, Appgree and Reddit, but was in fact a more hybrid on and offline initiative that used multiple channels of communication and organization (a strategy that worked much better and benefited from party leader Iglesias' already established television media presence). Podemos' electoral success enabled the project-initially presented as a 'citizen initiative'-to be consolidated and to institutionalize its processes and internal regulations, through both the Vistalegre I (2014) and Vistalegre II (2016) Meetings (Alabao, 2016, 2017a, 2017b; Flesher Fominaya, 2020a). During both these meetings, debate about opening institutionalization processes occupied a central place. This led to the consideration of proposals for the use of sortition to form certain party organs. Sortition partially worked in some local groups, but often led to major debates and scepticisms about its use (Costa Delgado & Moreno-Pestaña, 2019; Costa Delgado, 2017; Feenstra, 2017).

Podemos faced considerable difficulties consolidating horizontal organization forms. Despite experimentation attempts, Podemos obtained modest results when encouraging participation and horizontality (Deseriis & Vittori, 2019; Flesher Fominaya, 2020a; Gerbaudo, 2021; Gomez & Ramiro, 2019). Nonetheless, this experimentation served to take debate about political parties' internal democracy to the public sphere, and prompted some internal restructuring (or gesturing in this regard) in other Spanish political parties (Jaime-Castillo et al., 2018; Jiménez-Sánchez et al., 2018). Indeed Pedro Sánchez's revival as party leader of the PSOE was largely supported by his participatory roadshow to reconnect with party militants and adoption of 15-M style rhetoric about participation. 15-M cast a long shadow: in 2017, six years after the Acampada, Pedro Sánchez, in his closing speech for the PSOE's national conference, promised to 'represent' the participants of 15-M and to work for a system free of corruption and a judiciary free of political interference, assuring them that their unsatisfied aspirations for democracy would come (Noticias, 2017).

Experimentation as regards the political party structure also extended to other initiatives influenced by 15-M. Podemos' decision to not take part in the 2015 Regional/Local Elections opened a way for many electoral initiatives to proliferate. These initiatives varied from place to place, and from city to city (Feenstra & Tormey, 2023; Font & García-Espín, 2020; Font, 2017). Quasi political parties were created in some constituencies, while electoral platforms were thrown together in other cities (Romanos &

Sádaba, 2016; Marzolf & Ganuza, 2016). Many municipal initiatives adopted the principle 'to represent, not supplant'. In other words, they tried to go beyond classic party models by adopting a more modest form of leadership and more horizontal and open dynamics (Ordóñez et al., 2018). It is also here where technopolitics played a crucial role in devising collaborative electoral programmes or in promoting open processes to select representatives. The successful electoral results of 2015 in some towns and cities (e.g.such as Barcelona, Madrid, Zaragoza, Cádiz, Coruña, among many others) also allowed experimentation to directly shift to representative institutions since many activists were involved in parties, such as Barcelona en Comú, Ahora Madrid, Zaragoza en Común, Cádiz Sí Se Puede or Marea Atlántica (Lobera & Parejo, 2019; Font & García-Espín, 2020; Martínez & San Juan, 2020; Mota Consejero & Janoschka, 2022; Smith & Prieto Martín, 2021).

Democratic innovation in the institutions

The digitally enabled aspirations for democratic innovation of the hackers in the occupied squares and related movement spaces were given a once in a lifetime opportunity to put their aspirations into practice when several movement-related coalitions gained control of some of Spain's major cities. In all cases, the 15-M "hacktivists" joined the municipal governments to work on improving citizen participation through democratic innovations. In 2015, the establishment of municipal governments known as 'cities of change' (i.e. cities governed by 15-M related initiatives) led to different plural democratic innovations coming about in institutions themselves. Arguably the two most important examples were the digital platforms for participative democracy *Decide Madrid* and *Decidim Barcelona* (Barandiaran et al., 2017; Peña-López, 2017a).[8] These platforms seek to promote direct participation and deliberation channels through digital channels that also combine elements of presentiality (Peña-López, 2017b). Here, the idea is to extend participation in such a way that it is not restricted to representatives only, and at least part of the decision-making (or policies) about certain matters like participatory budgets or certain local policies include external political intervention channels. Decide Madrid has promoted participation opportunities both in the definition of participatory budgets and with the possibility of autonomously proposing proposals by citizens. In this way, those proposals that achieved the support of 1% of the population passed to the voting phase and, if approved, became binding decisions for the mayor's office (Hinojosa Navarro, 2019). Decidim Barcelona aims to facilitate the process by offering citizens the opportunity to put forward proposals and have them debated and voted on by users, which are then taken into account by the city council (Barandiaran et al., 2017; Bua & Bussu, 2021; Charnock et al., 2021). Both cases are paradigmatic examples of how citizen participation initiatives can be applied using the potential of technopolitical tools (Nez & Ganuza, 2020; Pina et al., 2022; Royo et al., 2020). Moreover, the philosophy of Decide Madrid and Decidim Barcelona is based on creating infrastructures or free open devices capable of encouraging participative democracy. The format is defined with a free open-source code that is capable of spreading to other locations and levels of government to transform or go into more depth with the democratic system. Both institutions have experimented with direct forms of direct participation. With the Decide Madrid platform, these advances obtained the 2018 UN Public Service Award for 'establishing more open, transparent, participative and inclusive governance models'.

In Madrid, other initiatives within institutions have involved the use of sortition and promoted deliberation for democratic regeneration, one of which is the Madrid City Observatory. This out-of-the-ordinary democratic experiment set up by the Madrid City Council was passed in 2019, and is defined as a citizens' assembly based on random selection that is designed to put forward proposals and to intervene in designing public policies (Ganuza & Mendiharat, 2020; Ganuza & Menendez-Blanco, 2020; Nez & Ganuza, 2020). However, the organ, made up of 49 randomly selected citizens, has not been well-established due to the change in the governing party that took place the same year it was passed.

This use of sortition, employed from democratic laboratories to drive mini-public or citizen jury initiatives, not only provides innovation in processes to select representatives but also appeals to deliberation as a central process towards democratic improvement (Fishkin, 1997). Deliberation has been a process encouraged from the very start of 15-M because it represents a movement that also seeks to put in practice the society it wishes to live in (Della Porta & Doerr, 2018; Flesher Fominaya, 2015a); hence, the claim for a series of principles to be fulfilled to consolidate inclusive, plural and rational dialogue. In 2017, before the Madrid City Observatory, an initial form of sortition-deliberative experimentation was also encouraged to be put into practice when Medialab-Prado replicated the Belgian G1000 experiment. This led to a mini-public deliberative practice to be set up to develop participatory proposals (Navarro Cueva, 2017). This experiment was extremely novel and relevant, but was unable to reach either the number or the plurality of the desired participants (Nez & Ganuza, 2020).

Democratic imaginaries can also enter the institutions beyond formal mechanisms of participation and are not limited to digitally enabled hacker or technopolitical imaginaries. 15-M activists brought their political priorities and vision of democracy into the institutions with them in other ways. Feminists in 15-M became key players in local and national governments, gradually increasing the attention and focus on feminism in Podemos (Flesher Fominaya, 2020a), and from the first establishing feminist principles as key guiding principles in Barcelona en Comú and Ahora Madrid. Indeed the feminization of politics has been a noted key feature of the so-called 'new municipalism' in Spain (La Barbera et al., 2022; Roth & Shea Baird, 2017; Russell, 2019). Zechner (2020) provides a genealogy of the roots of autonomous-feminist experimentation and theorizing in the precarity and squatting movements of Spanish feminism in the early 2000s, and its development in 15-M, prior to its uptake in the new municipalist movements and policy developments in Barcelona.

The reclaiming of public space for the citizens, a key aspect of the Acampada's political raison d'etre, also played a key motivating force in many of the municipalist policies. As Barcelona mayor Ada Colau put it: 'Public space is the place, par excellence, for democracy: this space that belongs to all of us ... The more public space there is, and the better its quality, the better the quality of the democracy' (Gessen, 2018). Many leaders in new municipalist movements were explicitly committed not only to a feminist policy agenda but to a fundamental transformation of the way politics itself was conceived, moving away from a hyper-masculinized model characterized by authoritative voice, competition, conflict and arrogance to a collaborative form of engagement. As Colau said in the documentary about her election to mayor 'Alcaldessa' (Pau Faus, 2016), 'You can be in politics without being a strong, arrogant, super-confident male, who has the answer to everything and has no doubts. [...] I wanted to show that there are other ways of doing politics.' The municipalist governments of change adopted policies that were explicitly motivated by 15-M, especially its commons thinking and feminism, prioritizing care for the most vulnerable and, in Barcelona, developing a publicly owned energy company to supply energy to municipal buildings and the combat energy poverty.

Reclaiming representative democracy: A radical impact in deficient really existing democracy?

The political, social, and cultural laboratory of the 15-M acampadas was concerned with the central problematic of democracy. We have shown how these imaginaries and emerging forms of experimentation were later developed to impact democracy in many arenas. But from the beginning, 15-M was founded on a critique of really existing democracy's democratic deficits. 15-M activists juxtaposed 'real democracy' to 'really existing democracy'. In the wake of the crash, participants in the squares were not just experimenting and dreaming up alternative democratic imaginaries, they were also doing something much less radical: holding political representatives accountable for failing to uphold their end of the representative democracy bargain with regards to guaranteeing the application of constitutional rights and representing the rights and needs of citizens.

We want to suggest that social movement impact on democracy doesn't only mean calling for new reforms or implementing unprecedented procedural strategies. In the context of arguably grossly deficient 'really existing democracy', where constitutional rights are not upheld or prioritized, and are in fact eroded, the demand that elected representatives follow their own rules and uphold basic rights becomes a form of protest in itself. In this context calls for democratic regeneration, especially when these influence public awareness and public opinion, can be seen as a form of movement impact on democracy. The *democratic turn* of 15-M (Flesher Fominaya, 2015a) represented a 'reclaiming of democratic institutions' which we can see in numerous examples: including activists from the anti-Gag Law platform *No Somos Delito* holding assemblies in parliament in an attempt to bring the movement practices into the 'casa del pueblo' (house of the people); 15MpaRato's use of the civil law and courts to bring Rodrigo Rato and others to trial; or the transformation of electoral political campaigns by the movements for graphic liberation in Madrid and Barcelona (MLG, 2017).

One illustrative example of this comes from the renewed struggles over housing following the *acampadas*. Urban housing struggles in Spain, especially those that involve political squatting, have long offered a radical critique of *inter alia* speculation, gentrification, displacement of marginalized communities, the use of public space, lack of affordable public housing, and abusive mortgage and financing regimes and practices. In Spain's major cities, the network of urban squatted social centers provides a crucial resource for social movement organizing, and they played a key role in supporting the occupied squares during the 15-M camps (Flesher Fominaya, 2020a; Martinez & García, 2015). Housing struggles formed one of the most emblematic and powerful waves of action following the global crash, and they preceded 15-M, but were given a renewed energy and increased in scale following the occupations of the squares. In the wake of the crisis and its attendant foreclosures and evictions, housing struggles exploded. During this wave of housing struggles, a notable shift in language towards the constitutionally guaranteed right to housing took place, in keeping with the broader framing of a myriad of issues in 15-M within the central problematic of democracy (Flesher Fominaya, 2015b, 2020b). The fact that even radical housing movements adopted a rights-based approach, appealing to the Constitution, (D'Adda, 2021) is further evidence of the evolution towards hybridity and the 'democratic turn' that characterizes this movement and its consequences. In a context of global democratic backsliding and rising authoritarianism (Freedom House 2022, Economist Intelligence 2022, V-Dem Democracy Reports 2020–2022), this in itself may be a 'radical' approach and a significant impact on democracy.

Conclusion

Our proposal in this article has been that current dominant understandings of social movement impact on democracy (as democratization in the form of regime change and innovation in governing institutions) while important and necessary, can be fruitfully expanded on. We drew on a wide range of research on the paradigmatic case of the 15-M pro-democracy movement to highlight several further ways social movements' democratic impact might be explored. Building on excellent work by Della Porta (2020), Font & García-Espín (2020) and others, we recognize and develop analysis on the key contribution of 15-M to democratic innovation in the institutions (arena 6). We argued that democratic imaginaries that shape policy and political visions (and not just procedural innovations) are also important influences on institutions. But we also argue for other forms of democratic innovation and impact beyond institutions: namely an increase in citizen participation through increased mobilization and intensification of movement social capital; transformations in public opinion; transformation of the electoral landscape; promoting democratic innovation within social movements and civil society organizations; and experimenting with party forms. Finally, we consider whether reclaiming representative democracy might be a radical act considering the deficiencies of really existing democracy and the decline of citizen trust and engagement. We are not suggesting that social movement impacts are monolithic, they always combine with a range of different factors to produce their effects. The point is not that they alone produce outcomes, but rather that without them, the same outcomes would not have been likely or possible. While direct impacts of movements are notoriously difficult to 'prove', the 15-M case study has generated a wealth of robust research that suggest that a much more open approach to social movement impacts on democracy is warranted.

What is clear from our analysis is that in 15-M, the experimentation of the occupied squares carries over into innovation attempts that are not limited to institutional governing arenas. Yet much of the literature considers democratic innovation or impact of social movements in this narrow way (see Elstub & Escobar, 2017 for a review). When we widen our gaze beyond formal institutional forms of democratic innovation, we are better able to evaluate the impact of social movements on democracy. We have analyzed several arenas to demonstrate how multiple democratic imaginaries and alternatives nurtured in the squares led later to concrete impacts on Spanish democracy both within and beyond governing institutions. Although we have engaged with contemporary literature on models of democracy, we have shown that neither activists nor their *democracy innovation repertoires* (Flesher Fominaya, 2022) correspond neatly to these classical ideal types. Ideal types enable us to have an indication of the diversity of imaginaries present in the movement, and how these are expressed in myriad combinations and synergies in specific initiatives and experiments. Our treatment of these models was by no means exhaustive: while we focused here on technopolitical imaginaries and their role in several arenas of democratic impact, we also highlighted the importance of feminist democratic imaginaries in the movement. Had space allowed, we could have developed more discussion on urban commons frameworks and right to the city, environmental/Anthropocene imaginaries, etc. These frameworks have also motivated the implementation of democratic initiatives in these diverse arenas as scholarship has shown (e.g. Zechner, 2020 in the case of the urban commons). The laboratory of the *Acampada* continued to develop in multiple arenas in Spain, 'occupying' the courts, the unions, the workplaces, the media, movement spaces, political parties and governing institutions.

The case of 15-M's impact on democracy also leads us to some specific theoretical insights. The first is that the opposition made between deliberation and contention as two alternative forms of political engagement (see Talpin, 2015) is not upheld for pro-democracy movements. In this case, deliberation and participation in the squares became not only a prefigurative experiment but a form of protest against a deficient really existing democracy, *making deliberation in the occupied squares itself a form of contention*.

The second is that previous findings from research on the Global Justice Movement of the inverse relationship between loosely organized groups and willingness to engage in institutionalized processes (Della Porta, 2009) is also not upheld for the 15-M movement. Instead, as has been noted earlier (Flesher Fominaya, 2015a, 2020a; Martínez, 2016) the movement's democratic turn represented a form of hybrid autonomy, where autonomous groups actively sought to reclaim and engage with parliament (framed as 'the house of the people'), the electoral process, and democratic institutions. This process was facilitated by the continuity between movement and institutional actors, but also by the adoption of elastic frames that enabled activists to overcome their cognitive dissonance, such as a belief in digital democratic imaginaries that would 'overcome' some of the tensions and barriers between citizens and representatives. The willingness to adopt a more hybrid form of autonomy also meant that even experimental spaces, actors and initiatives nevertheless influenced (directly and indirectly) institutionalized processes, thereby increasing the movement's impact on democratic innovation (even if the outcomes might not be what was desired or expected).

Pro-democracy movements like 15-M, which is an evolution of a rich tradition of autonomous movements in Spain, seem to have some characteristics and dynamics that distinguish them from more narrowly defined or focused movements. The ability to create cohesion across diversity, a hallmark of autonomous movements active in the Global Justice mobilizations, was taken even further in 15-M. Framing the movement around a central imaginary and problematic of democracy was an inclusive means of integrating a wide range of issues and participants; highly politicized 'radical' and less politicized actors; and more loosely organized and more institutionally organized groups, working towards common goals. Pro-democracy movements differ from more narrowly defined movements in this regard, and this elasticity of both identity requirements (anyone can join) and issue framing (almost any issue can be integrated into the pro-democracy framing) potentially enables a wide range of impacts on democratic innovation. Navigating between openness and elasticity and maintaining a cohesive and reciprocally constituted movement across diversity is a key challenge and one the 15-M movement has handled remarkably well despite internal debates and differences.

The analysis here has also been concerned with providing a more robust understanding of the term 'democratic laboratory,' a metaphor that has been applied often to 15-M and other autonomous pro-democracy movements. In what sense are pro-democracy movements laboratories? The 15-M political laboratory was a space that originated in the occupied squares and extended into numerous other arenas. The *acampadas* served as chrysalides and crucibles (Flesher Fominaya, 2020a) in which different political traditions and political action repertoires cross-pollinated. The laboratories were spaces that combined different political action repertoires to experiment in aid of a clear goal, 'real democracy', but a goal that was reflected in a variety of democratic imaginaries. Activists were receptive to a wide range of proposals, visions, and strategies. Despite this heterogeneity, they shared a desire to delve deeply into the problematic of democracy as a means of experimenting with different forms of political action (direct action, voting, deliberation, consciousness raising, pedagogical work, creative forms of protest, sortition, etc.). Rather than attempting to find and agree on closed formulas or solutions, participants opted for creative experimentation, in which democracy was an open horizon and continual work in progress. This openness, plurality and experimentation extended beyond the squares into diverse arenas and spaces, from street mobilization and new movement collectives, platforms and initiatives, to experimenting with party forms, or trying to transform representative institutions to bring them closer to citizens in a meaningful way, or to reclaim them for their original purposes to serve citizens and uphold democratic values. It is this combination of experimentation and non-predefined form or result that makes the laboratory metaphor an effective one for understanding the impact and role of 15-M on democracy over the last decade.

Innovation experiments are not necessarily long-lasting or 'successful' and the dream of transforming representative democracy and institutional sclerosis is very far from being fulfilled. 'Real democracy' is a horizon that always moves out of reach whenever you approach it. Institutional initiatives can be reversed by changes in government, and there are still important barriers to effective citizen uptake and lasting political cultural change in parties and institutions. Cultural change is the most important aspect of lasting political change, and it takes a long and sustained effort to achieve. The case of 15-M shows us, however, that social movements driven by a strong pro-democracy ethos can provide a creative laboratory that can yield democratic innovation experiments that can potentially move us in that direction.

Our argument here is not merely purposive with respect to developing new lines of research. We also want to argue that adopting this broader approach to democratic impact provides a more balanced assessment of movement outcomes, particularly with regard to success or failure. Movements like 15-M and other 'occupy' movements are often disparaged as having served no purpose because they failed to deliver regime change or a radical transformation of governing structures. Our analysis highlights that adopting such restrictive criteria to evaluate movement outcomes is counter-productive and leads us away from a nuanced understanding of the role of social movements in democratic innovation, which can take many forms. Although less dramatic and structural than regime change or institutional reform, these impacts are nevertheless important, as we hope to have shown.

Notes

1. **Notes.**
   See a wealth of references and discussion of the debate between elite driven versus populist/movement driven transitions to democracy in Tilly (1993/1994).
2. In June 2011 the *acampadas* were lifted by the 15 M activists who decided to move to the neighborhoods after a series of lengthy debates in the general assemblies. For more on this process in Madrid, see Flesher Fominaya (2020a).
3. Más Madrid is itself an offshoot of 15-M. It is a political party resulting from the split between the founders of Podemos, a so-called 'movement-party' that emerged in the wake of 15-M (see Della Porta, Fernández, et al., 2017; Flesher Fominaya, 2020a). Mónica García's popularity and influence has increased greatly during the pandemic, where she has spoken out against abuses and corruption in health care provision and policy, as well as calling attention to working conditions and patient conditions resulting from mismanagement and underfunding. As such, she embodies participatory/deliberative, contentious, institutionalized and monitory forms of democratic innovation.
4. We are indebted to Revilla-Blanco et al. (2015) for compiling this information, which was reverified by Flesher Fominaya. The original source is from the Ministry of the Interior and the data is available at www.interior.gob.es under 'nuarios y estadísticas'. Data from 2013 does not include Catalonia.
5. Podemos is a new political party that sought to channel 15 M support and demands and quickly rose to prominence after 2014 before declining. At the time of writing it is a minority partner in the PSOE LED government in Spain. It forms part of a coalition that is currently the fourth parliamentary party, with Podemos holding 26 seats of the 35 seats of the coalition (out of 350 total).
6. Ciudadanos is a conservative pro-Spanish unity (and anti-Catalan independence) party whose declining fortunes recovered as a result of the political space opened up by Podemos and 15-M.
7. See also their webpage: https://15mparato.wordpress.com/ 15MpaRato is also related to the Xnet project, which can be found here: https://xnet-x.net/en/.
8. You can see their respective webpages here: https://decide.madrid.es/and https://decidim.barcelona.

Acknowledgements

The authors would like to thank Priska Daphi and the anonymous reviewers for their helpful feedback on this manuscript, which greatly improved it. We also want to thank Simon Tormey for early discussions about the special issue as a whole.

Disclosure statement

No potential conflict of interest was reported by the authors.

ORCID

Cristina Flesher Fominaya http://orcid.org/0000-0002-6129-2313
Ramón A. Feenstra http://orcid.org/0000-0002-4775-8762

References

15MpaRato. n.d. https://xnet-x.net/docs/15MpaRato-dossier-english.pdf

Alabao, N. (2016). "Qué Tiene Que Ver La Democracia Interna de Podemos Con El Cambio En España?" *Ctxt.Es*, December 21, https://ctxt.es/es/20161221/Politica/10199/Podemos-Vistalegre- Iglesias- Errejon- anticapitalistas- proporcionalidad.htm.

Alabao, N. (2017a). "Historia de Dos Vistalegres." *Ctxt.Es*, February 11, https://ctxt.es/es/20170208/Politica/11066/vistalegre-2-podemos-iglesias-errejon.htm.

Alabao, N. (2017b). "Por Qué Hay Una Cultura Política de Guerra En Podemos?" *Ctxt.Es*, February 5, https://ctxt.es/es/20170201/Firmas/10954/podemos-vistalegre-iglesias-errejon-guerra.htm.

Alberich-Nistal, T. (2012). Antecedents, achievements and challenges of the Spanish 15M movement. In B. Tejerina & I. Perugorría (Eds.), *From social to political. New forms of mobilization and democratization* (pp. 93–111). Argitalpen.

Amenta, E., & Caren, N. (2004). The legislative, organizational, and beneficiary consequences of state-oriented challengers. In D. Snow, S. Soule, H. P. Kriesi, & H. McCammon (Eds.), *The Blackwell Companion to Social Movements* (pp. 461–488). Blackwell.

Antena 3 Noticias. (2017). Sánchez asegura que el PSOE "representará" al movimiento del 15-M y trabajará para formar una "mayoría alternativa". https://www.antena3.com/noticias/espana/sanchez-asegura-que-psoe-representara-movimiento-15m_20170618594662830cf26e79abb6d189.html

Barandiaran, X., Calleja, A., Monterde, A., Aragón, P., Linares, J., Romero, C., & Pereira, A. (2017). Decidim: Redes políticas y tecnopolíticas para la democracia participativa. *Recerca*, 21(1), 137–150. https://doi.org/10.6035/Recerca.2017.21.8

Barbas, A., & Treré, E. (2022). The rise of a new media ecosystem: Exploring 15m's educommunicative legacy for radical democracy. *Social Movement Studies*, 1–21. Online first. https://doi.org/10.1080/14742837.2022.2070738

Barber, B. (2003). *Strong democracy: Participatory politics for a new age*. University of California Press.

Bermejo, Y. (2017). Future democracies: Laboratory of collective intelligence for participatory democracy. https://archive.org/details/FutureDemocraciesLCPD

Betancur Nuez, G., & Santos, F. G. (2023). La configuración del campo de estudio de los movimientos sociales en España (1980-2020). *RES Revista Española de Sociología*, 32(1), 145. https://doi.org/10.22325/fes/res.2023.145

Blee, K. M. (2012). *Democracy in the making: How activist groups form*. Oxford University Press.

Bosi, L., Giugni, M., & Uba, K. (Eds.). (2016). *The consequences of social movements*. Cambridge University Press.

Breines, W. (1989). *Community and organization in the new left 1962-1968: The great refusal*. Rutgers University Press.

Bua, A., & Bussu, S. (2021). Between governance-driven democratisation and democracy-driven governance: Explaining changes in participatory governance in the case of barcelona. *European Journal of Political Research*, 60(3), 716–737. https://doi.org/10.1111/1475-6765.12421

Burnheim, J. (1985). *Is democracy possible?: The alternative to electoral democracy*. California: University of California Press.

Burnheim, J. (2006). *Is democracy possible? The alternative to electoral democracy*. Sydney University Press.

Calvo, K., & Romeo, A. (2022). *15-M mobilizations and the penalization of counter-hegemonic protest in contemporary Spain, social movement studies*. Online first. https://doi.org/10.1080/14742837.2022.2061943

Candón Mena, J., Montero Sánchez, D., & Calle Collado, Á. (2018). Discourses and practices of radical democracy. The 15M movement as a space of mobilization. *Partecipazione e Conflitto, 11* (2), 571–598. https://doi.org/10.1285/i20356609v11i2p571

Casanueva, A. (2021). Can chants in the street change politics' tune? Evidence from the 15M movement in Spain April 22, 2021. Available at SSRN: https://ssrn.com/abstract=3831874.10.2139/ssrn.3831874

Casas-Salleras, A., Davesa, F., & Congosto, M. (2016). La cobertura mediática de una acción «conectiva»: la interacción entre el movimiento 15-M y los medios de comunicación. *REIS Revista Española de Investigaciones Sociológicas, 155*, 73–96. https://doi.org/10.5477/cis/reis.155.73

Casero-Ripollés, A. (2020). Alternative media and social movements in Europe's digital landscape. In C. Flesher Fominaya & R. Feenstra (Eds.), *Routledge handbook of contemporary European social movements: Protest in turbulent times* (pp. 326–340). Routledge.

Casero-Ripollés, A., & Feenstra, R. A. (2012). The 15-M movement and the new media: A case study of how new themes were introduced into Spanish political discourse. *Media International Australia, 144*(1), 68–76. https://doi.org/10.1177/1329878X1214400111

Casero Ripollés, A., & López-Meri, A. (2015). Redes sociales, periodismo de datos y democracia monitorizada. In F. Campos-Freire & J. Rúas-Araújo (Eds.), *Las redes sociales digitales en el ecosistema mediático* (pp. 96–113). Sociedad Latina de Comunicación Social.

Charnock, G., March, H., & Ribera-Fumaz, R. (2021). From smart to rebel city? Worlding, provincialising and the Barcelona model. *Urban Studies, 58*(3), 581–600. https://doi.org/10.1177/0042098019872119

Chilton, P. (1994). Mechanics of change: Social movements, transnational coalitions, and the transformation processes in Eastern Europe. *Democratization, 1*(1), 151–181. https://doi.org/10.1080/13510349408403385

Chironi, D., & Fittipaldi, R. (2017). Social movements and new forms of political organization: Podemos as a hybrid party. *Partecipazione e Conflitto, 10*, 275–305. https://doi.org/10.1285/i20356609v10i1p275

Clemens, E. S. (1998). To move mountains: Collective action and the possibility of institutional change. In A. Giugni, D. McAdam, & C. Tilly (Eds.), *From contention to democracy* (pp. 109–123). Rowman and Littlefield.

Coleman, G. (2012). *Coding freedom: The ethics and aesthetics of hacking*. Princeton University Press.

Costa Delgado, J. (2017). Resistencias a la introducción del sorteo entre el asamblearismo y la institucionalización: el caso de Podemos en Cádiz. *Daímon, 72*(72), 221–237. https://doi.org/10.6018/daimon/293951

Costa Delgado, J., & Moreno-Pestaña, J. L. (2019). Democracy and sortition: Arguments in favor of randomness. In C. Flesher Fominaya & R. Feenstra (Eds.), *Routledge handbook of contemporary European social movements: Protest in turbulent times* (pp. 100–111). Routledge.

Cruells, M., & Ezquerra, S. (2015). Procesos de voluntad democratizadora: La expresión feminista en el 15-M. *ACME: An International Journal for Critical Geographies, 14*(1), 42–60. https://142.207.145.31/index.php/acme/article/view/1133

D'Adda, G. (2021). Urban mobilizations and municipal policies to un-make housing precarity: The Barcelona experiments. *City*, 1–24. https://doi.org/10.1080/13604813.2021.1981696

Della Porta, D. (2009). *Democracy in social movements*. Palgrave Macmillan.

Della Porta, D. (2020). *How social movements can save democracy*. Polity.

Della Porta, D., & Doerr, N. (2018). Deliberation in protests and social movements. In A. Bächtiger, J. Dryzek, J. Mansbridge, & M. Warren (Eds.), *The Oxford handbook of deliberative democracy* (pp. 391–406). Oxford University Press.

Della Porta, D., & Felicetti, A. (2017). IX democratic innovations and social movements. In The Hertie School of Governance (Berlin) (Ed.), *The governance report 2017* (pp. 127–142). Oxford University Press.

Della Porta, D., & Felicetti, A. (2019). Innovating democracy against democratic stress in Europe: Social movements and democratic experiments. *Representation, 58*(1), 67–84. https://doi.org/10.1080/00344893.2019.1624600

Della Porta, D., Fernández, J., Kouki, H., & Mosca, L. (2017). *Movement parties against austerity*. Polity.

Deseriis, M., & Vittori, D. (2019). Platform politics in Europe| the impact of online participation platforms on the internal democracy of two Southern European parties: Podemos and the five star movement. *International Journal of Communication, 13*, 5696–5714. https://ijoc.org/index.php/ijoc/issue/view/15

Diani, M. (1997). Social movements and social capital: A network perspective on movement outcomes. *Mobilization: An International Quarterly, 2*(2), 129–147. https://doi.org/10.17813/maiq.2.2.w6087622383h4341

Economist Intelligence Unit (2022) Democracy Index 2021: The China Challenge, Report available: https://www.eiu.com/n/campaigns/democracy-index-2021/

Elstub, S., & Escobar, O. (2017). A typology of democratic innovations. Conference Paper, Political Studies Association 2017, Glasgow. Retrieved from https://www.psa.ac.uk/sites/default/files/conference/papers/2017/A%20Typology%20of%20Democratic%20Innovations%20-%20Elstub%20and%20Escobar%202017.pdf

Faus, P. (2016). *Film Alcaldessa*. Nanouk Films.

Feenstra, R. (2015). Activist and citizen political repertoire in Spain: A reflection based on civil society theory and different logics of political participation. *Journal of Civil Society, 11*(3), 242–258. https://doi.org/10.1080/17448689.2015.1060662

Feenstra, R. (2017). Democracia por sorteo en las nuevas formaciones políticas: Un debate con rastros de la teoría política clásica y contemporánea. *Daímon, 72*(72), 205–219. https://doi.org/10.6018/295601

Feenstra, R., & Keane, J. (2014). Politics in Spain: A case of monitory democracy. *VOLUNTAS: International Journal of Voluntary and Nonprofit Organizations, 25*(5), 1262–1280. https://doi.org/10.1007/s11266-014-9461-2

Feenstra, R., & Tormey, S. (2023). From social mobilisation to institutional politics: Reflecting on the impact of municipalism in Madrid and Barcelona. *Social Movement Studies, 22*(1), 80–98. https://doi.org/10.1080/14742837.2021.1993181

Feenstra, R., Tormey, S., Casero-Ripollés, A., & Keane, J. (2017). *Refiguring democracy: The Spanish political laboratory*. Routledge.

Fishkin, J. S. (1997). *The voice of the people: Public opinion and democracy*. Yale University Press.

Flesher Fominaya, C. (2007). Autonomous movements and the institutional left: Two approaches in tension in Madrid's anti-globalization network. *South European Society & Politics, 12*(3), 335–358. https://doi.org/10.1080/13608740701495202

Flesher Fominaya, C. (2011). The Madrid bombings and popular protest: Misinformation, counterinformation, mobilisation and elections after '11-M'. *Contemporary Social Science: Journal of the Academy of Social Sciences, 6*(3), 1–19. https://doi.org/10.1080/21582041.2011.603910

Flesher Fominaya, C. (2014). *Spain's marches of dignity, 22M, 2014: Not anti-politics*. Open Democracy. https://www.opendemocracy.net/en/can-europe-make-it/spains-marches-of-dignity-22m-2014-not-antipolitics/

Flesher Fominaya, C. (2015a). Debunking spontaneity: Spain's 15-M/Indignados as autonomous movement. *Social Movement Studies, 14*(2), 142–163. https://doi.org/10.1080/14742837.2014.945075

Flesher Fominaya, C. (2015b). Redefining the crisis/redefining democracy: Mobilizing for the right to housing in Spain's PAH movement. *South European Society & Politics, 20*(4), 465–485. https://doi.org/10.1080/13608746.2015.1058216

Flesher Fominaya, C. (2017). European anti-austerity and pro-democracy protests in the wake of the global financial crisis. *Social Movement Studies, 16*(1), 1–20. https://doi.org/10.1080/14742837.2016.1256193

Flesher Fominaya, C. (2019). The Diffusion of Protest following the 2007-2008 Global Crash. *The Brown Journal of World Affairs, 26*(1), 59–72. https://bjwa.brown.edu/26-1/the-diffusion-of-protest-following-the-2007-2008-global-crash/

Flesher Fominaya, C. (2020a). *Democracy reloaded: Inside Spain's political laboratory from 15-M to podemos*. Oxford University Press.

Flesher Fominaya, C. (2020b). *Social movements in a globalized world*. Bloomsbury Publishing.

Flesher Fominaya, C. (2022). Reconceptualizing democratic innovation: "Democratic innovation repertoires" and their impact within and beyond social movements. *Democratic Theory, 9*(2), 78–100. https://doi.org/10.3167/dt.2022.090205

Font, J. (2017). Nuevos mecanismos participativos: un concepto, distintas realidades. Recerca. *Recerca Revista de pensament i anàlisi, 21*(21), 131–136. https://doi.org/10.6035/Recerca.2017.21.7

Font, J., & García-Espín, P. (2020). From Indignad@s to Mayors? Participatory dilemmas in Spanish municipal movements. In C. F. Fominaya & R. Feenstra (Eds.), *Routledge Handbook of Contemporary European Social Movements* (pp. 387–401). Routledge.

Freedom House, (2016). Freedom in the world 2016: Anxious dictators, wavering democracies: Global freedom under pressure, 3. https://freedomhouse.org/sites/default/files/FH_FITW_Report_2016.pdf

Freedom House (2022). Freedom in the World 2022. The Global Expansion of Authoritarian Rule. https://freedomhouse.org/sites/default/files/2022-02/FIW_2022_PDF_Booklet_Digital_Final_Web.pdf

Galdón Corbella, C. (2018). Interacción entre los Movimientos Sociales yel Feminismo: Estrategias Feministas en la Acampada de la Puerta del Solde Madrid. In Comité Organizador Noviembre Feminista 2016 (Ed), *Comité Organizador Noviembre Feminista 2016Comité Organizador Noviembre Feminista 2016* (pp. 229–240). Instituto de Investigaciones Feministas. Universidad Complutense de Madrid.

Gámez Fuentes, M. J. (2015). Feminisms and the 15M movement inSpain: Between frames of recognition and contexts of action. *Social Movement Studies, 14*(3), 359–365. https://doi.org/10.1080/14742837.2014.994492

Gamson, W. (1990). *The strategy of social protest*. Dorsey Press.

Ganuza, E., & Mendiharat, A. (2020). *La democracia es posible: El sorteo cívico y la deliberación para rescatar el poder de la ciudadanía*. Consonni.

Ganuza, E., & Menendez-Blanco, M. (2020). Te ha tocado? El sorteo llega a la política de Madrid. Recerca. *Revista de Pensament i Anàlisi, 25*(1), 95–110. https://doi.org/10.6035/Recerca.2020.25.1.6

Garrido, P. (2017). *Spain: The end of two-party dominance*. IPE (Investment & Pensions Europe Editorial). Retrieved from https://www.ipe.com/reports/special-reports/outlook-foreurope/spain-the-end-of-two-party-dominance/10019246.article

Gelb, J., & Hart, V. (1999). Feminist politics in a hostile environment. In M. Giugni & D. McAdam. & C. Tilly (Eds.), *How social movements matter* (pp. 149–181). University of Minnesota Press.

Gerbaudo, P. (2016). *The mask and the flag: The rise of citizenism in global protest*. Hurst Publishers.

Gerbaudo, P. (2021). Are digital parties more democratic than traditional parties? Evaluating podemos and movimento 5 stelle's online decision-making platforms. *Party Politics, 27*(4), 730–742. https://doi.org/10.1177/1354068819884878

Gessen, M. (2018). Barcelona's experiment in radical democracy, *The New Yorker*, August 6, 2018. Retrieved from https://www.newyorker.com/news/our-columnists/barcelonas-experiment-in-radical-democracy

Giugni, M. G. (1994). The outcomes of social movements: A review of the literature. Working paper no. 197. Center for the Study of Social Change. New School for Social Research. Available at: https://archive-ouverte.unige.ch/unige:112909

Giugni, M. G. (1998). Was it worth the effort? The outcomes and consequences of social movements. *Annual Review of Sociology, 24*(1), 371–393.

Giugni, M. (2004). Personal and biographical consequences. In D. Snow, S. Soule, H. P. Kriesi, & H. McCammon (Eds.), *The Blackwell Companion to Social Movements* (pp. 489–507). Blackwell.

Giugni, M. (2008). Political, biographical, and cultural consequences of social movements. *Sociology Compass, 2*(5), 1582–1600. https://doi.org/10.1111/j.1751-9020.2008.00152.x

Giugni, M., McAdam, D., & Tilly, C. (Eds.). (1998). *From contention to democracy*. Rowman and Littlefield.

Gomez, R., & Ramiro, L. (2019). The limits of organizational innovation and multi-speed membership: Podemos and its new forms of party membership. *Party Politics*, 25(4), 534–546. https://doi.org/10.1177/1354068817742844

González-Bailón, S., Borge-Holthoefer, J., & Moreno, Y. (2013). Broadcasters and hidden influentials in online protest diffusion. *The American Behavioral Scientist*, 57(7), 943–965. https://doi.org/10.1177/0002764213479371

Groves, T., Townson, N., Ofer, I., Herrera, A., & Parishes, N. (2017). *Social movements and the Spanish transition*. Palgrave Macmillan.

Günther, R., & Montero, J. R. (2009). *The politics of Spain*. Cambridge University Press.

Gunther, R., Sani, G., & Shabad, G. (1988). *Spain after Franco: The making of a competitive party system*. Univ of California Press.

Gutierrez, B. (2017). Madrid as democracy lab, open democracy, Available at: https://www.opendemocracy.net/en/democraciaabierta/madrid-as-democracy-lab/

Habermas, J. (1996). *Between facts and norms. Contributions to a discourse theory of law and democracy*. MIT Press.

Hinojosa Navarro, G. A. (2019). Un intento de ciberdemocracia en España: El portal participativo 'Decide Madrid' del Ayuntamiento de Madrid. *Estudios sobre el Mensaje Periodístico*, 25(2), 883. https://doi.org/10.5209/esmp.64814

Hipsher, P. (1998). Democratic transitions and social movements outcomes. In M. Giugni, D. McAdam, & C. Tilly (Eds.), *From contention to democracy* (pp. 149–168). Rowman and Littlefield.

Hughes, N. (2011). 'Young people took to the streets and all of a sudden all of the political parties got old': The 15M movement in Spain. *Social Movement Studies*, 10(4), 407–413. https://doi.org/10.1080/14742837.2011.614109

Ibarra Güell, P., Martí Puig, S., Cortina-Oriol, M., & Sribman, A. (2018). *Nuevos Movimientos Sociales: De la calle a los ayuntamientos*. Icaria.

Jaime-Castillo, A. M., Coller, X., & Cordero, G. (2018). New parties and new ways of candidate selection in Spain. In X. Coller, G. Cordero, & A. M. Jaime-Castillo (Eds.), *The selection of politicians in times of crisis* (pp. 226–242). Routledge.

Jeppesen, S. (2021). Intersectional technopolitics in social movement and media activism. *International Journal of Communication*, 15(23), 1961–1983.

Jiménez-Sánchez, M., Coller, X., & Portillo-Pérez, M. (2018). Mps of traditional parties' perceptions on candidate selection in times of political crisis and reform. In G. Cordero & X. Coller (Eds.), *Democratizing candidates selection. New methods, old receipts?* (pp. 147–171). Palgrave.

Johnston, H., & Almeida, P. (Eds.). (2006). *Latin American social movements: Globalization, democratization, and transnational networks*. Rowman & Littlefield.

Kaldor, M., & Selchow, S. (2013). The 'bubbling up' of subterranean politics in Europe. *Journal of Civil Society*, 9, 78–99.

Keane, J. (1998). *Civil society: Old images, new visions*. John Wiley & Sons.

Keane, J. (2009). *The life and death of democracy*. Simon & Schuster.

Keane, J. (2013). *Democracy and media decadence*. Cambridge University Press.

Keane, J. (2022). *The shortest history of democracy*. Black Inc.

Kitschelt, H. (2006). Movement parties. In R. S. Katz & W. J. Crotty (Eds.), *Handbook of party politics* (pp. 278–291). Sage.

Kroll, A. (2011). How Occupy wall street really got started. In S. van Gelder (Ed.), *This changes everything: Occupy wall street and the 99% movement* (pp. 16–21). Berrett-Koehler Publishers.

La Barbera, M., Espinosa-Fajardo, J., & Caravantes, P. (2022). Implementing intersectionality in public policies: Key factors in the Madrid city council, Spain. *Politics & Gender*, 1–28. https://doi.org/10.1017/S1743923X22000241

León, P. S. (2010). Radicalism without representation: On the character of social movements in the Spanish transition to democracy. In G. Alonso & D. Muro (Eds.), *The politics and memory of democratic transition* (pp. 109–126). Routledge.

Levy, S. (1984). *Hackers: Heroes of the computer revolution*. O'Reilly.

Lobera, J. (2015). De movimientos a partidos: La cristalización electoral de la protesta. *Revista Española de Sociología, 24*, 97–105. https://recyt.fecyt.es/index.php/res/article/view/65424

Lobera, J., & Parejo, D. (2019). Streets and institutions? The electoral extension of social movements and its tensions. In U. Gordon & R. Kinna (Eds.), *Routledge handbook of radical politics* (pp. 314–325). Routledge.

Maeckelbergh, M. (2009). *The will of the many: How the alter globalization movement is changing the face of democracy*. Pluto Press.

Manin, B. (1997). *The principles of representative government*. Cambridge University Press.

Martínez, M. A. (2016). Between autonomy and hybridity: Urban struggles within the 15M movement in Spain. In H. Thorn, M. Meyer, & K. Thorn (Eds.), *Urban uprisings* (pp. 253–281). Palgrave.

Martinez, M., & García, A. (2015). Ocupar las plazas, liberar edificios (the occupation of squares and the squatting of buildings). *ACME: An International Journal for Critical Geographies, 14*(1), 157–184. Available at. https://acme-journal.org/index.php/acme/article/view/1145

Martínez, M. A., & San Juan, E. D. (2020). Just rekindle hope? Social and political impacts of the 15M movement in Spain. *Revista Latinoamericana Estudios de la Paz y el Conflicto, 1*(1), 13–38. https://doi.org/10.5377/rlpc.v1i1.9514

Marzolf, H., & Ganuza, E. (2016). ¿Enemigos o colegas? El 15M y la hipótesis Podemos. *Empiria Revista de metodología de ciencias sociales*, (33), 89–110. https://doi.org/10.5944/empiria.33.2016.15865

Mattoni, A. (2018). From data extraction to data leaking. Data-activism in Italian and Spanish anti-corruption campaigns. *Partecipazione e Conflitto, 10*(3), 723–746. https://doi.org/10.1285/i20356609v10i3p723

McCorley, C. (2013). Structure, agency and regime change: A comparative analysis of social actors and regime change in South Africa, Zambia and Zimbabwe. *Journal of Contemporary African Studies, 31*(2), 265–282. https://doi.org/10.1080/02589001.2013.781321

Meyer, D. (1999). How the cold war was really won. In M. Giugni, D. Adam, & C. Tilly (Eds.), *How social movements matter* (pp. 182–203). Minnesota University Press.

Moreno Pestaña, J. L. (2017). Los desafíos del sorteo a la democracia, los desafíos de la democracia al sorteo. *Daímon, 72*(72), 7–21. https://doi.org/10.6018/daimon/303241

Mota Consejero, F., & Janoschka, M. (2022). Transforming urban democracy through social movements: The experience of Ahora Madrid. *Social Movement Studies*, 1–18. Online first. https://doi.org/10.1080/14742837.2022.2028615

Movimiento de Liberación Gráfica (MLG). (2017). *Y al final ganamos las elecciones*. Verkami.

Navarro Cueva, F. (2017). El G1000 de Madrid: un ejemplo de sorteo y deliberación como complemento de la representación. *Recerca Revista de pensament i anàlisi, 21*(21), 151–158. https://doi.org/10.6035/Recerca.2017.21.9

Nez, H. (2021). What has become of the Indignados? The biographical consequences of participation in the 15M movement in Madrid (2011–19). *Social Movement Studies*, 1–18. https://doi.org/10.1080/14742837.2021.1977113

Nez, H., & Ganuza, E. (2020). Del 15M a las instituciones: Las políticas participativas de Ahora Madrid (2015-2019). *Encrucijadas: Revista Crítica de Ciencias Sociales, 19*(1), 1–19. https://recyt.fecyt.es/index.php/encrucijadas/article/view/80208

Nicolau Gómez, E. (2023). Feminism and Protest Camps in Spain: From the Indignados to Feminist Encampments. In C. Eschle & A. Bartlett (Eds.), (pp. 115–134). Bristol: Bristol University Press.

Norris, P. (2014). *Democratic deficit: Critical citizens revisited*. Cambridge University Press.

Oberschall, A. (2000). Social movements and the transition to democracy. *Democratization, 7*(3), 25–45. https://doi.org/10.1080/13510340008403670

Ordóñez, V., Feenstra, R. A., & Franks, B. (2018). Spanish anarchist engagements in electoralism: From street to party politics. *Social Movement Studies, 17*(1), 85–98. https://doi.org/10.1080/14742837.2017.1381593

Pateman, C. (1979). *Participation and democratic theory*. Cambridge University Press.

Peña-López, I. (2017a). Citizen participation and the rise of the open source city in Spain. *IT For Change*. Available at: https://opendocs.ids.ac.uk/opendocs/handle/20.500.12413/13006

Peña-López, I. (2017b). Decidim. Barcelona. *IT For Change*. Available at: https://opendocs.ids.ac.uk/opendocs/handle/20.500.12413/13284

The People's Health Movement. (n.d.) Spain: Marea Blanca, A Rising Tide against Privatization. https://phm-na.org/resisting-privatization/spain-marea-blanca-rising-tide-against-privatization/

Pina, V., Torres, L., Royo, S., & Garcia-Rayado, J. (2022). Decide madrid: A Spanish best practice on e-participation. In T. Randma-Liiv, R. Nurske, V. Lember (Eds.), *Engaging citizens in policy making* (pp. 152–165). London, UK: Edward Elgar Publishing.

Polletta, F. (2012). *Freedom is an endless meeting: Democracy in American social movements.* University of Chicago Press.

Portos, M. (2021). *Grievances and public protests: Political mobilisation in Spain in the age of austerity.* Palgrave Macmillan.

Postill, J. (2018). *The Rise of Nerd Politics: Digital Activism and Political Change.* Pluto Press.

Raeburn, N. C. (2004). *Changing corporate America from inside out: Lesbian and gay workplace rights* (Vol. 20). University of Minnesota Press.

Rama, J., Cordero, G., & Zagórski, P. (2021). Three is a Crowd? Podemos, Ciudadanos, and Vox: The end of bipartisanship in Spain. *Frontiers in Political Science*, *95*(3), 1–16. https://doi.org/10.3389/fpos.2021.688130

Revilla-Blanco, M., Garrido, A., Martínez, I., Molina, C., More, H., & Rodríguez, K. (2015). Consecuencias Inesperadas de Las Acciones de Protesta: Reconfiguración Ideológica y Electoral En España (). Unpublished paper.

Revilla-Blanco, M., & Molina-Sánchez, C. (2021). Ciclo de protesta y cambios en el sistema de partidos español: 15M, Mareas y nuevos partidos. *Forum Revista Departamento de Ciencia Política*, *20*(20), 206–232. https://doi.org/10.15446/frdcp.n20.88762

Romanos, E. (2016). Immigrants as Brokers: Dialogical Diffusion from the Spanish Indignados to Occupy Wall Street. *Social movement studies*, *15*(3), 247–262. https://doi.org/10.1080/14742837.2015.1095084

Romanos, E., & Aguilar, S. (2016). Is Spain Still Different?. In O. Fillieule & G. Accornero (Eds.), *Social Movement Studies in Europe: The State of the Art* (pp. 338–355). New York: Berghahn.

Romanos, E., & Sádaba, I. (2022). The evolution of contention in Spain (2000-2017): An analysis of protest cycles. *Revista Española de Investigaciones Sociológicas (REIS)*, *177*, 89–110. https://doi.org/10.5477/cis/reis.177.89

Romanos, E., & Sádaba, I. (2015). La evolución de los marcos (tecno) discursivos del movimiento 15M y sus consecuencias. *Empiria Revista de metodología de ciencias sociales*, *0*(32), 15–36. https://doi.org/10.5944/empiria.32.2015.15307

Rosanvallon, P. (2008). *Counter-democracy: Politics in an Age of Distrust.* Cambridge University Press.

Roth, L., Monterde, A., & Calleja, A. (2019). *Ciudades democráticas. La revuelta municipalista en el ciclo post-15M.* Icaria.

Roth, L., & Shea Baird, K. (2017). Municipalism and the Feminization of Politics. *ROAR Magazine*, 6. Available at. https://roarmag.org/magazine/municipalism-feminization-urban-politics/

Royo, S., Pina, V., & Garcia-Rayado, J. (2020). Decide Madrid: A critical analysis of an award-winning e-participation initiative. *Sustainability*, *12*(4), 1674. https://doi.org/10.3390/su12041674

Rubio-Pueyo, V. (2017). *Municipalism in Spain. From Barcelona to Madrid and Beyond.* Rosa-Luxemburg-Foundation.

Rucht, D. (1999). The impact of environmental movements in western society. In M. Giugni, D. McAdam, & C. Tilly (Eds.), *How Social Movements Matter* (pp. 204–224). University of Minnesota Press.

Russell, B. (2019). Beyond the local trap: New municipalism and the rise of the fearless cities. *Antipode*, *51*(3), 989–1010. https://doi.org/10.1111/anti.12520

Sampedro, V. (Ed.). (2005). *13-M: Multitudes Online.* La Catarata.

Sampedro, V., & Lobera, J. (2014, 1). The Spanish 15- M Movement: A Consensual Dissent?. *Journal of Spanish Cultural Studies, 15*(2), 61–80. https://doi.org/10.1080/14636204.2014.938466

Sánchez, J. L. (2013). *Las diez mareas del cambio*. Roca editorial.

Sandoval, S. (1998). Social Movement and Democratization: The Case of Brazil and the Latin Countries. In M. Guigni, D. McAdam, & C. Tilly (Eds.), *From Contention to Democracy* (pp. 169–202). Rowman and Littlefield.

Santos, B. D. S. Y., & Avrtizer, L. (2004). Introducción: para ampliar el canon democrático. In B. Santos (Ed.), *Democratizar la democracia* (pp. 35–74). Fondo de Cultura Económica.

Sartori, G. (1999). En defensa de la representación política. *Claves de Razón Práctica, 91*, 2–6.

Schneiberg, M., & Lounsbury, M. (2008). Social movements and institutional analysis. In R. Greenwood, C. Oliver, K. Sahlin, & R. Suddaby (Eds.), *The SAGE handbook of organizational institutionalism* (pp. 650–672). Sage.

Schudson, M. (1998). *The good citizen. A history of the American civic life*. Martin Kessler Books.

Siapera, E. (2016). Digital Citizen X. XNet and the Radicalisation of Citizenship. In A. McCosker, S. Vivienne, & A. Johns (Eds.), *Negotiating Digital Citizenship: Control, Contest and Culture* (pp. 95–113). Rowman and Littlefield International.

Siapera, E. (2017). Reclaiming citizenship in the post-democratic condition. *Journal of Citizenship and Globalisation Studies, 1*(1), 24–35. https://doi.org/10.1515/jcgs-2017-0003

Simsa, R., & Totter, M. (2017). Social movement organizations in Spain: Being partial as the prefigurative enactment of social change. *Qualitative Research in Organizations and Management: An International Journal, 12*(4), 280–296. https://doi.org/10.1108/QROM-01-2017-147.0

Sintomer, Y. (2012). Selección aleatoria, autogobierno republicano y democracia deliberativa. *Enrahonar: quaderns de filosofía, 48*, 133–156. https://doi.org/10.5565/rev/enrahonar.131

Sintomer, Y. (2017). Sorteo y política: ¿de la democracia radical a la democracia deliberativa?. *Daímon, 72*(72), 25–43. https://doi.org/10.6018/daimon/295531

Smith, A., & Prieto Martín, P. (2021). Going Beyond the Smart City? Implementing Technopolitical Platforms for Urban Democracy in Madrid and Barcelona. *Journal of Urban Technology, 28*(1–2), 311–330. https://doi.org/10.1080/10630732.2020.1786337

Staggenborg, S. (1988). The consequences of professionalization and formalization in the pro-choice movement. *American sociological review, 53*(4), 585–605. https://doi.org/10.2307/2095851

Staggenborg, S. (2013). Institutionalization of social movements. In B. Klandermans & D. McAdam. London: Blackwell. pp. 181–182, D. A. Snow, D. della Porta (Eds.), *The Wiley-Blackwell Encyclopedia of Social and Political Movements* (pp. 181–182). London: Blackwell.

Subirats, J. (2015a). *Ya nada será lo mismo: Los efectos del cambio tecnológico en la política, los partidos y el activismo juvenil*. Centro Reina Sofía.

Subirats, J. (2015b). Todo se mueve. Acción colectiva, acción conectiva. *RES Revista Española de Sociología, 24*, 123–131. https://recyt.fecyt.es/index.php/res/article/view/65427

Talpin, J. (2015). Democratic Innovations. In D. della Porta & M. Diani (Eds.), *The Oxford handbook of social movements* (pp. 781–792). Oxford University Press.

Tarrow, S. (1989). *Democracy and Disorder: Protest and Politics in Italy, 1965–1975*. Clarendon Press.

Tarrow, S. (1995). Mass mobilization and elite exchange: Democratization episodes in Italy and Spain. *Democratization, 2*(3), 221–245. https://doi.org/10.1080/13510349508403440

Tejerina, B., & Perugorría, I. (2012). Continuities and Discontinuities in Recent Social Mobilizations. From New Social Movements to the Alter-Global Mobilizations and the 15M. In B. Tejerina & I. Perugorría (Eds.), *From Social to Political. New Forms of Mobilization and Democratization* (pp. 93–111). Argitalpen.

Thompson, M. (2021). What's so new about New Municipalism?. *Progress in human geography, 45*(2), 317–342. https://doi.org/10.1177/0309132520909480

Tilly, C. (1993/1994). Social movements as historically specific clusters of political performances. *Berkeley Journal of Sociology, 38*(1), 1–30.

Tilly, C. (2004). *Social Movements, 1768–2004*. Routledge.

Tilly, C., & Wood, L. J. (2015). *Social Movements 1768-2012*. Routledge.

Tindall, D. B., Cormier, J., & Diani, M. (2012). Network social capital as an outcome of social movement mobilization: Using the position generator as an indicator of social network diversity. *Social Networks*, 34(4), 387-395. https://doi.org/10.1016/j.socnet.2011.12.007

Toret, J. (2013). Tecnopolítica: la potencia de las multitudes conectadas. El sistema red 15M, un nuevo paradigma de la política distribuida. *IN3 Working Paper Series*. https://tecnopolitica.net/sites/default/files/1878-5799-3-PB%202.pdf

Tormey, S. (2015). *The end of Representative Politics*. Polity.

Tormey, S., & Feenstra, R. (2015). Reinventing the political party in Spain: The case of 15M and the Spanish mobilisations. *Policy Studies*, 36(6), 590-606. https://doi.org/10.1080/01442872.2015.1073243

Trujillo, G. (2018). Queering the Indignadxs movement in spain: Conflicts, resistances and collective learnings. In J. DeFilippis, M. Yarbrough, & A. Jones (Eds.), *Queer Activism After Marriage Equality* (pp. 187-194). Routledge.

Van Reybrouck, D. (2016). *Against elections: the case for democracy*. Random House.

Whittier, N. (1995). *Feminist Generations: The Persistence of the Radical Women's Movement*. Temple University Press.

Whittier, N. (1997). Political generations, micro-cohorts, and the transformation of social movements. *American sociological review*, 62(5), 760-778. https://doi.org/10.2307/2657359

Whittier, N. (2004). The consequences of social movements for each other. In D. Snow, S. Soule, & H. Kriesi (Eds.), *The Blackwell companion to social movements* (pp. 531-551). Blackwell Publishing Ltd. https://doi.org/10.1002/9780470999103

Zechner, M. (2020) HETEROPOLITICS Refiguring the Common and the Political, European Council Report ERC-COG-2016-724692 D3.6, Available https://ikee.lib.auth.gr/record/325747/files/Case%20Studies%20in%20Spain.pdf

What has become of the Indignados? The biographical consequences of participation in the 15M movement in Madrid (2011–19)

Héloïse Nez

ABSTRACT
This article examines the biographical consequences of participation in 15 M by following the trajectories, from May 2011 to November 2019, of individuals who took part in the movement in Madrid. Based on a field study combining observations and repeat interviews, this follow-up of the trajectories of forty Indignados (22 in the period 2013–15 and 18 to 2019) reveals considerable biographical impacts on both representations and individual practices in the political, personal and professional spheres. These impacts were particularly salient among those who had experienced biographical disruptions, whether in relation to political socialization or a drop in social status, and those who had mobilized in an intense and lasting way. However, 15 M had also had a profound influence on the biographies of those with an activist background and those who had been less involved in the movement. This microsociological approach gives us a better understanding of the biographical trajectories of the Indignados and provides an account of the transformations in collective action in Madrid over the past ten years. The main legacy of 15 M is therefore that it created a new generation of activists who are now involved in a multitude of activist microspheres and institutional settings.

It was a ticking time bomb that just suddenly exploded. It was like the Big Bang. First, there was nothing, and then the galaxies formed, and then different systems within the galaxies, their planets, and then all of a sudden it was something so big I don't think it could go on like that any more (Marcos, aged 22, student).[1]

Like this participant, who was part of the Puerta del Sol assembly and his neighbourhood assembly for almost two years, many of the Indignados I met during this field study told me that the 15 M movement had marked a watershed in their lives and in Spanish society more generally. This movement emerged in Spain following a demonstration that took place on 15 May 2011 organized by groups associated with the platform 'Democracia Real Ya!' (DRY, Real Democracy Now!). Tens of thousands of people took to the streets to protest against the government's management of the 2008 economic crisis and its social consequences as well as the failings, more broadly, of the country's representative political system. As the demonstration drew to a close, a few dozen people stayed on and set up camp for the night in Puerta del Sol, a symbolic square in the heart of the capital. This square was to host a self-managed camp for almost a month, which organized itself into assemblies. More camps sprang up in the plazas of other Spanish cities, and the assemblies were decentralized to the neighbourhoods. Adell (2011), a sociologist and specialist in the Madrid protests, estimated that by the end of 2011, almost 7 million people had participated in some way or another in 15 M.

This mobilization has been analysed in the scientific literature as a pivotal moment, the biggest upheaval in Spanish politics and society since the transition to democracy at the end of the Francoist dictatorship (Cruells & Ibarra, 2013; Tejerina & Perugorría, 2018). A number of researchers have focused on the 'Spanish political laboratory', analysing the consequences of 15 M both for political culture (Flesher Fominaya, 2020; Sampedro & Lobera, 2014) and for institutional and party practices (Feenstra et al., 2016; Romanos & Sádaba, 2016). According to Tejerina et al., the impact on the political socialization of those who took part in 15 M, as with other Occupy movements, has been 'one of the most important outcomes of this cycle of mobilizations and we suggest that this practice will have impact long after these mobilizations wane' (Tejerina et al., 2013, p. 554). This hypothesis, which can only be tested through a study of the participants' trajectories before, during and after the movement, marked the starting point for this study. It examines the biographical consequences of participation in 15 M through an analysis of the trajectories from May 2011 to November 2019 of individuals who took part in the movement in Madrid.

Although 15 M has been the subject of numerous publications, few have focused on the effects of the mobilization from a biographical perspective. In her thesis, Razquin (2014) reconstructed the trajectories to March 2012 of twenty-four individuals who had taken part in one of the 15 M assemblies. She showed the importance of academic and activist capitals in relation to understanding the rationales for entry into and exit from the movement. Smaoui's (2017) comparative study of the Barcelona Indignados and the Nuit Debout protestors in France indicated that the newcomers to collective action had found the mobilizations an intense political experience. They had suddenly become aware of power relationships and, despite their different backgrounds, all ended up behaving rebelliously. However, he pointed out that 'only a longitudinal survey will be able to tell us more about the biographical effects of such participation (in terms of continued involvement with affinity and activist networks, learning redeployed in other spaces of conflict, practices implemented to politicize daily activities, disinhibited relationships with conflict, etc.)' (p. 125). In a recent article, Prado Galán and Fersch (2021) developed this approach, conducting sixteen interviews with former Indignados in Valladolid six years on from 15 M. They showed that the forms of sociability experienced in the camp had impacted longer-term participation. However, their analysis was limited by their *a posteriori* entry into the field, resulting in substantial biases in the participant selection process. Indeed, the authors acknowledged that 'a main obstacle to accessing interviewees was the dormant state of the movement' (p. 6). They had recruited using Facebook announcements, a mailing list that was still active and a public commemoration of the anniversary of 15 M in 2017, so it is likely those they interviewed would have been among the most engaged both during and after the camp, making it more difficult to access those whose engagement was less intense and/or more ephemeral. Betancor and Prieto (2018) also sought to analyse the biographical impacts of 15 M and focused on young people because of their greater likelihood of involvement in future mobilizations. Based on 30 interviews conducted between 2012 and 2015 mainly in Madrid, they distinguished several types of participants according to whether or not they had previous activist experience and whether or not they had always attended their respective 15 M assemblies. Their conclusion on the emergence of a new generation of activists profoundly marked by the Indignados experience and destined to play a key role in the development of new collectives, however, remained at the hypothesis stage given the short temporal distance of their survey.

The aim of this study was to extend the analysis of the biographical consequences of participation in 15 M outlined by these early studies by mobilizing the sociology of social movements literature on 'activist careers' and by conducting a combination of observations and repeat interviews in the Madrid region. The paper begins by outlining the theoretical (part 1) and methodological (part 2) frameworks of the research. The main results are then presented, first in relation to the changes in representations of the social world that can impact all spheres of life (part 3) and second in relation to the redeployment of learning from the assembly and the mobilization in a variety of professional, activist and institutional arenas (part 4). Finally, the conclusion shows how the findings provide information on the biographical futures of the Indignados and on the transformations in collective action in Madrid over the last ten years.

Analysing the effects of a social movement through activist careers

The literature on the effects of social movements distinguishes three types of consequences, namely political, cultural and biographical (Bosi & Uba, 2009; Giugni, 2008). While, as several state of the arts have shown (McAdam, 1999; Fillieule, 2005; Giugni, 2004; Vestergren et al., 2017), the biographical perspective is a developing research area, there are still fewer studies conducted on the biographical effects of participation than on the political consequences in terms of impact on public policies. The biographical approach is characterized by its focus on individual rationales for activist participation in a context in which an organizational approach has long been the preferred option. It examines participation as a vector of political socialization through an analysis of how this experience can transform individual representations and practices. Studies in this area have focused mainly on the student protesters of the 1960s in the United States (in the tradition of McAdam, 1988) and, to a lesser degree, on the 1968 activists in Europe (Fillieule & Neveu, 2019; Pagis, 2014). They have shown that activist participation has a lasting influence on people's life trajectories in the political, professional and personal spheres. One of the main consequences of social movements is thus thought to be 'the production of activists able to reinvest the energies in a great variety of movements during many years' (Neveu, 2019, p. 106).

The literature on activists' biographical futures has been marked by McAdam's (1988) pioneering study of the Freedom Summer campaign, which was mounted in Mississippi in 1964 as part of the civil rights movement. Two decades on from the event, McAdam analysed the campaign registration files and conducted a survey using a questionnaire and interviews with volunteers who did and did not actively participate in the campaign. He showed that those who had become actively involved in this high-risk militant action – mainly privileged white students – had been fundamentally transformed by the experience. The vast majority had discovered activism during this campaign. For some, the event had marked the beginning of their involvement, while for others, its was an extension of previous activities. The most immediate consequence of these individuals' participation in Freedom Summer was political in nature. Many had been radicalized from conventional liberals into extreme leftists. Their stay in Mississippi had strongly challenged their adherence to the American political system and changed their relationships to religion, school and family. These Freedom Summer volunteers had gone on to become heavily involved in the New Left social movements of the 1960s and 1970s. Their participation had also impacted their professional and personal lives because all the choices they had made (e.g., profession, partner) had taken on a political significance.

Building on this baseline study as well as on Becker's work (1963), French sociologists have developed the concept of 'activist careers' to analyse the effects of participation in a variety of social and political organizations (Fillieule & Mayer, 2001). Fillieule (2001) proposed to use the tools of symbolic interactionism, in particular the concepts of career and life trajectory, to account for the multiplicity of forms of participation throughout the life cycle and the withdrawal from or extension of these involvements. Participation in collective action is thus understood as a process that develops over time and is therefore not definitively determined by original position or socialization. The 'career' concept allows us to reflect on the association between individual trajectories and the contexts in which they take place by focusing both on an analysis of the collective conditions of the action and on the meaning that the individuals in question attribute to it. However, this perspective should not obscure the fact that the rationales for participation are very often part of collective trajectories and that they rarely manifest without the canvassing of existing groups or organizations (Sawicki & Siméant, 2009). It is also important to relate the biographical effects of participation to the intensity of participation in protest events (Pagis, 2014) and to the individual's social trajectory, in particular by analysing how logics of upward or downward social mobility mark activist careers (Leclercq & Pagis, 2011).

Studies in this area have proposed a variety of methodologies for understanding the biographical consequences of participation. Microsociological analyses through life stories reveal, like the statistical macrosociological approach that is predominant in American research, what participation produces in the medium and long term, but they also, more especially, provide an understanding of the contexts and social logics involved in cases where participation contributes to influencing individual life trajectories. However, the biographical narrative method is not without its problems, because it gives retrospective meaning to the sequence of events selected by the interviewee. It is therefore important to connect the life stories not just to the contexts to which they refer but also to the respondents' characteristics in order to distinguish the regularities and typical trajectories beyond the singularity of individual trajectories (Fillieule & Mayer, 2001). The problem of retrospective analysis can also be mitigated through direct observation of practices and repeat in situ interviews (Leclercq & Pagis, 2011). This was the methodological approach adopted here.

A longitudinal field study in Madrid

The analysis was based on a field study conducted over nine years in the Madrid region. The study began at the end of May 2011 and took place first in the Puerta del Sol area and then in one of the city neighbourhoods (Carabanchel) and a suburban town (Parla) located in the south of Madrid, whose population was socially mixed but predominantly working-class. The analysis focused mainly on the data from two rounds of interviews, which were conducted in 2013–15 and 2019. Based on contacts established during my observations, I conducted the first round of interviews with forty Indignados in order to investigate the initial biographical effects of their participation. Without claiming to be representative, which is not the aim of ethnographic interviews (Beaud, 1996), respondent selection was based on ensuring the sample contained a variety of sociodemographic and political profiles, a range of participation histories before and after 15 M and an assortment of types and levels of involvement in 15 M. The objective was to take into account the heterogeneous nature of a movement that comprised 'collectives and individuals with different ideological and sociodemographic characteristics and different forms and degrees of involvement' (Lobera, 2015, p. 100). I thus interviewed twenty-three men and seventeen women, aged between 16 and 69, with a range of social backgrounds and professional profiles (see Table 1 in the appendices). Some of them had been involved since the early days in Puerta del Sol (a few had belonged to organizations that had preceded 15 M, such as Juventud sin futuro (JSF) and ¡Democracia real ya!), some had joined the movement when the assemblies were decentralized to the neighbourhoods, and some had only become involved a year or two later, often through the assemblies on housing. Their reasons for participation were extremely diverse, including the need to resolve a personal crisis (such as eviction) and a desire to continue or reactivate their activism. Some reported that they had been active for only a month or two, some for between a few months and a year, and some were still actively involved in 15 M in 2013–15. One of the criteria for selecting respondents in the first round of interviews was the diversity of their trajectories after the peak of the mobilization. The sample therefore included those who had ceased involvement, those who had continued participating in the 15 M assemblies and those who had become involved in other spaces, such as political parties (notably the Podemos Party, which was created in January 2014) or local initiatives (self-managed squatted social centres, barter markets, and so on).

In November 2019, I conducted a second round of interviews with almost half of the people I had met in the first round (18 out of the original 40) in order to understand the biographical effects of their engagement over a longer period. The selection of interviewees for this round was again based on ensuring a diversity of social situations and engagement trajectories before, during and after 15 M (see Table 2 in the appendices). Most of these repeat interviews were conducted in Parla, where I have maintained the majority of my contacts in recent years for scientific, friendship and family reasons. I balanced the proportion of women (9) and men (9) in this second round and prioritized those who had not been activists prior to 15 M in order to examine the impact of the movement on newcomers to collective action. To this end, I also recontacted five Indignados in Carabanchel who had no previous experience of engagement.

This longitudinal approach, which is still relatively rare in research on the biographical consequences of engagement (Vestergren et al., 2017), is one of the main contributions of this article. The study method nevertheless has a number of limitations, such as the relatively short temporal distance and more importantly the absence of a control group comprising non-15 M-participants, which would have enabled me to verify whether the changes observed were indeed linked to participation in the social movement (Giugni & Grasso, 2016; McAdam, 1988). My longitudinal study of 15 M was based on regular observations carried out between 2011 and 2019. My first observations, in 2011 and 2012, comprised around sixty assemblies and fifteen or so demonstrations and other protest actions that took place during the Puerta del Sol camp and decentralization of the movement to the neighbourhoods (Nez, 2012). Owing to professional commitments in France, my field trips were ad hoc (lasting a few days to several weeks) but very regular (twenty trips over the nine years, including ten between 2011 and 2012). At the beginning, I stayed in a shared house in Carabanchel, hence why I chose to observe this particular neighbourhood assembly. During one of the 'Indignados marches' in Aranjuez in July 2011, I met and formed friendships with a few members of the Parla assembly (and indeed married one of them), which explains my attachment to this area. Beyond the effects of 15 M on my own life journey, setting out the context in which the research was conducted provides an understanding of how I managed, despite the intermittent nature of the observations (Badimon, 2017), to develop bonds of trust with the interviewees and gain access to many informal discussions (such as the 'after-meeting drinks' discussions) and everyday conversations. This detailed knowledge of the movement in Madrid allowed me to distinguish different Indignados profiles in line with Siméant's (2001) methodological recommendations: 'Only ethnographic immersion allows us to judge the exemplarity of certain observed trajectories' (p. 57). The fact that I conducted the interviews mainly with people I had met in Puerta del Sol, Carabanchel and Parla (I also asked these people for other contacts to diversify the engagement profiles) allowed me to triangulate the interview discourses with the observations. Cross-checking what the participants had said in the interviews with the observations made at the beginning of the movement a number of years before partially controlled for 'biographical illusion', which is linked to problems associated with memory and discourse reconstructed a posteriori (Bourdieu, 1986). These interviews were also accompanied by observations carried out both in the 2013–2014 period at the Eko collective squat, which had been set up by the Indignados in Carabanchel (Nez, 2017), and from 2015 onwards within the Podemos circle in Parla (Nez, 2015).

The comprehensive approach was adopted for the interviews, which takes into account in both their implementation and their analysis the strong reflexivity of the individuals involved. The interview schedule used in 2013–15 thus aimed to reconstruct the individual's participation history, to talk about their trajectory (personal, professional and political) and their family and friends and to understand, from their point of view, any learning and changes that had taken place as a result of their participation in 15 M. The interview schedule in 2019 began by going back over the evolution of their personal situation and participation and then focused on their perception of the evolution of the social and political panorama in Spain generally and in the Madrid region specifically, explicitly tackling the subject of 15 M's legacy. In line with the ethnographic interview methodological approach, which always forms part of a field study (Beaud, 1996),

I personally fully transcribed all the interviews (which lasted between one and four hours). The two sections that follow present the main results from the comparative analysis of all the interviews and the in-depth study of each one.

'There is another truth': changes in representations of social reality

One of the main elements that emerged from the comparative analysis of the interviews concerned 15 M's impact on the participants' ways of looking at the social world. Many respondents told me how they had been forced to question everything they had previously taken for granted. Their perception of politics had thus changed through, for example, their questioning of the two-party system or of the professionalization of a field dominated by experts. This change was summed up by Evelyn (aged 41, unemployed), who had been intensely involved first in Puerta del Sol and then in her neighbourhood: '[15 M] challenged stuff people took for granted [...], it broke with a lot of discourses that were already flawed ... on the transition, on the monarchy. Before it'd never even occurred to us the transition could've been done differently [...]. It was like a taboo subject'. Their representations of capitalism, social movements, the police and the media had also been transformed by their participation in the movement. This corresponds with the findings of studies that have highlighted a transformation of political culture associated with 15 M, particularly concerning 'the culture of transition' (Flesher Fominaya, 2020; Sampedro & Lobera, 2014). Compared to these macro-sociological analyses, this biographical approach was able to show that these changes varied in degree depending on the individual's profile, notably in relation to their social trajectory and political socialization. The changes were highly visible when the individuals had not previously participated in activism and/or when they had experienced a drop in social status, but they also manifested in Indignados with an activist background who had experienced favourable economic conditions. These transformations in their perceptions of the social world had impacted all or at least some of the spheres in their lives (political, professional and personal).

The changes were particularly noticeable when participation in 15 M had marked a break with previous socializations (Leclercq & Pagis, 2011). This was exemplified by Victor, who had no previous experience of politics and came from a right-wing family. This photographer claimed that no one in his circle of family and friends would ever have told him about the Puerta del Sol camp, which he had stumbled upon 'by chance' at the age of 33. His parents (an engineer and a teacher) had taught him 'not to give his opinion', but he had been attracted by the slogan 'they don't represent us'. He discovered through 15 M 'that [he] had been told many lies': 'I realized that the politicians, the media and the police were all corrupt. [...] I realized that the police repressed rather than acted to resolve social problems and protect the majority of society. [...] I realized there was a lot of media blocking'. Victor believed that the movement was 'making society rethink politics and question whether it makes sense to vote every four years instead of having a much more constant level of engagement and whether it makes sense that politicians can win elections and then not keep any of their election promises. It makes us rethink the perception there's not much we can do about it'. Two to three months after discovering the social movement, Victor decided to devote all his professional time 'to documenting everything to do with 15 M' and to 'campaign by telling the story that nobody talks about'. This was a radical political and professional change for Victor, who had no history of any activist engagement and who had chosen to specialize in artistic studio photography rather than politically engaged documentary photography. When I met him two years later, he fully identified with 15 M ('it's my movement') and had photographed all the demonstrations, especially the scenes of police repression, which had already cost him three trials and a fine. When I asked him about what he had learned by participating, he answered: 'I've learned to think politically, to make my own judgements, to not just blindly trust what I'm told'. He believed that 15 M had changed everything in his life: 'Your way of working, your way of life, your way of thinking, your ideology, your way of understanding social relations, money, everything'. At the time, he was looking for a way to combine his activism and his profession and still get paid.

Changes in social representations and biographical trajectories were also strongly in evidence when individuals had experienced a drop in their social status. These individuals questioned everything that they had previously taken for granted because their living conditions had suddenly deteriorated with the economic crisis. This phenomenon has been highlighted by Johsua in her research on anti-capitalist activists: 'These disruptions are likely to reveal the arbitrariness of the social world and its rankings and the domination logics that underlie them, contributing to 'subjective breaks with 'the self-evident''' (Johsua, 2015, p. 87). A number of the individuals I interviewed at the Eko squat in 2014, who had been prompted to join 15 M a year or two after it had begun when they were faced with a housing problem, had reviewed their perceptions of the social world in relation to their drop in social status. This was the case with Mónica (aged 47), a concierge from a working-class background (mother a seamstress, father a craftsman). Her life had been turned upside down when her husband Javier, a sound and lighting manager with a company, had been made redundant during the crisis and then set up his own company, which had subsequently gone bankrupt. This couple, who had enjoyed a good standard of living until then, had first become involved in 15 M some time after the movement had started, when they were amusing themselves having their pictures taken in Puerta del Sol with 'those crusties'. In May 2013, they went to a housing assembly at the Eko after meeting some squatter neighbours, because they could no longer continue living in their flat (there was no gas or electricity) and were threatened with eviction. Although Mónica had no previous experience of activism, she began to participate in all the Indignados actions and demonstrations. When I met her in 2014, she told me that 15 M had changed her way of looking at things: 'It's as if it opened your eyes to the real problems'. Her representations of the social movement, especially of squats and squatters, had completely changed. The 'troublemakers' and 'the poor' had become their 'neighbours' and 'benefactors' who had pointed them towards 'the only place where we had a bit of hope'. This change was commensurate with their downward social trajectory: 'Suddenly you realize what it's like to be poor'. A year on from entering the Eko, Mónica and Javier had formed extremely radical views on squatting, which had led them to distance themselves from the housing assembly. They were helping other people find squats and considered squatting in their own apartment if they were to be evicted. When I interviewed the couple for the second time, in 2019, their social situation and discourse had not changed. They were still involved in occupancy issues and were ready to squat in their apartment once evicted. Mónica believed that 15 M had transformed them and shown them 'another truth': 'We've become different people on every level'.

She spoke of an 'inner revolution' linked to a new 'way of living and interacting' and came back again to what 15 M had meant in terms of 'openness [...] to other people and other ideas, and to other ways of life, with not much money, not much security, not much work'. While her professional life had not been impacted to any great extent, the effects on her personal and political life were considerable. As a result of her contact with the social movement, she had reviewed her lifestyle, including even her eating habits (she had become a vegetarian), and had developed an 'anarchist consciousness', which had led her to question the capitalist system.

While changes in perceptions were more salient among those who had political socializations that were far removed from the social movement and conflicting social trajectories, they were nevertheless also visible in individuals who were more politicized and enjoyed privileged social situations. Clara and Ruben, a couple who had only recently settled in Parla when 15 M first emerged, were a good example of this. At 38 and 35, they both worked in publicly listed companies, one as a lawyer, the other as an accountant. During my first interview with them in 2014, they told me that they were comfortable financially, as indeed were all those who still met in the local assembly: 'We all work, we've all got homes, none of us are affected by education problems, we've got an iron constitution'. Clara, who came from a working-class family in Asturias (mother a cook, father an employee in a state-owned company) that had always encouraged her to participate in protests, had been involved with the student movement as well as with environmental NGOs. Ruben, who came from a more conservative family (father a lathe turner, mother a cleaner) and region (Ávila), had only taken part in the bigger demonstrations. Both were intensely involved in 15 M, first in Puerta del Sol (notably on the legal committee) and then in their own city, where they were very active in the assembly until its dissolution at the end of 2013. Clara and Ruben believed that '15 M's opened us up enormously, it's changed us'. This extract from our second interview in 2019 sums up the extent of the changes to their way of thinking and acting in the social movement and in their daily lives:

Me What did 15M change for you?

Ruben It's changed a lot.

Clara Everything, everything, everything. The way we think about life, our consumption habits of course, our beliefs, our values. [...]

Ruben Ultimately it changes the way you see things, the way you look at everything.

Clara At life, at people, everything. It's as if you put on different glasses and see the world in a different way. [...]

Ruben Before I always found it difficult to communicate with people, now it's a bit easier. You can relax ... you can go to a self-managed centre, before you'd say that's foreign to me, I wasn't used to going there ... now you can go to those places no problem [...].

Clara Learning to create networks, to be happy in a different way as well. With fewer things ... [...] In terms of conversation, of reflection, of thought, of always asking yourself questions ... everything, everything, everything, it's a complete change.

Ruben Right down to what we eat, we've gone vegetarian.

Clara and Ruben thus revealed transformations both in their perceptions of the world (in particular with regard to questioning their prejudices about the squatter movement) and in their social, political and consumer practices. They stressed this last point because they believed their power as consumers was a determining factor in the capitalist system. With 15 M, they had decided to boycott supermarkets, switch electricity companies, wear vegan shoes and only buy from organic producers. Like many former Indignados, they belonged to a local consumer group and as such subscribed to a prefigurative conception of politics aimed at transforming their lifestyles (Yates, 2015). Although they had 'slowed down a bit' by 2019, they were still involved in numerous collectives that tackled environmental, feminist and animalist issues. However, there was a total disconnect between these changes and their professional lives, as Ruben explained: 'Unfortunately, we work in areas that are far removed from everything 15 M stands for'. They did not feel they would be able to engage in strike action, but the money they earned allowed them to support many social and political projects that were important to them.

While Clara's trajectory shows that changes in representations can happen when people have an activist experience, a number of the activists I interviewed rejected the idea of an 'awakening' with 15 M. This was the case with Julio (aged 25), an autonomist activist who looked on the assemblies as a 'way of life', and Javi (27), a lawyer who was sceptical about the slogan 'now or never'. Their discourses evidenced the affinities between 15 M and the autonomist and squatter movements (Flesher Fominaya, 2015; Martínez & García, 2018). Nevertheless, other activists did claim their lives had been transformed with the Indignados. Despite the fact they had already formed a critical view of the world before 2011, the movement nevertheless had a lasting impact on them. José (aged 69, journalist), for example, who had a long activist trajectory in trade unionism and social movements, was so intensely involved in 15 M that he had reviewed his accommodation type (moving from a shared flat to a squat) and talked of a change in his 'life system'. Alberto (aged 57), who had long been involved in the autonomist and squatter movements, believed that 15 M had 'awakened consciousnesses and even revived those of us who were asleep'. This was also the case with Natalia (aged 37, teacher), who had been very involved in the squats but had been disengaged for a few years. When 15 M emerged, however, she had become involved on a daily basis in the Puerta del Sol camp and subsequently in the assembly in Parla. The 15 M movement had substantially impacted not just her activist life (she had been an active participant from its inception) but also her personal life. She had broken up with her partner because she was disappointed that he would not get involved and had gone on to find a new partner and friends in the movement. Similarly, when I asked Lola (aged 23, student), who was very involved first in the student movement and then in the emergence of the Podemos Party, if there was a 'before 15 M' and an 'after 15 M', she had answered without hesitation: 'For me and for everyone else, for me and for the political history of this country. 15 M is the biggest thing that's happened here in … I don't know, since the transition. [...] It changes the way we understand politics'. She believed the main learning experience from 15 M 'for all organized people' had been 'learning to work and build with real people who don't fit into the moulds the activists previously had for them'. The section that follows shows how, through learning accumulated from the assembly and the mobilization, 15 M was a major political experience for both the newcomers to collective action and the seasoned activists alike.

'I learned how to do politics': learning from the assembly and the mobilization

When I asked the respondents about what they had learned from 15 M, all of them talked about the experience they had gained from the assembly. Learning to (no longer be afraid to) speak in public came up repeatedly, especially among the women, particularly those with few qualifications, even when they had an activist background. This had been the main learning from 15 M for Elena (aged 28, healthcare assistant), a 'lifelong activist' who had been involved with the Juventudes Comunistas since the age of 18: 'I used to be really embarrassed when I spoke in public, when I expressed myself in public, and that's been great for me. To be able to speak in public and say what I think, what I feel'. There was a lot of learning linked to the assembly's practice among those who had not been familiar with this kind of organizational structure, such as Marcos (aged 22, student), who had learned 'patience, to listen to people, to collaborate with people, to be much more open, how to work with other people who think differently'. He nevertheless bemoaned, as many did, the slowness of consensus decision-making. Those with an activist background said that the main thing they had learned from the 15 M assemblies was to listen to and work with different people. This learning was highlighted by all the activists, regardless of their generation and the movements they had been involved in. The interview I conducted in 2013 with Rafa (aged 23) and Emilio (aged 63), two journalists involved in the 'Periódico del 15 M', exemplified the idea of a joint venture between people from different backgrounds. Rafa, who had come from the student and right to housing movement, responded to the 'learning' question with a single word 'listening'. Indeed, he repeated it several times and then said: 'The most important thing is to listen to other people who think differently from you'. Emilio, who described himself as a 'somewhat sectarian' anarchist, had learned that he could work respectfully with people he never would have thought he had any affinity with. He thus talked about 'relinquishing the flag' and believed that 15 M had made him 'a better person'.

Beyond the assembly's practice, there was a great deal of learning accumulated from the collective action. Several first-time demonstrators claimed to have 'learned how to do politics', referring to the skills of debating, mobilizing in the streets, putting pressure on elected representatives and creating systemic alternatives. Miguel (aged 32, unemployed), who had no previous activist experience and had been involved in Parla's assembly for over a year, told me he had 'learned that you can fight, don't let them walk all over you'. Many trajectories were thus marked by a process of empowerment 'that links up an individual dynamic of self-esteem and skills development with a collective commitment and transformative social action' (Bacqué & Biewener, 2013). By participating in 15 M, the respondents had become aware of their individual and collective ability to change their social reality. These empowerment trajectories were conspicuous among the newcomers to collective action, who had learned they no longer needed to be afraid because they realized that a problem that they had perceived to be specific to them (such as the threat of eviction) was in fact shared by many others and could therefore be solved collectively. This is similar both to the concept of agency as used by Butler (2004), where a capacity to act and self-emancipate from forms of domination is expressed through a denouncement of injustices, and to the concept of cognitive liberation developed by

McAdam: 'Before collective protest can get under way, people must collectively define their situation as unjust and subject to change through group action' (McAdam, 1982, p. 29).

The case of Gabriela illustrates this well. This 33-year-old cleaner from Ecuador had gone along to a housing assembly at the Eko in spring 2012 on the advice of a social worker because she could no longer meet her mortgage payments as her husband was unemployed. In 2014, she told me that at the start she had been 'petrified' when she had gone to see her bank manager but that 15 M had shown her that it was in fact a 'scam' and that she was not the guilty party. She had learned how to organize sit-ins, demonstrations and assemblies and how to negotiate with the banks by 'demanding a solution' from them. The trajectories of the newcomers to collective action thus revealed processes of political subjectivation, which were particularly marked when they were confronted with forms of dispossession through a loss of income and/or housing (Butler & Athanasiou, 2013). These empowerment trajectories also applied to those Indignados with activist profiles who had become aware through 15 M of the possibility of effecting concrete change. Like a number of other activists, Amalia (aged 36, psychologist), who was actively involved in a political party (Izquierda Unida), a trade union and international solidarity NGOs, had thus changed her activist representation and practices: 'I was campaigning on theoretical stuff, or on ideologies [...]. Activism was almost like having a faith, practising a faith, but deep down you think it's impossible because everything always just stays the same and there's no way to change things. Suddenly, a movement that's so big, so broad, and that also achieves real things [...]. This is the first time I've thought we can really change the system'.

Despite the variety of their trajectories, the Indignados had all acquired a great deal of knowledge and know-how related to the assembly and the collective action, which they had then redeployed in a diverse range of political and professional spaces. Elena (aged 28) showed, for example, how learning to speak in public had been useful to her both in her militant activities after 15 M (in the 'white tide' protest in Madrid for public health and then in the Podemos circle in Parla) and in her professional life, that is in the many projects she undertook alongside her job as a healthcare assistant, such as 'Tuppersex' parties and presenting her own radio programme. On a political level, the Indignados were redeploying their learning in a range of organizations, which were thus marked by the influence of 15 M. Activists from the Podemos circle in Parla told me, for example, how they had drawn inspiration from the way in which the Indignados assemblies operated but that they had streamlined the meetings to make them more efficient. Experience in the social movement had proved useful in the institutional sphere for those who had joined the municipal council in 2015 and then the government team in 2019. Camila, a 22-year-old student in 2011 who had gone on to become an elected representative (Podemos) in Parla's municipal council in 2019, told me how her participation in 15 M had impacted her 'way of doing politics, in a more participative way, more empathetic' and added that she had 'a lot of respect for people who organize and mobilize themselves to get things done, because I've lived it'. A number of the Indignados also pointed out the similarities between the organizational structure of 15 M and that of other social movements that they had subsequently become involved in, such as the 'white tide' and 'green tide' (state education) protests and the 8 M feminist movement. Its influences were even visible in collectives that were initially far removed from the principles of 15 M. For example, Ariel (aged 31, software developer), who had been involved in a small anti-capitalist, revolutionary organization for the past decade, had learned from 15 M that more attention should be paid to internal democracy, *micromachismos* (everyday sexism) and the feminization of language. The activist trajectory of Luis, a 16-year-old high school student at the time of 15 M, had also been marked by this first political experience in the Parla assembly, which had led to his subsequent involvement in libertarian groups at university and then back in his home town, although he had reviewed his relationship to pacifism in the interim.

The learning acquired from the assembly and the collective action could also be reused in the professional sphere. Juan (aged 27), who went to the Puerta del Sol camp every day and whom I met at the general assemblies, stopped participating when he emigrated to the United States in the summer of 2011 to do a doctorate in biotechnology. Although he had no history of activism and his family was opposed to 15 M, Juan had been marked by this participation experience that was as intense as it was brief. While he did not continue with any political activity, he listed (in our interview two years later) the lessons he had learned from his participation that he valued in his professional sphere, such as 'getting stuck in', 'appearing in public' and 'I don't need to be a prominent figure to share what I know'. Other people's professional lives had changed more radically since 2011. Isabel (aged 32), who considered herself to be 'a 15 M purist', believed that all the paid jobs she had had since 15 M had been 'because of my political birth in 15 M'. A former company sales manager, she was in the process of retraining as a community worker when the movement had first emerged, which gave her the opportunity to put her knowledge into practice by moderating large assemblies in Puerta del Sol. Eight years later, she told me how she had converted her know-how into her professional activities (notably the setting up of local participatory bodies in Madrid and the reception of asylum seekers) by specializing in participatory methods. Isabel said that she had 'found herself' with 15 M and that it had taught her 'a lot of things on a human level', such as 'to have patience, to take my time, to have more empathy, to take care of myself'. In 2014, Evelyn (aged 41), who was unemployed and tired of precarious jobs, told me that her participation in the 15 M assemblies had taught her a number of things that were useful for her cooperative project, like organizing meetings, but also that she had learned above all that it was possible to have 'a job that we enjoy and do in the way we like'. The 15 M movement thus represented a space for the acquisition not only of skills that could then be of value in other spaces but also of ways of seeing and reconsidering life on all levels.

Conclusion: a new generation of activists in militant microspheres and institutional spaces

This follow-up of the trajectories of forty Indignados in Madrid (22 in the period 2013–15 and 18 to 2019) highlights substantial biographical impacts on representations and individual practices in the political, personal and often also professional spheres. These impacts were particularly salient among those who had experienced biographical disruptions, whether in relation to political socialization or a drop in social status, and who had mobilized themselves in an intense and lasting way. However, 15 M had also profoundly impacted the trajectories of those with an activist background or who had been less involved in the movement. The methodology used in this study certainly had a number of limitations, above all the absence of a control group, which would have enabled me to verify whether the changes observed were actually linked to participation in the social movement. Other interviews conducted as part of a survey of the Podemos activists, some of whom had not participated in 15 M, showed that they may also have been influenced by the movement without even having taken part in it (Nez, 2015). The respondents in the present study also reported changes in their families' representations and practices. Natalia, for example, had noted a clear difference from the time when she had been mobilized in the squats: 'In my family, the discourse has changed a lot, before I was a radical, now they tell me you're right, it's just we couldn't see it'. It seems possible therefore that 15 M also had an influence on people who had not participated directly in the movement. There is no doubting the fact, however, that there was a considerable change in the perceptions of the social world and the political, personal and professional practices of those who had participated in the Indignados assemblies and actions. Beyond the mobilization itself, they had politicized all aspects of their daily lives and transformed their lifestyles (Yates, 2015). The findings of this study thus confirm that there is evidence of biographical effects of participation in social movements in contexts outside that of the United States in the 1960s (Giugni & Grasso, 2016).

This micro-sociological approach gives us a better understanding of the biographical futures of the Indignados and, in addition, provides an account of the transformations in collective action in Madrid over the last ten years. While most of the respondents remembered with some nostalgia that 'we were all there' and valued the fact that 15 M had succeeded in bringing together a very diverse range of people fighting very different battles, they also recognized that it was difficult to work together in such a heterogeneous movement. The vast majority of those interviewed in 2019 had thus continued their activism in much smaller affinity groups. These activist microspheres were marked by a division between 'horizontal' and 'vertical' conceptions of politics that was very present in 15 M (Feenstra et al., 2016). Some of the Indignados I followed had become involved in partisan organizations, mainly in the Podemos and Izquierda Unida Parties, and a few had become elected representatives in the municipal councils. Some had mobilized in social organizations as diverse as a feminist committee, an anti-racist libertarian collective, a local group campaigning against bullfighting and a Latin American women's association combatting gender-based violence. Some of the collectives were only very loosely formalized and comprised barely a dozen people who all knew one another through friendship and family networks and who were committed to concrete actions such as fundraising for animal shelters or artistic interventions in the public space. These Indignados were aware, as Ruben pointed out, that they had thus limited their sphere of action and influence: 'We have withdrawn into more closed groups'. Isabel, for example, regretted the fact that 'we've gone back to what we had before 15 M a bit, I mean, everyone in their own area, on their own cause'. However, some Indignados had demonstrated that it was far more pleasant and sustainable to participate in this way, because the more unifying movement had generated many interpersonal and political conflicts. These conflicts were found to be among the disengagement from 15 M factors, along with the emotional toll and variations in biographical availability over time. Most of the trajectories were in fact marked by phases of engagement and disengagement, which were linked in particular to activist fatigue and even exhaustion. The many immediate effects of 15 M on the participants' personal lives, such as separation from a partner and exam failure, had also contributed to the rationales for exiting the movement. However, among the 18 people interviewed in 2019, only three mentioned an almost total disengagement, which had been mainly for biographical reasons. Two of them, who had been activists as a couple in their 15 M local assembly and then in the Podemos circle in Parla, had got divorced and gone on to meet new partners who were far removed from the social movement. The other, a first-time demonstrator in Carabanchel, had found a job that had left him little time for collective action, although he had managed to resolve the housing problem that had prompted his involvement in the first place. These 'disengaged' Indignados had not withdrawn completely, however, because they continued to participate in some demonstrations and said they were ready to re-mobilize at any moment.

My findings here differ from those presented by Accornero (2018), whose longitudinal study of the trajectories of students who had engaged with far-left organizations during the dictatorship in Portugal showed that their disillusionment with the revolutionary project had led to widespread disengagement. However, my interviews also revealed disappointment that the 15 M ideals had not been achieved. The comprehensive approach adopted in this study has thus provided an understanding of how the Indignados themselves perceived the legacy of 15 M. When the second round of interviews were conducted in November 2019, after the re-run of several legislative elections in Spain and just before the new left-wing coalition government was formed, most people were very critical of 15 M's impact, condemning the lack of legislative changes that could improve social situations. The disappointment around 15 M's lack of institutional opportunities was palpable, especially among the first-time demonstrators and those in difficult social situations. A number of Indignados had nevertheless changed their electoral behaviour, often choosing the new option proposed by the Podemos Party and maintaining it over time despite their disillusionment. Others had remained sceptical about the idea of effecting change through elections, going so far as to say that 'Podemos killed off 15 M'. Although they lamented the limited transformations at the macro level, with the notable exception of the end of the two-party system, many Indignados highlighted the multiple effects of 15 M in Spanish society more broadly, for example, in terms of political conversations in everyday life and 15 M's influence on other social movements. There was not total disenchantment therefore, which may explain the differences between the findings of this study and those of Accornero. In addition, unlike Accornero's far-left activists in Portugal, whose redeployment prospects were severely limited under the dictatorship, the Indignados were able to easily and quickly redeploy all the knowledge and know-how they had acquired during 15 M into other political and/or professional spaces. Emilio, the 'old anarchist' who wondered 'if we had a life before that', succinctly summed up the general feeling of those interviewed and indeed the main idea defended in this article when he said that '15 M's legacy' was that it had 'created thousands of new activists who will go on to do other things'.

Note

1. All data extracts and all quotations from Spanish or French sources have been translated into English. Pseudonyms are being used to protect interviewee's identities. The ages and professions indicated are those given at the time of 15 M.

Acknowledgments

I would like to thank all the people who kindly gave their time to be interviewed and who shared their experiences with enthusiasm. My thanks also to the anonymous reviewers of this article for their helpful suggestions.

Funding

This research, which was conducted without funding, benefited from occasional help with transport costs from my successive research laboratories (Lavue and then Citeres). This article has been translated from French by Clare Ferguson with funding from Citeres.

References

Accornero, G. (2018). 'I wanted to carry out the revolution': Activists' trajectories in Portugal from dictatorship to democracy. *Social Movement Studies, 18*(3), 1–19. https://doi.org/10.1080/14742837.2018.1560258

Adell, R. (2011). La movilización de los indignados del 15M. Aportaciones desde la sociología de la protesta. *Sociedad y Utopía, 38,* 141–170.

Bacqué, M.-H., & Biewener, C. (2013). *L'empowerment, une pratique émancipatrice ?* La Découverte.

Badimon, M. E. (2017). Observer le militantisme par intermittence?: Les effets de la discontinuité sur le terrain. *Politix, n° 118*(2), 209–232. https://doi.org/10.3917/pox.118.0207

Beaud, S. (1996). L'usage de l'entretien en sciences sociales. Plaidoyer pour l'entretien ethnographique. *Politix, 35,* 226–257. https://doi.org/10.3406/polix.1996.1966

Becker, H. S. (1963). *Outsiders. Studies in the Sociology of Deviance.* Free Press.

Betancor, G., & Prieto, D. (2018). El 15M y las juventudes: Entrada y salida en los espacios activistas e impactos biográficos del activismo. *Pensamiento al Margen, 8,* 161–190.

Bosi, L., & Uba, K. (2009). Introduction: The Outcomes of Social Movements. *Mobilization: An International Quarterly, 14*(4), 409–415. https://doi.org/10.17813/maiq.14.4.m1408k812244744h

Bourdieu, P. (1986). L'illusion biographique. *Actes de la recherche en sciences sociales, 62-63,* 69–72. https://doi.org/10.3406/arss.1986.2317

Butler, J. (2004). *Undoing Gender.* Routledge.

Butler, J., & Athanasiou, A. (2013). *Dispossession. The Performative in the Political.* Polity.

Cruells, M., & Ibarra, P. (Ed.). (2013). *La democracia del futuro. Del 15M a la emergencia de una sociedad civil viva.* Icaria Editorial.

Feenstra, R. A., Tormey, S., Casero-Ripollés, A., & Keane, J. (2016). *La reconfiguración de la democracia. El laboratorio político español.* Editorial Comares.

Fillieule, O. (2001). Propositions pour une analyse processuelle de l'engagement individuel. *Revue française de science politique, 51*(1–2), 199–217. https://doi.org/10.3917/rfsp.511.0199

Fillieule, O. (2005). Temps biographique, temps social et variabilité des rétributions. In O. Fillieule (Ed.), *Le désengagement militant* (pp. 17–47). Belin.

Fillieule, O., & Mayer, N. (2001). Devenirs militants. *Revue française de science politique, 51*(1), 19–25. https://doi.org/10.3917/rfsp.511.0019

Fillieule, O., & Neveu, E. (Ed.). (2019). *Activists forever? Long-term impacts of political activism.* Cambridge University Press.

Flesher Fominaya, C. (2015). Debunking Spontaneity: Spain's 15-M/ Indignados as autonomous movement. *Social Movement Studies, 14*(2), 142–163. https://doi.org/10.1080/14742837.2014.945075

Flesher Fominaya, C. (2020). *Democracy Reloaded. Inside Spain's Political Laboratory from 15-M to Podemos*. Oxford University Press.

Giugni, M. (2004). Personal and Biographical Consequences. In D. A. Snow, S. Soule, & H. Kriesi (Eds.), *The Blackwell Companion to Social Movements* (pp. 489–507). Blackwell.

Giugni, M. (2008). Political, biographical, and cultural consequences of social movements. *Sociology Compass, 2*(5), 1582–1600. https://doi.org/10.1111/j.1751-9020.2008.00152.x

Giugni, M., & Grasso, M. T. (2016). The biographical impact of participation in social movement activities: Beyond highly committed New Left activism. In L. Bosi, M. Giugni, & K. Uba (Eds.), *The Consequences of Social Movements* (pp. 88–105). Cambridge University Press.

Johsua, F. (2015). *Anticapitalistes. Une sociologie historique de l'engagement*. La Découverte.

Leclercq, C., & Pagis, J. (2011). Les incidences biographiques de l'engagement. *Sociétés contemporaines, 84*(4), 5–23. https://doi.org/10.3917/soco.084.0005

Lobera, J. (2015). De movimientos a partidos. La cristalización electoral de la protesta. *Revista Española de Sociología, 24*, 97–105.

Martínez, M., & García, Á. (2018). Converging movements: Occupations of squares and buildings. In B. Tejerina & I. Perugorría (Eds.), *Crisis and social mobilization in contemporary Spain. The M15 Movement* (pp. 95–118). Routledge.

McAdam, D. (1982). *Political process and the development of the black insurgency, 1930–1970*. University of Chicago Press.

McAdam, D. (1988). *Freedom Summer*. Oxford University Press.

McAdam, D. (1999). The biographical Impact of Activism. In M. Giugni, D. McAdam, & C. Tilly (Eds.), *How social movements matter* (pp. 119–146). University of Minnesota Press.

Neveu, E. (2019). Life Stories of Former French Activists of "68": Using Biographies to Investigate the Outcomes of Social Movements. In O. Fillieule & E. Neveu (Eds.), *Activists Forever? Long-Term Impacts of Political Activism* (pp. 84–107). Cambridge University Press.

Nez, H. (2012). Délibérer au sein d'un mouvement social. *Participations, 4*(3), 79–101. https://doi.org/10.3917/parti.004.0079

Nez, H. (2015). *Podemos. De l'indignation aux élections*. Les Petits matins.

Nez, H. (2017). La politisation par l'occupation. Pratiques quotidiennes et trajectoires d'empowerment dans un squat madrilène. *Politix, 117*(1), 63–89. https://doi.org/10.3917/pox.117.0063

Pagis, J. (2014). *Mai 68, un pavé dans leurs histoires. Evénement et socialisation*. Presses de Sciences Po.

Prado Galán, L., & Fersch, B. (2021). Where did the Indignados go? How movement sociality can influence action orientation and ongoing activism after the hype. *Social Movement Studies, 20*(1), 2–19. https://doi.org/10.1080/14742837.2020.1722627

Razquin, A. (2014). *Tomar la palabra en el 15M: Condiciones sociales de acceso a la participación en la asamblea* [Unpublished doctoral dissertation]. Universidad de Cádiz.

Romanos, E., & Sádaba, I. (2016). From the Street to Institutions through the App: Digitally enabled political outcomes of the Spanish Indignados movement. *Revista Internacional de Sociología, 74*(4), e048. https://doi.org/10.3989/ris.2016.74.4.048

Sampedro, V., & Lobera, J. (2014). The Spanish 15-M Movement: A consensual dissent? *Journal of Spanish Cultural Studies, 15*(1–2), 61–80. https://doi.org/10.1080/14636204.2014.938466

Sawicki, F., & Siméant, J. (2010). Decompartmentalizing the sociology of activism. A critique of recent tendencies in French studies. *Sociologie du travail, 52*(1), e83–125. https://doi.org/10.4000/sdt.16032

Siméant, J. (2001). Entrer, rester en humanitaire. Des fondateurs de Médecins sans frontières aux membres actuels des ONG médicales françaises. *Revue française de science politique, 51*(1–2), 47–72. https://doi.org/10.3917/rfsp.511.0047

Smaoui, S. (2017). *Faites place. Novices en lutte.* Textuel.

Tejerina, B., & Perugorría, I. (Ed.). (2018). *Crisis and Social Mobilization in Contemporary Spain. The M15 Movement.* Routledge.

Tejerina, B., Perugorría, I., Benski, T., & Langman, L. (2013). From Indignation to Occupation: A New Wave of Global Mobilization. *Current Sociology, 61*(4), 377–392. https://doi.org/10.1177/0011392113479738

Vestergren, S., Drury, J., & Chiriac, E. H. (2017). The biographical consequences of protest and activism: A systematic review and a new typology. *Social Movement Studies, 16*(2), 203–221. https://doi.org/10.1080/14742837.2016.1252665

Yates, L. (2015). Rethinking prefiguration: Alternatives, micropolitics and goals in social movements. *Social Movement Studies, 14*(1), 1–21. https://doi.org/10.1080/14742837.2013.870883

Appendix 1: The numerical results

As a complement to the method section, the two tables below synthesize the sociodemographic and political profiles of those who took part in the two rounds of interviews. They include indications of the modes of engagement of each individual before, during and after 15M based on Prado Galán and Fersch's (2020) categorization. These overviews are nevertheless simplistic compared with the various phases of engagement and disengagement presented in greater detail in the article.

Table 1. Presentation of respondents who participated in the first round of interviews only

No	Respondent	Sex	Age	Profession	Engagement before 15M	Participation in 15M	Engagement in 2013–15
1	Victor	M	33	Photographer	None	Medium (Sol)	High
2	Marcos	M	22	Student	None	High (Sol/Arganzuela)	None
3	Javi	M	27	Lawyer	High (civil disobedience collective)	High (Sol)	High (Legal Sol)
4	Emilio	M	63	Journalist	High (anarchist, CGT)	High (Sol/Villaverde)	High (Periódico 15M)
5	Rafa	M	23	Journalist	Medium (student movement)	High (Sol/Lavapiés)	High (Periódico 15M)
6	Inés	F	40	Unemployed (cultural project manager)	High (neighbourhood associations)	High (Sol)	High (review committee)
7	Juan	M	27	Student	None	Medium (Sol)	None
8	Ariel	M	31	Software developer	High (anti-capitalism group)	Low (Sol/Carabanchel)	High (anti-capitalism group)
9	Paula	F	26	TV producer	High (neighbourhood association movement, Okupa, JSF)	Medium (Sol/El Retiro)	High (Podemos)
10	Evelyn	F	41	Unemployed (accountant)	Low ~ High (local mobilization)	High (Sol/Carabanchel)	Medium (Carabanchel)
11	Lucía	F	31	Telemarketer	Low (anarchist, CNT)	Low ~ High (Carabanchel)	High (Carabanchel)
12	Julio	M	25	Performer	High (student movement, autonomous, Okupa)	High (Sol/Carabanchel)	High (Carabanchel, autonomous collective)
13	Adriana	F	45	Unemployed (cleaner)	None	None ~ High (Carabanchel)	Medium (Carabanchel)
14	Pablo	M	33	Consultant	High (student movement, Izquierda Unida, DRY)	High (Sol/Carabanchel)	High (Carabanchel)
15	Salvador	M	64	Retired (bricklayer)	High (labour movement, CGT, PCE)	High (Parla)	High (CGT)
16	Eduardo	M	30	Unemployed (healthcare assistant)	High (student movement, anti-fascist group, Okupa)	High (Sol/Parla)	Low
17	Pilar	F	29	Librarian	Medium (local community movement)	Medium (Parla)	Medium (local community movement)
18	Lola	F	23	Student	High (student movement, JSF)	High (Sol)	High (Podemos)
19	José	M	69	Retired (journalist)	High (CCOO, anti-racism collective)	High (Carabanchel)	High (Carabanchel)
20	Alberto	M	57	Unemployed (screen printer)	High (libertarian activist, Okupa)	High (Sol/Moratalaz/Carabanchel)	High (Carabanchel)
21	Amalia	F	36	Educational psychologist	High (International solidarity NGO, Izquierda Unida, CCOO)	High (Carabanchel)	High (Carabanchel/Izquierda Unida)
22	Fernando	M	36	Unemployed (scaffolder)	None	None ~ High (Carabanchel)	High (Carabanchel)

Notes

1. Low = occasional participation in non-political associations, demonstrations, protest events; Medium = recurrent participant in associations, protest event association, protest events; High = member of/collaborator in political organizations, unions, social movements. Regarding 'Engagement before 15M': Low ~ High = high level of engagement in the period immediately prior to 15M; High ~ Low = disengaged following a period of engagement (often as a young activist). Regarding 'Participation in 15M': None/Low ~ High = participation began a substantial time after the camps (one or more years after).
2. JSF and DRY are acronyms for Juventud Sin Futuro and ¡Democracia Real Ya!, two organizations that preceded 15M and that called for people to join the demonstration on 15 May 2011. Izquierda Unida is a left-wing coalition that includes the Spanish Communist Party (PCE). Comisiones Obreras (CCOO) is a trade union with historical links to the PCE. The CGT and CNT are anarchist trade unions, and Okupa is a squatter movement that sets up squatted self-managed social centres.
3. The respondents' main areas of participation in 15M are shown in parentheses (Carabanchel, Parla, etc.) and the committees that still existed at the time of interview (Legal Sol, Periódico 15M, etc.).

Table 2: Presentation of respondents who participated in both rounds of interviews

No	Respondent	Sex	Age	Profession	Engagement before 15M	Participation in 15M	Engagement in 2019
1	Javier	M	42	Unemployed (sound and lighting manager)	High (Okupa) ~ None	None ~ High (Carabanchel)	Medium (Okupa)
2	Mónica	F	45	Concierge	None	None ~ High (Carabanchel)	Medium (Okupa)
3	Elena	F	28	Healthcare assistant	Medium (Izquierda Unida)	High (Parla)	None
4	Miguel	M	32	Unemployed (warehouseman)	None	High (Parla)	None
5	Natalia	F	37	Primary school teacher	High ~ Low (Okupa)	High (Parla)	High (local collectives)
6	Esteban	M	51	Secondary school teacher	Low	High (Sol/Parla)	High (libertarian collectives)
7	Clara	F	37	Lawyer	Medium (NGO)	High (Sol/Parla)	High (feminist, environmental and animal rights movements)
8	Ruben	M	35	Accountant	None	High (Sol/Parla)	High (environmental and animal rights movements)
9	Luis	M	16	High school student	None	Medium (Parla)	High (libertarian groups)
10	Isabel	F	32	Unemployed (community worker)	None	High (Sol/Carabanchel)	High (feminist movement)
11	Gabriela	F	33	Cleaner	None	None ~ High (Carabanchel)	High (feminist association)
12	Manuel	M	44	Unemployed (surveyor)	None	None ~ High (Carabanchel)	None
13	Gloria	F	36	Freelance psychologist	Low	High (Parla)	Medium
14	Sergio	M	41	Library worker	Medium	High (Parla)	Medium
15	Camila	F	22	Student	Medium (NGO)	Low ~ High (Parla)	High (Podemos, municipal team)
16	Mario	M	24	Maintenance technician	Low	Medium (Sol/Parla)	Low
17	Andrés	M	36	Instructor	High (local community movement)	High (Sol/Parla)	High (Izquierda Unida, municipal team)
18	Dolores	F	49	Retired (secondary school teacher)	High ~ Low (feminist movement)	High (Parla)	High (libertarian and feminist collectives)

15-M movement and feminist economics: an insight into the dialogues between social movements and academia in Spain

Astrid Agenjo-Calderón ⓘ, Lucía Del Moral-Espín ⓘ and Raquel Clemente-Pereiro

ABSTRACT
This paper explores the relationship between the articulation of the 15-M movement in Spain and the expansion of Feminist Economics (FE) at the feminist base of this movement, in particular, in Feminism Committees (FC-15 M). We assert that this expansion was due to FE's capacity to explain the 2008 crisis beyond its economic-financial dimensions and to analyse the effects of the political-economic austerity measures on the sustainability of life. We claim that a differentiating feature of FE in Spain is its permeability to dialogue with social movements. Therefore, it has become more politicized and critical than other academic fields. This influence has also been reflected in the structure and contents of the most recent FE national conferences, which from 2013 on included not only the classic academic strand but also training and political action strands. In order to explore this development, our methodology includes interviews with key informants; document analysis of material generated in the conferences and the Feminism Committees of 15-M; questionnaires to activists, academics, and practitioners of FE; and informal observation as direct participants of the described processes and events. The paper begins with an introduction to FE thought and its connections with so-called 'Feminism for the 99%' and continues with a methodological section. The twofold results section analyzes the dialogues between FE and FC-15 M. It concludes with a summary of the key ideas presented and some final remarks.

1. Introduction

Feminist economics (FE) can be defined as a stream of heterodox economic thought but also as a proposal for political action (Agenjo-Calderón, 2019). On the one hand, it is constituted as an economic discourse with five main components (Power, 2013): incorporation of caring and unpaid labour as fundamental economic activities; use of well-being as a measure of economic success; analysis of economic, political, and social processes and power relations; inclusion of ethical goals and values as an intrinsic part of the analysis; and interrogation of differences by class, race-ethnicity, and other factors. On the other hand, FE is also a political practice committed to economic transformation and envisioning new scenarios where all people have access to a dignified life in conditions of justice and equity (Carrasco, 2014; Picchio, 2009; Pérez Orozco, 2014). This has favoured the multi-belongingness (Martínez, 2019) of feminist activists and feminist economists, a process that problematizes the relation between academia and activism and theory and practice. Indeed, this is a permanent issue within feminism (Araiza & González, 2017; Martínez, 2019).

The links between FE and the women's and grassroots feminist movements have been visible throughout the so-called three waves of feminism[1] (Agenjo-Calderón, 2021). And it can be seen even more clearly in what some authors already call the Fourth Wave (Baumgardner, 2011; Munro, 2013). This paradigm of the waves has received insightful critiques as a way of framing feminism. However, it also has significant potential as a metaphor to make visible continuity, inclusivity and multiplicity within feminist identity, discourse, and praxis (Evans & Chamberlain, 2015). The so-called fourth wave would refer to the emergence of a new feminist movement at the beginning of the 21st century, focusing on the empowerment of women, the use of internet tools, and intersectionality. A movement united around the world by slogans and hashtags such as #MeToo, #NosotrasParamos, the Spanish equivalent to #WeStrike, #VivasNosQueremos, #NiUnaMenos (in English 'NotOneLess' to face gender-based violence and murders). Likewise, in this context, a new radical feminist activism and militancy has taken shape. Arruzza, Bhattacharya and Fraser (2019) call it 'Feminism For The 99%' (in a clear analogy to the slogan of Occupy Wall Street and the 15-M movement). This Feminism For the 99% reclaims the historical roots of feminist struggles for workers' rights and social justice, and invites one to 'question that classless and naive look at women's relations [...] with the punitive power of the state' (Skulj, 2020, p. 1). It also recovers interest in redistributive issues and environmental concerns, seeking confluences with other anti-capitalist social movements. In this sense, we speak of a 99% engaged with questions of exclusion: gender, race, ethnicity, origin, sexual orientation, or gender identity. Nevertheless, it is also concerned with material objectives of a universal nature, such as the redistribution of income, the struggle against the sexual division of labour and the negotiation of power and difference (Alabao et al., 2018; Juris et al., 2012).

In Spain, this Feminism For The 99% has been increasingly visible since the beginning of the century. For example, it was already present within the anti-globalization movement and the World March of Women in 2000. Moreover, in 2002 General Strike when some feminist groups, inspired by historical processes such as the 'Women's Day Off' strike in Iceland in 1975, raised the need to rethink the labour strike as a political intervention for three reasons:

> (1) it does not reflect the experience of exploitation and unfair distribution of domestic and care work, mostly carried out by women in the 'non-productive' sphere of cohabitation units, (2) it marginalizes [...] certain jobs which are increasingly widespread and commonly grouped under the label of 'precarious' and (3) it does not pay any attention to precarious, flexible, invisible and undervalued work that is specifically feminized and/or migrant (sexual, domestic, care work, listening, etc.)
>
> (Precarias a la deriva, 2004, p. 22).

These reasons, based on the knowledge built through 'militant research processes' (Cruells & Ruiz, 2014), are rooted in FE approaches and would lead to the proposal of a 'care strike'. In the following years, these perspectives would be consolidated as a tool that recovers a historical form of struggle for redistribution, putting other forms of work and other relationships at the centre (Precarias a la Deriva, 2004). In this period prior to the 2008 crisis, the precariousness of existence and the feminization of work would be two central focuses of attention for some feminist groups (like *Precarias a la Deriva* or *Territorio Doméstico*, among others).

With the outbreak of the crisis in 2008, these concerns took on a new status. In the new context, numerous feminists began to articulate and make visible feminist readings of the crisis understood as systemic, economic, social and ecological (Carrasco, 2009; Gálvez & Torres, 2010; Perez Orozco, 2009). These concerns were also reflected in the *Jornadas Feministas Estatales* (National Feminist Meeting) in Granada in 2009, which was a critical moment in the evolution of the autonomous feminist movement in Spain. It was a space for feminist knowledge production and exchange that blurred the boundaries between activism and academia.

By 2011, the political dimension of this crisis was more than evident from a feminist perspective. In this context, the 15-M movement erupted as an open, continuous wave of political experimentation, determined to introduce politics into everyday life, building counter-power in defence of life (Galcerán, 2012). From the beginning, many 15-M feminist participants felt the need to unite and work together in thematic groups. These were called Feminism Committees (FC-15 M), where much of the previous knowledge about the functioning of the economic system, precariousness, and the crises were shared. As will be shown, we understand 15-M as a diffuse movement with very visible nuclei, such as the *acampadas* (protest camps), 15-M committees (among others FC-15 M), neighbourhood committees, and virtual spaces but which also had an influence that extended well beyond these arenas. This democratizing aspiration for mobilization has its roots, according to Flesher Fominaya (2020), in three ideational frameworks: Autonomy; Hacker Ethics and Technopolitical Imaginaries; and Feminism, which is interconnected with anti-militarist and environmentalist epistemologies and methodologies.

Departing from this ideational feminist framework, in this paper, we focus on the dialogues between academia (specifically Feminist Economics) and 15-M (specifically Feminist Committees-15 M). We propose two objectives: 1) exploring FE influence in the work of FC-15 M. We believe that these committees incorporated FE as an innovative contribution for explaining the causes and consequences of the crisis, decentralizing markets, and putting people's living conditions and care at the centre of political attention. However, we believe it is wise 'to be wary of a tendency of academics to overstate their own importance to struggles for social change' (Choudry, 2020, p. 32). Therefore, our second objective is: 2) exploring the effects of the 15 M on Feminist Economics. Specifically, our hypothesis is that FE, in Spain and especially since the crisis, has been more open to incorporating the contributions of social movements, in general, and feminist movements, in particular. This would have favoured the democratization and politicization of this current of thought and its academic spaces, specifically in the National FE conferences in so far as they reflect the evolution of the themes and methodologies addressed by feminist economists.

Based on these initial considerations, the central structure of this paper consists of a methodological section and a twofold results section where we analyze the connection between FE and CF-15 M. We conclude with a summary of the main ideas and some final remarks.

2. Methodology

When approaching the feminist movement, we find a particularly talkative research 'object' that questions its very own classification and qualification as a research object/subject (Martínez, 2019). Taking this into consideration is very relevant when designing and developing a study such as the one presented here.

It should be noted that not all of us (co-authors) work in academia, but we all have been part of the organization of at least one of the FE conferences held in the post-2011 period. In parallel, one of us (Astrid Agenjo-Calderón) had a very intense and prolonged involvement in a FC-15 M. This involvement and participation were not guided by research objectives. In fact, the activist, formative, and self-learning purposes were the main drivers of participation at that time. Despite this, it included a continuous process of informal observation and self-reflexivity, which is fundamental in the process of research (Simons, 2009); a provisional on-going critical-reflexive approach grounded in the contingency of our lives (Maxey, 1999), which questioned the boundaries between academia and activism. Guided by the principles of feminist epistemology and situated knowledge (Haraway, 1988; Harding, 2008; Longino, 2017), we consider that feminist movement accounts are a key source of knowledge. However, they are not infallible, given that they also depend on the research context and the changing relationship between the subject and the object of research (Martínez, 2019). As feminist researchers and academics, we experienced a blurring of times and spaces. Militancy, teaching, and the generation of knowledge converge in a feminist challenge 'bridging the academic/activist' divide (Eschle & Maiguashca, 2006).

To reach our objectives, we used methodological triangulation. Five semi-structured individual and group interviews were conducted. Three of them, individual interviews, were carried out in 2018 before the VI Conference with key feminist economists in the Spanish-speaking context. The interviewees reflected different generational positions, status and professional development both within and outside academia. One of them was herself an active member of a FC-15 M. The other two interviews were online group interviews carried out in 2020 with participants of two of these FC-15 M: One interview was conducted with two members of *Feminismos Sol* (Madrid) and the other one with two members *Setas Feministas* (Seville). Both FCparticipated in the post-2011 FE Conferences. All of these interviews were recorded and selectively transcribed.

In addition, fourteen standardized online questionnaires[2] with open and closed questions were also collected in 2018 before the VI Conference. The (intentional) sample was composed of people who had participated either as promoters, organizers, or attendees in different FE Conferences, and some of them were also part of FC-15 M. Care was also taken to collect the voices of people in different positions both within and outside academia, as reflected in the following Table 1.

The questionnaires collect information on the content, structure and work methodologies of the conferences. They also include information on personal, social or political events that influenced the trajectory of these spaces and the informants' relationship to them. This information allows us to advance in understanding the context in which the FE conferences spread from academia to the socio-political sphere.

In parallel, we analysed the documents generated by the FC-15 M: manifestos, presentations, articles, material for workshops, pamphlets and slogans. In addition, we

Table 1. Interviews.

LIST OF INTERVIEWS		
Semi-structured interviews		
Name / Group	Profile	Code or Name
Cristina Carrasco	Retired academic	CC
Lina Gálvez	Consolidated academic/ Positions of academic responsibility	LG
Amaia Pérez Orozco	Social consultant	APO
Feminismos Sol	2 founding members	FS1 – FS2
Setas Feministas	2 founding members	SF1 – SF2
Standardised interview (online questionnaire)		
Profile[3]	Number	Type of participation	Number
Academic	9	Organisers (Local committee)	5
Professional-consulting/EES	5	Organisers (Scientific Committee)	5
Activists-Participants in 15M-FC	11	Organisers (Political Action Committee)	8
		Participants	5

Source: Own elaboration

analysed the documents created around the organization, structure, development and subsequent evaluation of FE conferences, as well as documents related to internal management, dissemination, and advocacy (see Table 2 for details).

3. Dialogues and convergences between the Feminist Committees 15-M movement and Feminist Economics

15-M was a movement that appeared in response to the socio-economic consequences of the global economic crisis of 2008 and, in particular, to the disappointment and indignation generated by the austerity policies. These policies subordinated politics to economic interests and accentuated the lack of confidence in democratic institutions and the electoral system. Moreover, they intensified the lack of expectations in terms of employment and fundamental social rights, especially for young people. The main difference compared to previous, similar mobilizations, in addition to their greater convening power, was to turn the squares into an undefined meeting space for dialogue, enunciation and expression of ideas by civil society. (Bonet I Marti, 2015).

This movement irrupted in the continuity of state policies that, until then, had expropriated any possibility of political intervention beyond that of political parties and the ephemeral participation in elections (Galcerán, 2012). In this regard, 15-M marked a turning point, an exercise in participatory, horizontal and self-managed democracy; an unusual impulse towards social resistance and the will to envision a different future (Cruells & Ruiz, 2014; 2020 This was associated with the fact that the discursive DNA of the 15-M movement was formed by a double helix of anti-austerity and pro-democracy demands (Flesher Fominaya, 2020). In this sense, one of the specificities of the movement was a clearer 'will to democratize' (Cruells & Ezquerra, 2015) than in previous movements where it had already been somewhat present, at least in those which explicitly demanded greater equality and protection of minorities (della Porta & Diani, 2010).

From the beginning of 15-M, many feminist participants felt the need to unite in response to the absence of feminist demands and the persistence of patriarchal attitudes in the protest camps. They joined in a very visible way in thematic groups, termed

Table 2. Documents analysed from the FE conferences and the 15M-FCs.

Type	Document
Conference information and dissemination documents*.	• Call for papers • Conference program • Congress websites
Organisational documents and conference communication channels*.	• Minutes of preparatory meetings • Call-letters for the consolidation of the State Feminist Economics Network for the organisation of the congresses • Call letters to the congress organisers. • Participant data collection forms
Conference Outreach and Advocacy Documents*.	• Manifestos • Dossiers • Debate / action reports • Rapporteurships • Summary of contents • Minute books
Documents and materials related to the activity of some feminist commissions of the 15-M Movement (Feministes indignades, Feminismos Sol and Setas Feministas).	• Workshop proposals to congresses (Feminismos Sol, Feministes indignades and Setas Feministas) • Thematic dossiers (Feminismos Sol) • Dossiers and presentation (Feminismos Sol, Setas Feministas and Feministes indignades) • Leaflets, posters and actions' materials (Setas Feministas) • Articles (Setas Feminist mushrooms) • Photos and videos of workshops and actions (Setas Feministas)

The documents of all the conferences held were analysed:
- BILBAO 2005, I Conference. University of the Basque Country
- ZARAGOZA 2007, II Conference. University of Zaragoza
- BAEZA 2009, III Conference. Pablo de Olavide University
- MADRID 201, One-day Seminar. Complutense University of Madrid
- CARMONA 2013, IV Conference. Pablo de Olavide University
- VIC 2015, V Conference. University of Vic
- MADRID 2017, Conference. Self-managed (supported by UCM)
- VALENCIA 2019, VI Conference. Chair of Feminist Economics, University of Valencia.

Source: Own elaboration.

Feminism Committees (FC-15 M), in various parts of Spain: *Feminismos Sol* (Madrid), *Feministes indignades* (Barcelona), *Setas Feministas* (Seville), *#AcampadaObradoiro* (Santiago de Compostela), *Feministas bastardas* (Zaragoza) or the *Comisión Transfeminista* (Valencia). Feminists also collaborated in workgroups or simply by locating themselves in strategic places of the encampments and making occasional interventions (VV.AA, 2012). They arose out of the need for a 'space of their own' for women, dykes and trans feminists who participated in this pro-democracy movement which still had significant androcentric biases.

According to the reviewed literature and our interviews, the constitution of these FCs-15 M was seen, in general, as being an impromptu affair that divided the movement. Therefore, their work was not without difficulties and conflicts. One of the most notorious points of contention was the removal of the feminist banner 'The revolution will be feminist or it will not be' that had been hung in Puerta del Sol (Madrid). This incident highlighted the lack of a consensus in understanding feminism as a point of convergence of the 15-M movement (Cruells & Ruiz, 2014; Cruells & Ezquerra, 2015; Flesher Fominaya, 2020; Galcerán, 2012; Galdón, 2017; Gámez, 2015). The interviewees posit that 'Deep down, nobody wanted a feminist group to be created within the 15-M movement.' Everyone said, 'No, feminism [should be] transversal' (SF2) and even that the FCs could be 'counter-hegemonic' within the movement:

> *Feminismos Sol* was a counter-hegemonic group within 15-M [...], we, of course, we were within that maelstrom, and we grabbed things here and there, but this does not mean that there was a bidirectionality or that we had the same possibilities of being heard.
> (FS1)

The FCs-15 M interpreted these events as a sign of ignorance about their struggle and, in response, they offered feminist pedagogy and training using simple workshops (Calvo & Álvarez, 2015; Flesher Fominaya, 2020; Galcerán, 2012, Cruells & Ezquerra, 2015): [we] had to "go back to pedagogy, to very basic issues of the feminist movement" (FS2).

These workshops also provided spaces to think and make the diversity and plurality of feminisms visible (Gámez, 2015) as well as establish networks imbued with the experience of the 15-M movement itself. Developing spaces for collective reflection and learning and valuing processes of informal and non-formal learning is crucial for producing knowledge in movements (Choudry, 2020). In fact, in recent years, it has been argued that 15-M contributed to revitalizing feminism by allowing different feminist visions and generations to come into contact, engage in dialogue and work together (Flesher Fominaya, 2020; Galdón, 2017; Gámez, 2015). Likewise, there has been a reflection on how much the dynamics and roles of the feminist struggle impacted the 15-M movement both discursively and in the field of practices: horizontality, organization and participation in physical and virtual networks, self-care and openness to promote relational policies and intersectional strategies connecting diverse struggles for social and political equality (Cruells & Ezquerra, 2015; Gámez, 2015). Of particular interest to our case is the 'profound influence [in 15-M movement] of feminist discourse and its emphasis on the need to redefine the central task of politics as primarily caring for citizens and placing the interests of life before capital' (Flesher Fominaya, 2020, p. 119).

3.1. FE perspectives within 15-M Feminism Commissions: the crisis from a feminist gaze

The fact that these notions of 'politics as caring' and 'life before capital' are also crucial in feminist economic thought (Pérez Orozco, 2014), contributed to our interest with more in depth reserch of the politics of knowledge production between FC-15 M and FE. These committees gave way to an increasing interest in economic issues, both at macro and micro levels, in calling attention to how the productive and financial economy is sustained by the invisible exploitation of nature and women's domestic and care work.

> I learned about FE during the 15-M. In my old [feminist] group, we never talked about care work, about putting life at the centre ... all these concepts that I learned with FE and Ecofeminism (SF2).

> In Madrid, many in the feminist movement were keen to see what feminist economists had to say about the crisis (APO, personal communication).

As Gámez (2015, p. 326) argues:

> the initial tensions with other members of the protest camps made women realise that they had to give priority to making their vindications understood within the context of the current neoliberal crisis. Therefore, they focused on the links between capitalism and

patriarchy. In the face of quotidian precariousness, the materiality of the feminist slogan "the personal is political" was clearer than ever.

In this sense, Galcerán (2012) also stresses that the contributions of feminist economists to 15-M were central in bringing the organization of care in a context of commodification and incessant precarization of living conditions to the forefront.

> During the Seville campouts [...] I remember people who heard for the first time the concept of the 'care economy', who heard about the (economic) iceberg[4] for the first time, about circuits, about reproductive work. And seeing older women passing by nodding their heads. (SF2)

> What was really important to me was that, on the first anniversary of 15-M, academia went out into the street. Because it was a time when university professors taught in the street and Lina [Galvez] talked in a discussion about Feminist Economics in the Incarnation Square. We could also hear Amaia [Perez Orozco] ... I remember it as something rather more powerful when academia approached the street than when I approached academia (SF1).

This favoured a better understanding of the crisis as systemic or multidimensional, encompassing the economy, ecology and social reproduction. It is also a denunciation of how structural adjustments 'rescue' financial institutions and large companies while increasing precariousness and the individualization of risk. This strongly impacts the women performing most of the invisible work that makes life possible (Galcerán, 2012; Gámez, 2015).

A central point made by feminists in 15-M was to make visible how household units bear the impact of economic adjustments and cuts in health, education and family support. They either modify or reduce consumption or deploy 'survival strategies' (Pérez Orozco, 2014). The video *A Feminist in the Market* made in 2012 by *Setas Feministas* (and presented at the 2013 FE Conference) collects many of these survival strategies, which generally involve more unpaid work for women, via the testimonies of diverse women. Also, Feminismos Sol Manifesto *The Euro or Life* stated: '(The euro pact) will not solve the crisis but will aggravate it. It is in the homes where the crisis is absorbed, paid and "solved",' unjustly falling on women, who do magic to keep the household afloat' (El Euro o la Vida, Manifesto *Feminismos Sol*, June 2011).

Likewise, FC-15 M generated reflection regarding the issues of debt and austerity from a feminist perspective. For example, at the end of 2012, *Feminismos Sol* created a study and workgroup on debt audit and disobedience to address androcentric biases and hostilities:

> The Economic Commission of 15 M was a very hostile environment for feminist proposals. And from that hostility of the group, from the lack of permeability of feminist proposals within these economic debate environments, which were mixed, very masculinized and very unkind, the need to generate a debate group on the debt, to try to analyse the debt from a feminist perspective arises within the Commission of Feminismos Sol
>
> *(FS1).*

As we will address in the next section, this group also participated in and presented their conclusions at the IV FE Conference in 2013.

FCs-15 M work created a collective process of reinterpreting reality, formulating new values and making social conditions that had previously gone unnoticed into issues worthy of attention and general action (Choudry, 2020). As the social movement scholar has pointed out, the importance of constantly 'revisit[ing] and rethink[ing] not only the politics of producing knowledge, but also what and who that knowledge is for' (Choudry,

2020, p. 32). In this sense, it is worth noting that the FCs-15 M influenced the movement's practices by raising the need to overcome the sexual division of labour and transcend the struggles of egos and competition in the camps for building a sustainable activism compatible with life. In this sense, they promoted a debate on self-care, the care of the participants and of the process itself, as opposed to the traditional male militant style that pays little attention to the body, gestures and positioning (Galcerán, 2012).

The care work strikes are a clear example of this centrality of care. These strikes (already called for in previous years) were called in the two general strikes of 2012 and contributed to the incorporation and recognition of increasingly diverse subjects in the mobilization, encouraging the participation and inclusion of historically left out-groups (Cruells & Ruiz, 2014).

It is important to highlight that the FCs-15 M were connected with and inspired each other continuously thanks to social networks, meetings and, also, FE conferences:

> There was a lot of communication, so when suddenly a FC from one part of the country came up with a proposal, there were times when you copied and copylefted it and promoted it.
> *(FS2)*
>
> The interesting thing about the [FE] conferences or any meeting we had was weaving these networks, these ties and communicating with each other and inviting each other to learn to listen to each other's realities and points of view
> *(SF1).*

This interconnection materialized, for example, in the publication of the monograph "R-evolving: Feminisms in the 15-M Movement" (VV.AA, 2012), in which FCs-15 M from different cities collaborated. In this publication, three horizons for future work were proposed: to transversalize feminist discourses in neighbourhood and town assemblies, to create and maintain feminist networks, and to delegate and share tasks and responsibilities of the feminist struggle with *compañeros* (male comrades).

Thus, over time, the discourses of the 15-M movement incorporated a certain recognition of feminist proposals and perspectives, in particular the cognitive frameworks of 'life' and 'precariousness' developed in FE (Cruells & Ezquerra, 2015; Cruells & Ruiz, 2014). Feminist groups themselves also continued to deepen and share knowledge about FE. For example, in Madrid, the '*Eje de precariedad y Economía Feminista*' emerged, an autonomous work group born from the feminist struggle that organized the 2014 Women's Day March (in which the *Feminismos Sol* study and workgroup on debt audit and disobedience participated), still in force today. In Seville, *Setas Feministas* stated that their agenda 'revolved more around the problems of the precarization of life, a feminist critique of the economy, and direct action in the street' (Setas Feministas, 2014, p.1). They transferred this agenda to the '*Asamblea de Mujeres Diversas*' of the 2014 Women's Day March and to the 'feminist coven' performance on 1 May 2014, which was called the 'Procession of the Archconfraternity of the Holiest Rebellious Pussy and the Holy Burial of Social-Labour Rights' (for which three activists were later tried in court).

FE frameworks also permeated collectives and practices that could be considered part of the '15-M network' as well as the creation and success of municipalist platforms in different cities. In this sense, an emerging topic of debate for feminisms was the reception or even appropriation of these frameworks and the danger of emptying or depoliticizing them. Another debate is developing around the identification of FE to a single field, care work, which could reduce its transformative potential:

the meaning of care work has been used so extensively that it has reached a point where it has even been emptied of its content so that care work became everything and, in the end, it was nothing. [...] and then there is an identification all the time of FE as meaning only care work. In other words, issues such as precariousness, it's as if they have been lost, blurred ... everything that has to do with the FE of sustaining lives in terms of diversity, the meaning of health, the meaning of education, what it would mean to completely transform the organization of the economy so that lives are effectively sustained [...] this has also been lost.

(FS2)

This risk, the hypertrophy of the concept, as well as its idealization, has been criticized by part of FE (academic and activist) and, according to Pérez-Orozco (2014), has led to an increasing use of the notion of Sustainability of Life.

3.2 The influence of the 15 M-movement on Spanish FE: The 'political pillar' of the conferences

Our analysis of the expansion of FE in Spain identifies several crucial influences, which in turn are linked to the socio-political and economic context of the time:

• The rise and subsequent institutionalization of feminism, enacting specific laws for equality and the increased presence of gender issues at the academic and political level.

• The consolidation of Critical Economics in general, and FE in particular, in international academia, through the creation of networks, organizations and publications throughout the world. In Spain, the 'Jornadas de Economía Crítica' (Critical Economics Conference), held since the 1980s, were a meeting point where the need to have more space for feminist economists arose and gave rise to national conferences, specifically for FE.

• The influence of social movements, particularly the student movement for a critical economy, the feminist movement itself, and, as we expand upon in this article, the 15-M movement and the anti-austerity struggles.

These influences are reflected in Figure 1. This compiles the development of the FE in Spain chronologically in relation to relevant socio-political milestones and social movements linked to it, as well as similar spaces in the western international context.

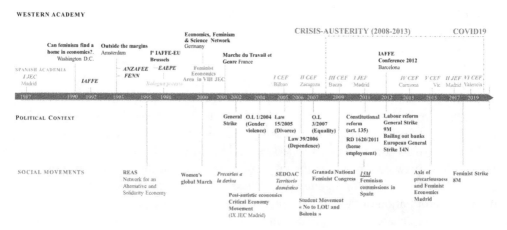

Figure 1. Timeline in Spanish FE.
Source: Own elaboration.

Regarding the influence of social movements on FE, Carrasco (2014, p. 36) states that:

> FE has developed, and continues to do so, in an on-going exchange between academic institutions and the various social movements, which could not be otherwise, since it is presented to us as a theoretical body, but also as a political roadmap.

Both Carrasco and Pérez-Orozco (2014) point out that, based on this influence, visions have emerged within FE that seek to liberate the discursive economic space from what Gibson-Graham (2006) call 'capital-centrism'. These authors integrate three central elements 1) the 'use of a new language' that allows for identifying the existing economic diversity; 2) a 'politics of the subject' around how subjects are constructed that contributes to fostering other possible economies; 3) a 'politics of collective action' that offers feminist alternatives to the existing capitalist model (Gibson-Graham, 2006). These three elements make it possible to dialogue with other non-academic discourses coming from social movements, as well as other worldviews that confront capitalist epistemology with different grassroots epistemologies. For example, decolonial feminisms; ecofeminisms and decrecentist ecological proposals; the popular, social and solidarity economy; alter/anti-capitalism; and feminist reflections on "buen vivir". This has resulted in the consolidation of multiple spaces for research, learning and collective creation in the field of FE. One of these spaces are the national FE Conferences. Although their emergence predated 15-M, the movement represented a qualitative shift in the evolution of these conferences.

Their origin dates back to the 1980s when a group of critical economists began to meet in the Critical Economics Conferences to discuss new emerging proposals in heterodox economics. This included those that specifically examined gender issues; however, the spaces provided remained nonetheless insufficient for many feminist economists.

> The specific need [of the FE Conferences] has to do with the fact that [...] heterodox economics in general leaves FE a little aside; it did not give it a place. We often criticize that mainstream economics, neoclassical economics, has not admitted the postulates of FE. But the reality is that heterodox economics has not been very permeable to the postulates of FE either, especially because it is based on very productivist postulates and is therefore quite removed from the main postulates of FE so that gap was there and had to be addressed in some way (LG, personal communication).

From the Critical Economics Conferences onwards, 'the need to have more space and more time for our topics' (CC, personal communication) began to take shape. The first FE Conference, Bilbao 2005, was organized and, from then on, they take place every two years. 2011 was a significant turning point in terms of the relevance of the academic sphere. On 12 May 2011, three days before the 15-M foundational demonstration, a FE Congress was organized open to 'students, researchers, activists, trade unionists ... economists or not, feminists interested in economic issues' to prepare for the International Association for Feminist Economics (IAFFE) Conference 2012 that would take place in Barcelona. At that conference, an informal meeting of the network of Spanish feminist economists was organized in Plaza de Catalunya at the same time as a meeting of the 15-M movement, which was attended by well-known feminist economists. There, it was agreed to expand the national conferences to three key branches: research (academic-activist), workshops (theoretical-academic and practical experiences) and political debate/social action (to strengthen the network and generate policy proposals).

Thus, from 2013, the FE Conferences opened themselves explicitly, becoming 'to some extent, less academic and more linked to the feminist movement, social movements, the social and solidarity economy … and less strictly to the university' (APO, personal communication). Not only did they focus on the above mentioned three branches, but also arranged space for democratic meetings and artistic interventions. As a declaration of principle, the conference poster itself (Image 1) reproduces an image of *Setas Feministas* Committee at a demonstration.

This permeability to social movements is also visible in the evolution of the conferences' structure (Table 3). From 2009 onwards, there has been an evident increase in the number and diversity of the themes and an incorporation of emerging topics connected to the socio-economic alternatives linked to the FE. In terms of the conferences' structure, spaces designed from a social transformation rather than an academic perspective have been included: workshops and training sessions, artistic interventions and assembly spaces.

The interviews and questionnaires carried out with conference participants and organizers, highlight how this evolution was strongly influenced by the socio-political context, particularly by the crisis; the resistance and alternatives that arose in response to it; and the increasing engagements of feminist groups:

Image 1. Poster IV FE Conference, Carmona 2013.
Source: Pablo de Olavide University

Table 3. Evolution of the thematic areas and structure of FE conferences.

	TEMATIC TOPICS	AREAS OF CONFERENCE
BILBAO 2005	1. Living and working conditions (8) 2. Public policies (8) 3. International economy (8)	Presentations of academic papers Plenary Sessions
ZARAGO-ZA 2007	1. Fundamentals of Feminist Economics (1) 2. Labour market (2) 3. Living conditions (2) 4. Public policies (2) 5. Science and Technology (1)	Presentations of academic papers Plenary Sessions
BAEZA 2009	1. Times and work 2. Public policies 3. International economy	Presentations of academic papers Plenary Sessions
CARMONA 2013	1. Public policies (9) 2. Conciliation and co-responsibility (4) 3. Education (2) 4. Sustainability and feminist thinking (11) 5. Works (2) 6. Economic Crisis (3) 7. Time and work in the provision of care (4) 8. Taxation and budgets (4) 9. Dependence and care (2) 10. Entrepreneurs and jobs in companies (5) 11. Development and cooperation (6) 12. Labour and the labour market (2) – Training: 7 Debate/political action: 8	Presentations of academic papers Training Political Action Plenary Sessions Assembly Artistic interventions
VIC 2015	1. The labour market (19) 2. Care (8) 3. Welfare status and public policies (14) 4. Living conditions, models and collective imaginaries (10) 5. Economic alternatives (18) – Training: 5 Debate/political action: 12	Presentations of academic papers Training Political Action Plenary Sessions Assembly Artistic interventions
VALENCIA 2019	1. Care (21) 2. Dismantling neoliberalism (16) 3. Ecofeminism (21) 4. Public policies (22) 5. Gender-focused budgets (11) 6. Feminist resistances and change strategies (25)	Presentations of academic papers Training Political Action Plenary Sessions Assembly Artistic interventions Division by topic, not by blocks

Source: Own elaboration.

There was a very important moment for the EF, which were those years in which the crisis exploded with the [slogan] 'they do not represent us', with a rejection of the official policy. And therefore, many people from social movements who were looking for alternatives found the proposals of FE attractive. Then, FE, not only the conferences but FE in general, made a very important leap, and 300 people started to come to the FE Conferences (CC, personal communication).

It is also worth noting that other currents of critical economic thought, such as social economy, environmentalism, degrowth, agroecology and food sovereignty have shown interest in and have incorporated FE principles and approaches. '[There is] much interest in how to put FE in practice' by 'people who do feel a connection with FE but to do other things' (APO, personal communication).

Indeed, Astrid Agenjo-Calderón recalls how she explained to the movement's assemblies how the organization of the Feminist Economics Conference in 2013 was evolving.

As we pointed out in the previous section, the FCs-15 M were among the groups that approached the FE Conferences and actively participated in them. For example, *Setas Feministas* presented a video, and *Feministes Indignades* and the austerity debt work/study group from *Feminismos Sol* offered workshops:

> I wouldn't even have shown up there, but they told us that, for the first time, the FE Conferences was opening up and that they were going to have workshops and spaces for activists, not necessarily linked to academia. From then on, sessions were scheduled for several weeks […] meetings to share FE topics. And from then on, a lot of people became interested in attending the conference in Carmona. (FS1)

> Work was done throughout the year [by *Feminismo Sol*] to warm up for the Carmona [Conference], which linked up with other networks created due to the National Feminist Meeting in Granada in 2009 (APO, personal communication)

In the questionnaire responses there seems to be a broad consensus that the FE Conferences: 1) have strengthened their ties with social movements and the feminist movement; 2) have acquired a more interdisciplinary character; 3) have incorporated new themes and emerging interests; and 4) that the current structure of the conference in three branches is interesting and enriching. This evolution is regarded as positive by the majority of our informants. They also consider that there has been a good presence of militant and activist voices, breadth and variety of topics dealt with and importance given to each of its different components (Research – Training workshops – Political debate/social action, small group meetings and larger democratic meetings).

The proceedings of the conferences themselves underline this openness, cross-contamination and the intention to generate not only academic understandings but also political proposals:

> Some 400 people from the world of academia, civil society and social movements met in Vic in early July 2015 to discuss and reflect on the progress made in the field of Feminist Economics in recent years, as well as its potential to generate alternatives to the multi-dimensional and civilizational crisis in which we have been immersed for so long (V FE Conference, Vic 2015 Proceedings Book).

This has led to an increase in the number of participants and proposals submitted over the last 15 years as the following figure (Figure 2) shows, except for the Zaragoza FEC.

This evolution, however, has not been free from tensions. This can be seen in the lack of consensus about whether it is important for the EF conferences to maintain the

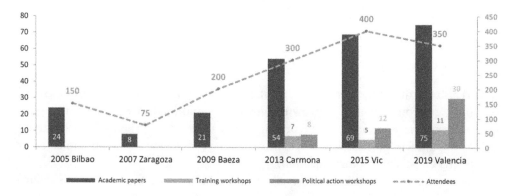

Figure 2. Number of proposals submitted and attendees.

academic character with which they began. Although half (13) of the questionnaire respondents agree with this idea, one informant completely disagrees, and the rest do not consider it relevant. When asked about the future of these conferences, the responses focus on two scenarios: 1) to configure a space for debate and reflection, collective construction and generation of proposals, and 2) to articulate and link different areas related to FE, within and outside academia.

Cristina Carrasco aptly summarizes what has been analysed in this section, starting from the idea that these conferences are a privileged source for learning about and understanding FE's research/action agendas in Spain.

> The [FE] conferences have evolved from being more economics centred to more interdisciplinary and perhaps from being more analytical to more political. I think it is good to be analytical and political simultaneously, but not political without analytical; we are not going to simply repeat pre-existing slogans. We are going to analyse the world because we want to transform it (CC, personal communication).

4. Discussion and conclusions

Feminist Economics is a line of thought and political action that has expanded and gained visibility in Spain within and beyond academic environments. This process may be associated with the emergence of a new wave of radical feminist activism at the beginning of the 21st century. FE and these struggles converged and expanded in the 15-M movement, a movement that set out to unveil the capital-life conflict: 'If austerity policies neglect people's material needs by placing capital before life, as some activists succidnctly put it, the camp inverted that formula, putting life before capital' (Flesher Fominaya, 2020, p. 128). Feminist Committees-15 M not only incorporated and disseminated FE concepts and explanation through workshops, artistic interventions and collective reflection and learning spaces, but also produced knowledge from within people's, particularly women's, everyday experiences.

In this article, we approach these processes from our situated position as feminist academics and activists, trying to articulate different forms of knowledge. The analysis of documents, interviews and questionnaires shows that, within the crisis context, there has been a back-and-forth process in the relations between FE and FC-15 M. FE has been permeable to and overlapped with the knowledge, demands and practices generated by social movements. This has fostered a democratization and politicization of FE and its academic spaces in Spain, blurring, or at least problematizing, the boundaries between academia and activism spaces, which is a hallmark of FE in Spain, as has become evident in the FE Conferences held since 2011.

Exploring the evolution of these conferences is helpful to address this reciprocal influence: how social movements, particularly FC-15 M, have incorporated FE frameworks and how the FE conferences changed their trajectory to a more political one. Our analysis posits that this reciprocal influence has been due to: the capacity of FE to explain the multidimensionality of the so-called 'economic-financial crisis'; to problematize the political-economic measures applied in response to it; and to generate a theoretical framework that is intertwined with the struggles around the sustainability of life (the housing movement, universal basic income, domestic work and so on).

Thus, based on discourses and practices that exceed the strictly academic, FE has also been articulated by subjects that are usually excluded from the generation of knowledge and that embodied practices that transcend what is usually understood as 'economics'. The political character of FE and the activist and academic multi-belonging of many feminist economists has been a crucial link between the 15-M movement and the EF Conference. The commitment to the sustainability of life has also promoted intersectionality in the struggles and in those spaces that claim to be an alternative to the current economy, and rejects the various facets of the heteropatriarchal, ecocidal and racist capitalist system. All this reveals how the academic-activist linkages reinforced FE potential: clarifying the new configurations of the systemic and civilizational crisis; confronting emerging scenarios of uncertainty and instability; and designing novel forms of social solidarity and moving towards a critical-transformative feminist project in terms of justice and equity.

(1) Decolonial feminists question this paradigm for fundamentally reflecting a Western Eurocentric genealogy of feminism (Medina, 2013). This paper does not address the complexity of this debate, although we consider it essential to point this out.
(2) The table reflects the multiple positions occupied by some people (coherently with the notion of multi-belonging that was previously described); hence the sum will be greater than 14.
(3) See endnote 2.
(4) The economic iceberg refers to the division between the productive economy (visible) and the reproductive economy (invisible), and the sexual division of labor between the two spaces.

Acknowledgements

We would like to thank the availability and generosity of all the women who have agreed to be interviewed and to dialogue and reflect with us, in particular Cristina Carrasco, Lina Gálvez, Amaia Pérez Orozco, as well as the activists of Setas Feministas and Feminismos Sol - Grupo Deuda. We would also like to express our gratitude for those who have contributed to the development of the Feminist Economics Congresses in Spain and, last but not least, to the people who put FE in practice and show us that it is possible to build a more just world.

Disclosure statement

No potential conflict of interest was reported by the author(s).

ORCID

Astrid Agenjo-Calderón http://orcid.org/0000-0002-2203-8435
Lucía Del Moral-Espín http://orcid.org/0000-0001-6733-5831

References

Agenjo-Calderón, A. (2019). Genealogía del pensamiento económico feminista: Las mujeres como sujeto epistemológico y como objeto de estudio en economía [Genealogy of feminist economic thought: Women as epistemological subject and as object of study in Economics]. *Revista de Estudios Sociales, 75*, 42–54. https://doi.org/10.7440/res75.2021.05

Agenjo-Calderón, A. (2021). *Economía Política Feminista. Sostenibilidad de la vida y econom'ía mundial. [Feminist Political Economy. Sustainability of life and world economy]*. Catarata / Fuhem ecosocial.

Alabao, N., Cadahia, L., Cuenca, G., Castejón, M., Adelantado, A., Llaguno, T., & Montero, J. (2018). *Un feminismo del 99% [A feminism for the 99%]*. Lengua de trapo.

Araiza, A., & Gonz'ález, R. (2017). La Investigación Activista Feminista. Un diálogo metodológico con los movimientos sociales [Feminist activist research. A methodological dialogue with social movements]. *Empiria. Revista de Metodología de las Ciencias Sociales, 38* (September–December), 63–84.

Arruzza, C., Bhattacharya, T., & Fraser, N. (2019). *Feminism for the 99%: A Manifesto*. Verso.

Baumgardner, J. (2011). *Is there a fourth wave? Does it matter? Excerpt from F'em: Goo Goo, Gaga and Some Thoughts on Balls*. Seal Press. http://www.feminist.com/resources/artspeech/genwom/baumgardner2011.html

Bonet I Marti, J. (2015). Movimiento del 15-M: undefined fuerza politizadora del anonimato [15-M movement: The politicising power of anonymity]. *ACME: An International E-Journal for Crtical Geographies, 14*(1), 104–123.

Calvo, C., & Álvarez, I. (2015). Limitaciones y exclusiones en la institucionalización de la indignación: Del 15-M a Podemos [*Limitations and exclusions in the institutionalisation of indignation: From 15-M to Podemos*. *Revista Española de Sociología, 24* (June), 115–122.

Carrasco, C. (2009). Mujeres, sostenibilidad y deuda social. *Revista de educación* Nº Extraordinario 2009, 169–194.

In *Con voz propia. La economía feminista como apuesta teórica y política [With a voice of its own. Feminist Economics as a theoretical and political bet]* (La Oveja Roja). Carrasco, C. Ed., 2014.

Choudry, A. (2020). Reflections on academia, activism, and the politics of knowledge and learning. *International Journal of Human Rights*, 24(1), 28-45. https://doi.org/10.1080/13642987.2019.1630382

Cruells, M., & Ezquerra, S. (2015). Procesos de voluntad democratizadora: undefined expresión feminista en el 15-M [*Processes of democratising will: Feminist expression in 15-M*]. *ACME: An International E-Journal for Critical Geographies*, 14(1), 42-60.

Cruells, M., & Ruiz, S. (2014). Political intersectionality within the spanish indignados social movement. In Intersectionality and Social Change *(Research in Social Movements, Conflicts and Change)*, Vol. 37 (Emerald Group) (pp. 3-25).

della Porta, D., & Diani, M. (2010). *Social movements. An Introduction*. Wille- Blackwell.

Eschle, C., & Maiguashca, B. (2006). Bridging the academic/activist divide: Feminist activism and the teaching of global politics. *Millennium*, 35(1), 119-137. https://doi.org/10.1177/03058298060350011101

Evans E., & Chamberlain P. (2015). Critical waves: Exploring feminist identity, discourse and praxis in western feminism. *Social Movement Studies*, 14(4), 396-409. https://doi.org/10.1080/14742837.2014.964199

Flesher Fominaya, C. (2020). *Democracy reloaded. Inside Spain's Political Laboratory from 15-M to Podemos*. Oxford University Press.

Galcerán, M. (2012). Presencia de los feminismos en la puerta del sol madrileña [Feminist presence in puerta del sol, Madrid]. *Youkali*, 12, 31-36.

Galdón, C. (2017). Feminismo como indicador de coherencia revolucionaria. Una aproximación al feminismo en el movimiento 15M [*Feminism as an indicator of revolutionary coherence. An approach to feminism in the 15M movement*]. *Atlánticas. Revista Internacional de Estudios Feministas*, 2(1), 220. https://doi.org/10.17979/arief.2017.2.1.2010

Gálvez, L., & Torres, J. (2010). Desiguales. Hombres y mujeres en la crisis financiera *[Unequal. Men and women in the financial crisis]*. Icaria.

Gámez, M. J. (2015). Feminisms and the 15m movement in Spain: between frames of recognition and contexts of action. *Social Movement Studies*, 14(3), 359-365.

Gibson-Graham, J. K. (2006). *A Postcapitalist Politics. Is There Life after Capitalism?*. University of Minnesota Press.

Haraway, D. (1988). Situated knowledges: the science question in feminism and the privilege of partial perspective. *Feminist Studies*, 14(3), 575-599. https://doi.org/10.2307/3178066

Harding, S. (2008). *Sciences from Below: Feminisms, Postcolonialities, and Modernities*. Duke University Press.

Juris, J. S., Ronayne, M., Shokooh-Valle, F., & Wengronowitz, R. (2012). Negotiating Power and Difference within the 99%. *Social Movement Studies*, 11(3-4), 434-440. https://doi.org/10.1080/14742837.2012.704358

Longino, H. E. (2017). Feminist epistemologyIn: Greco, J., Sosa, E. (Eds.), *The Blackwell guide to epistemology* (pp. 325-353). Blackwell Publishing.

Martínez, M. (2019). *Identidades en proceso: Una propuesta a partir del análisis de las movilizaciones feministas contemporáneas*. CIS - Centro de Investigaciones Sociológicas. https://elibro-net.bibezproxy.uca.es/es/lc/ucadiz/titulos/124019

Maxey, I. (1999). Beyond boundaries? Activism, academia, reflexivity and research. *Area*, 31(3), 199-208. https://doi.org/10.1111/j.1475-4762.1999.tb00084.x

Medina, R. (2013). Feminismos periféricos, feminismos-otros: Una genealogía feminista decolonial por reivindicar [Peripheral feminisms, feminisms-other: Adecolonial feminist genealogy to be reclaimed]. *Revista Internacional de Pensamiento Político*, 8, 53-79.

Munro, E. (2013). Feminism: A fourth wave? *Political Insight*, 4(2), 22-25.

Perez Orozco, A. (2009). Global perspectives on the social organisation of care in times of crisis: Assessing the situation. *UN-INSTRAW Working Paper, 5*.

Pérez Orozco, A. (2014). Subversión Feminista de La Economía: Aportes Para Un Debate Sobre El Conflicto Capital-Vida *[Feminist Subversion of the Economy: Contributions to a Debate About the Capital-Life Conflict]*. Traficantes de sueños.

Picchio, A. (2009). Condiciones de vida: Perspectivas, análisis económico y políticas públicas. *Revista de Economía Crítica, 7*(1), 27–54.

Power, M. (2013). A social provisioning approach to gender and economic life. In D. Figart & T. Warnecke (Eds.), *Handbook of research on gender and economic life* (pp. 7–17). Edward Elgar.

Precarias a la deriva. (2004) . A la deriva por los circuitos de la precariedad femenina *[Drifting through the circuits of female precariousness]*. Traficantes de Sueños.

Setas Feministas (3 May 2014). "Amenazadas y danzantes", *periódico Diagonal*. Available at http://mujerdelmediterraneo.heroinas.net/2014/05/amenazadas-y-danzantes.html

Simons, H. (2009). *Case study research in practice*. Sage.

Skulj, A. I. (2020). Estado Penal y populismo punitivo. reflexiones feministas sobre el devenir punitivista del feminismo [*The penal state and punitive populism. Feminist reflections on the punitivist future of feminism*]. *Viento Sur, 168* (February) , 77–85.

Precarias a la deriva (2005): undefined la precarización de la existencia a la huelga de cuidados.In *Estudios sobre género y economía*. In Vara, M. J. Ed.pp. 104–134. Akal

VV.AA. (2012) . *R-Evolucionando. Feminismos en el 15-M [R-Evolving. Feminisms in 15-M]*. Icaria.

Transforming urban democracy through social movements: the experience of Ahora Madrid

Fabiola Mota Consejero and Michael Janoschka

ABSTRACT
Between 2015 and 2019, the Spanish capital, Madrid, was governed by the movement party Ahora Madrid, a novel political actor strongly connected to anti-austerity and pro-democracy movements gathered under the umbrella of the Indignados, or '15 M', movement. Against the background of the party's abundant hopes for regenerating urban democracy at the beginning of its term, our research asks how and to what extent Ahora Madrid translated the movement's democratizing practices and expectations into concrete policies. Based on our own qualitative research involving government actors and social movements, our empirical findings demonstrate that the democratic innovations implemented responded to diverging visions of how to achieve 'real democracy', defined by different imaginaries and traditions of collective action within 15 M. While demonstrating the steady interaction between Ahora Madrid policy makers and the social movements they came from, the findings also reveal the policy agenda divisions that posed a challenge for the broadening and deepening of urban democracy. These divisions concerned vertical versus horizontal political logics, the individual versus collective nature of political subjects, and digital versus on-site political participation and deliberation. In addition to the tensions emerging among the various ideational frameworks for collective action (i.e. the autonomous tradition, technopolitics, and the institutional left), this study identifies an apparent divorce between the two intertwined goals of the 15 M: to fight neoliberal austerity and to seek participatory democracy. The empirical findings lead to highlight the internal accounts of the consequences of social movements, especially concerning the conditions for institutionalization.

Introduction

The emergence of social movements in response to austerity and the failure of institutional political representatives to respond to people's concerns may be considered a key outcome of the post-2008 financial, economic, and social crisis (Della Porta, 2015; Flesher Fominaya, 2014, 2015). Southern European countries were at the core of the structural adjustments, and their populations were severely affected by the deterioration of public welfare, the restructuring of public and private debt, soaring unemployment, and the social drama of skyrocketing foreclosures (Alexandri & Janoschka, 2018). Accordingly, social movements framed austerity policies as an authoritarian governance approach aimed at further naturalizing the various processes of neoliberalization (Gerbaudo, 2017; Hayes, 2017; Jessop, 2019).

In Spain, the crisis resolution mechanisms triggered intense protest, particularly since 2011, under the umbrella of the so-called Indignados, or 15-M, movement, which brought together the claims of different anti-austerity, anti-eviction, and pro-democracy struggles (Castañeda, 2012; Flesher Fominaya, 2020; Ordóñez et al., 2018). Soon after, citizen platforms and so-called 'movement parties' were established (Della Porta et al., 2017; Martín, 2015), initiating a citizen-led re-configuration of the political sphere, which was especially successful at the local level. Consequently, the country-wide municipal elections in May 2015 resulted in an electoral landslide, with local coalitions led by movement parties assuming the leadership of dozens of councils and, crucially, of the two largest cities, Madrid and Barcelona (Blanco et al., 2020; Font & García-Espín, 2020). In this regard, the electoral platform Ahora Madrid (Madrid Now) interrupted 25 years of consecutive liberal-conservative rule by the Partido Popular in the Spanish capital. The resulting high expectations for political change, including the regeneration of urban democracy and participatory governance, corresponded to a belief in the opportunity to build a 'democracy of the many', as advocated by the Real Democracy Now movement (Democracia Real Ya), a major organizer of the 15-M protest.

This article analyses the political shifts implemented by Ahora Madrid during the 2015–19 legislative term, with a specific focus on the participatory mechanisms introduced. It addresses the following question: How and to what extent did the government convert the 15-M movement's democratizing practices, experiences, and expectations into concrete policies? More specifically, what local democratic innovations were introduced, and to what extent did conflict and contradictions emerge between government and social movements during policy implementation? The research illustrates that in the introduction of democratic innovations, attempts were made to include different and even conflicting visions of 'real democracy' aligned with the various traditions, practices and imaginaries brought together under the political culture and collective identity of the 15-M movement (Flesher Fominaya, 2020). The resulting policy agenda divisions determined the unfolding of such experiments and demonstrated the conflicts emerging when institutional actors attempt to transform movement claims into reformist urban governance.

The article is structured as follows: First, a brief outline of the empirical research is presented. The next section frames theoretically the research by introducing a series of conceptual considerations on the political impact of social movements. This is followed by an overview of the anti-austerity and pro-democracy movements in Madrid and a nuanced account of the circumstances surrounding the electoral candidacy of Ahora Madrid. Then, an analysis of policies for citizen participation and democratic regeneration is carried out, providing in-depth comprehension of the main democratic innovations implemented and their connections with social movements. The final section critically reflects on the contradictions and political dilemmas faced by Ahora Madrid in its attempt to transform urban governance.

Research methods and data

This article is grounded in a wider empirical research project comparing Spanish cities that were (co-)governed from 2015 to 2019 by 'municipal movement governments'. However, the current article focuses only on Madrid. During data collection, consideration was given to analytical dimensions corresponding to four crucial spheres of urban governance: the co-management and use of public space, housing policies, local services, and participatory governance. Original qualitative research consisting of 38 semi-structured interviews and two focus groups was carried out between 2016 and 2019. While the theme of participatory governance was raised in all conversations and consultations, ten interviews focused exclusively on the transformation of local participatory governance. The research also included systematic analysis of public documents, policy reports, and website content, as well as participant observation.[1]

The aim of the interviews was to obtain an in-depth understanding of the logics motivating the actions of two different groups: (1) political and administrative actors (i.e. local councillors from both the government and opposition parties, public officials and consultants) and (2) activists and representatives of social movements and civic associations. Interviewees were selected by combining a positional approach (i.e. selecting individuals in positions of authority in the city council and local administration) with a reputational approach (i.e. identifying persons who were influential in their respective associative communities and fields of action). Additionally, movement activists and interviewees from civic associations were also selected based on their geographical location to obtain insights into actions carried out in different neighbourhoods. Interview and focus group guides were developed according to the research interests in each policy dimension. Table 1 provides an overview of all interviewee profiles and the interview content in relation to the field of participatory governance.

Table 1. Interviewee profiles and interview content.

Interviewee profiles	Interview content
Political and administrative actors – Councillors (government and opposition parties) – Public officials appointed by Ahora Madrid – Government consultants	- Comparison of previous and current participatory governance model - Regulatory reforms concerning citizen participation - Evaluation of existing mechanisms for citizen participation - Social inequalities and participation - Digital participation - Deliberative participation - Involvement of social movements in participatory mechanisms - Social and public co-management
Social movement activists and representatives of civic associations - Neighbourhood associations - Free culture and digital democracy activists - Local/neighbourhood assemblies - Housing struggles - Civic associations	- Comparison of previous and current participatory governance model - Regulatory reforms concerning social and public cooperation - Functioning and performance of local forums for participation - Social innovation and involvement in participatory mechanisms - Digital participation - Deliberative participation - Binding (politically rather than legally) nature of public consultations - Government transparency

The political impact of anti-austerity social movements

In the aftermath of the 2008 economic crisis, deep public dissatisfaction with austerity measures, especially since 2011, led to a wave of anti-austerity protests of which the appearance of movement parties in the Western world has been the most visible political outcome. In addition to theoretical reflections on the links between protest politics and institutional politics (Della Porta *et al.*, 2017), the conceptual debates on anti-austerity social movements have addressed alternative comprehensions of democracy, especially regarding the deliberative and participatory visions of emancipatory movements (Della Porta, 2015; Feenstra *et al.*, 2017; Gerbaudo, 2017; Tormey, 2015). For instance, the occupation of emblematic squares in the hearts of cities epitomizes a prefigurative model of direct and radical democracy. Moreover, collective action uses new information and communication technologies, including social media, to create individual experiences of immediacy and direct political engagement (Castells, 2012).

The Indignados, or 15-M, movement in Spain has been characterized by a reliance on an autonomous networking logic to shape the movement and mobilize against austerity and for democracy. These two goals are so strongly intertwined in the political culture of 15-M that they have given rise to a new democratic imaginary, which includes not only reform of the procedural elements of liberal democracy that impede 'real democracy' but also a substantive conception of democracy that includes greater equality and freedom, as well as participation (Flesher Fominaya, 2020, p. 23). On the other hand, the example of Spain has demonstrated that protest can alter the course of political demands and organization, resulting in a transformation of 'street politics' into 'party politics' (Ordóñez *et al.*, 2018), especially at the local level (as the examples of Ahora Madrid, Barcelona en Comù, and many others have shown). Electoral platforms and movement parties emerged under the conceptual umbrella of 'new municipalist experiences' with the aim of reconfiguring urban governance procedures (Thompson, 2021).

One of the most compelling challenges that the advent of 15-M and other 'occupy' movements brought to the field of social movements studies was that of assessing their consequences and their impact on democratic regeneration and the transformation of urban democracy. In fact, recent research on the institutional democratic innovations that occurred after 2015 has provided novel in-depth insights into the role that social movements can play in redefining urban democracy and participatory governance (Blanco *et al.*, 2020; Bua & Bussu, 2021; Font, 2017; Font & García-Espín, 2020; Ganuza & Menéndez, 2020; Iglesias & Barbeito, 2020; Janoschka & Mota, 2021; Martínez & Wissink, 2021; Navarro, 2017; Nez & Ganuza, 2020; Roth *et al.*, 2019). This article aims to contribute to this strand of research by adopting a broad perspective that considers both the intended and unintended policy outcomes of social movements (Giugni *et al.*, 1999; Meyer, 2021). An important assumption here is the existence of mutual influences between policy and protest: social movements, or actors' coalitions within social movements, can achieve some success in altering the substance of policies and even how policies are made, but changes in policy mean that the terrain on which social movements mobilize is constantly shifting (Meyer, 2003). Nonetheless, we find it useful to consider the linkage mechanisms that connect contention to outcomes of interest. In this regard, our analysis seeks to identify significant 'transferable innovations', that is, new forms of collective action and frameworks introduced by social movements (McAdam & Tarrow, 2010, p. 533), which may be traced from the protest cycle to the electoral stage and further to the governance process.

Such a perspective enables us to distinguish the repertoires of collective action for radical urban democracy, including pluralist visions, different traditions, and diverging collective interests, that left their footprints on the Ahora Madrid electoral programme and on institutional politics (Roth *et al.*, 2019). For example, in her analysis of the 15-M movement in Madrid, Flesher Fominaya (2020) finds that '15-M political culture does not form a neat and coherent alternative model of democracy, but rather what are known as *ideas fuerza*, or core ideational frameworks, that motivate action, or praxis' (p. 288). She identifies various ideational frameworks 'which are rooted in specific political movements traditions and imaginaries that come into tension with each other but can also combine synergistically' (Flesher Fominaya, 2020, p. 288). Consequently, we expect to find three main divides underpinning the ideas and policy propositions for regenerating and improving urban democracy: (i) the divide between vertical and horizontal forms of collective action; (ii) the divide that distinguishes individual from collective and deliberative forms of political participation; and (iii) the divide between digital and online mechanisms of participation and on-site civic engagement.

From 'street politics' to 'institutional politics'

The empirical analysis carried out in this paper is guided by the hypothesis that democratic innovations implemented by the Ahora Madrid government can be traced back to the political culture, practices, and repertoires of action of collective actors involved in the 15-M movement. This is why we briefly discuss significant aspects of the post-2011 protest cycle, thereby providing empirical evidence of the origin in social movements of the participatory policies implemented by Ahora Madrid.

At first glance, the initial dissent that gave birth to the movement was related to the No Les Votes (Do Not Vote for Them) campaign. This initiative called for an electoral boycott of all the traditional parties on the basis that they had been identified as responsible for legislating on curtailing copyright infringement on internet users and committing digital freedom in favour of media lobbies. Although this campaign is of secondary consideration in much of the academic discourse on the evolution of the Indignados movement, it is crucial for understanding the development of networks between several organizations, such as Juventud Sin Futuro (Youth Without a Future), Real Democracy Now, Anonymous, ATTAC, the Platform of Mortgage Affected People (PAH), who promoted the protest march on 15 May 2011 that gave birth to the 15-M movement (Flesher Fominaya, 2014). One feature of 15-M was its widespread and innovative use of digital technologies, which was stimulated by free culture activists (Fuster Morell, 2012; Romanos & Sádaba, 2016). Even more significantly, a technopolitical or cyberactivist's ideational framework combined with other movement traditions facilitated the establishment of specific networks for collective action (Flesher Fominaya, 2020).

However, once the Indignados occupied the squares, the camps became the main visible expression of protest. In line with events taking place elsewhere across the globe, these camps were democratic experiments with popular assemblies, horizontal self-organization, and decentralized mutual aid networks. Combined with the transparency and horizontal rationalities of citizen participation, they generated spaces of interaction that did not conform to the logics of institutionalized political organizations, so trade unions and political parties were widely banned from the camps (Feenstra, 2015; Flesher Fominaya, 2014, 2015).

The occupation of public space and the practice of direct democracy based on face-to-face communication and deliberation changed people's perceptions of local democracy and the right to the city. As a result of intense discussions, the initial Acampada Sol was soon decentralized, which extended participatory experiences across many neighbourhoods (Perrugoría & Tejerina, 2013). Two forms of assembly coexisted for a long time after the camp in Sol was lifted. On the one hand, the Asamblea General Sol (AGSOL) persisted in trying to maintain the Acampada's general assembly on the previous basis of pure autonomous assembly, inclusiveness, and individual participation. On the other hand, the Asamblea Popular de Madrid (Popular Assembly of Madrid; APM) emerged after 15-M as a coordinating group that meets with representatives of each neighbourhood assembly and takes decisions as a body. Ultimately, it was a revitalization of the more traditional popular neighbourhood assemblies under the coordination of the Federation of Madrid Neighbourhood Assemblies (FRAVM) and a network of more 'radical' squatted centres. Different tensions emerged between these two forms of *asamblearismo* (individual and inclusive *versus* mediated and restricted participation), and between the institutional left (more vertical and formalized) and autonomous collective actors (who were more horizontal and non-formalized). Additionally, there was an apparent opposition between the face-to-face assembly model, which is rooted in place – specifically, in neighbourhoods and autonomous social centres – and the technopolitical vision of cyberspace as open to everybody without geographical restrictions (Flesher Fominaya, 2020, p. 145).

While we contend that these divisions within 15-M had an impact on the composition of the Ahora Madrid government and the design of its participatory policies, we also argue that this influence was to a certain extent mediated by hybrid political experiments that saw the establishment of movement parties and electoral platforms seeking to transform the institutions (Feenstra, 2015). The platform Municipalia emerged in Madrid on the horizon of the 2015 municipal elections. Its remit was to negotiate a strategy to 'take back the institutions' and 'put them at the service of the majority and for the common good' (Ordóñez et al., 2018, p. 89). Municipalia comprised activists from different social movements and organizations (including participants from parties such as the ecologist party EQUO; movement parties such as the then recently founded Podemos; local factions of Izquierda Unida, a coalition of left-wing organizations under the leadership of the Communist Party; cultural centres; social cooperatives; and civic associations). In this regard, Municipalia can be considered as a space that facilitated the preparation of an electoral programme to reclaim the city, social rights, and public services, in opposition to the existing austerity governance. It also intended to pursue a radically different political ethos based on honesty, responsiveness, and political inclusion through citizen participation (Rubio-Pueyo, 2017). However, *Municipalia* soon became Ganemos Madrid (Let's Win Madrid) and later the electoral platform Ahora Madrid. It gained support from Podemos, which decided to withdraw its own candidates in favour of the emerging local initiative (Font & García-Espín, 2020). Consequently,

Ahora Madrid can be considered a movement party insofar as it was a coalition of political activists who originated from social movements and tried to apply the organizational structures and strategic practices of those movements in the arena of electoral competition (Kitschelt, 2006, p. 280). By the same token, Ahora Madrid can also be considered part of the 15-M movement in Madrid, as evidenced by the overlapping membership and the organizational and activist links (Della Porta et al., 2017).

An electoral programme to transform urban democracy

When it came to drafting an electoral programme, Ahora Madrid purposely attempted to apply the prefigurative experimentation with democratic praxis (forms of action, ideational frameworks, and strategic practices) developed within 15-M. First, they introduced themselves as 'ordinary citizens doing wonderful things' (Ahora Madrid, 2015). Second, the Metropolitan Programme was drawn up over several months in a participatory and collaborative way through tables and discussion forums convened by Ganemos Madrid and involving consultation with the sectoral and territorial circles (assemblies) of Podemos. Third, once the drafting of the Metropolitan Programme was completed, citizens' suggestions for the concrete implementation of the measures were collected through workshops in all the districts of Madrid, which gave rise to the district citizen programmatic proposals. This process was enriched by the establishment of a web platform for collecting citizens' suggestions.[2]

One of the four areas structuring the electoral programme was entirely devoted to shaping a 'democratic, transparent, and efficient government', which was deliberately pursued through citizen participation in opposition to the 'Madrid of despotism' of the Popular Party (Ahora Madrid, 2015). During the liberal-conservative era in Madrid, an elitist conception of citizen participation prevailed, which was almost exclusively electoral and strongly influenced by economic interests in terms of policy making (i.e. building companies). The rare participatory processes were mostly the result of neighbourhood protest movements (e.g. the so-called Movimiento por la Dignidad del Sur [Movement for the Dignity of the South of the City]), as was the case with so-called Integral District Plans for Investment, which were drawn up in the 2000s by the regional government in the districts of Usera and Villaverde at the southern periphery of the municipality (Walliser, 2008). Innovative experiments that evolved over time, such as the self-organized public space *Campo de la Cebada* in the city centre or collective urban garden initiatives, primarily resulted from a lack of administrative coordination rather than from a strategy for collective approaches to public engagement. It is against this background that Ahora Madrid proposed novel ideas about urban governance, involving participatory approaches, and advocated for structural and transversal changes to achieve territorial cohesion, ecological transformation, gender equality, the inclusion of minorities, and, more generally, the recovery of welfare for all citizens. Accordingly, commitments to establish a proper model of citizen participation, achieve greater transparency and responsiveness from local government, and replicate democratic innovations from the previous protest cycle were at the core of their electoral promises (Ahora Madrid, 2015).

In this environment, Ahora Madrid evoked widespread hope for political change, attracting more than 500,000 votes in the city, which was equivalent to 31.85% of the electorate. More importantly, the number of elected councillors associated with the progressive political spectrum enabled the movement to take control of local government, ousting the liberal-conservative Partido Popular for the first time in a quarter of a century. At that point, the success of Ahora Madrid and similar platforms in other cities was conceived as the rise of a 'new municipal agenda' in Spain, aimed at designing new participatory politics structured around free, self-empowered, and active citizens (Delclós, 2015; Russell, 2019).

Realizing transferable democratic innovations: challenges and contradictions

Among the Spanish cities that have been governed by new municipalist candidacies, Madrid is probably the most enmeshed in the 15 M movement, as the social and political background of the city councillors and the participatory policies implemented since 2015 show (Font, 2017; Font & García-Espín, 2020; Nez & Ganuza, 2020). However, only twenty of the fifty-seven members of the city council were from the government of Ahora Madrid, which meant that the latter did not rule with a majority but had to rely on the nine votes of the traditional social democratic party, the Spanish Socialist Labour Party (PSOE), to pass bills, crucial policy documents, and budget plans. Additionally, the new council had to face the immediate consequences of recentralization pursued by the national state, which had reduced and partially suspended local autonomy.

After the formation of the government, the local executive was organized into ten departments, each one led by a candidate from the Ahora Madrid primaries' list, which represented the plurality of the traditions and activism within the social movements. In an attempt to restructure government action, the responsibility for citizen participation was shared between the Department of Transparency and Citizen Participation and the Department of Territorial Coordination and Associative Promotion (later re-named Territorial Coordination and Public–Social Collaboration). The councillors appointed to coordinate these two areas reveal the influence of the previous protest cycle on the composition of the new government. The Department of Transparency was directed by Pablo Soto, who was well known in the free digital culture movement. This department conceived its role as to 'initiate decision-making mechanisms by direct and individual participation of citizens' (public official appointed by Ahora Madrid).

The councillor responsible for the Department of Territorial Coordination, Nacho Murgui, had been active in neighbourhood movements and was also the president of the FRAVM. Hence, the aims of the department were to decentralize local democracy by transferring responsibilities to the city districts and to ensure the effective participation of civic associations in governance processes by implementing innovative forms of co-management. A public official we interviewed explained this as follows:

> Participatory policy in Madrid has a territorially defined dimension, which is simultaneously individual and collective. However, the use of the platform Decide Madrid [Madrid Decides] also introduces a dimension of digital democracy. In other words, there are two different driving forces, and this is a novel and unconventional approach. (Public official appointed by Ahora Madrid).

Ultimately, each government area responsible for citizen participation had contrasting comprehensions of how democracy, participation, and deliberation should work in practice. On the one hand, individual and direct citizen participation was mostly conceived from the technopolitical imaginary that developed within 15-M, which greatly influenced the participatory policies implemented by the Department of Transparency. Such policies were also supported by a series of innovative 'laboratories of participation' (ParticipaLab). These were held in Madrid's MediaLab, a public centre belonging to the Department of Culture, which had hosted part of the free culture protest movement during the previous municipal mandates. On the other hand, democratic innovations introduced by the Department of Territorial Coordination were more specifically connected to the autonomous tradition, which is rooted in local urban movements (Flesher Fominaya, 2020), and to the neighbourhood assemblies of the leftist tradition, which had expanded in Madrid during the seventies (Castells, 1977).

As Font (2017) noted, the overall result of the participatory policies devised and implemented by the Ahora Madrid city council has been the most ground-breaking of all the achievements of new municipalist governments in Spain (p. 134). However, despite the apparently straightforward implementation of electoral promises, multiple contradictions and readjustments occurred over time. These revealed various tensions among social movement organizations despite their close ties to the government. The following analysis addresses the underlying dynamics of the corresponding political processes by characterizing the main democratic innovations conceived of and implemented in Madrid. In this regard, the four mechanisms described below were crucial.

(1) *The online platform Decide Madrid (Madrid Decides)*

Decide Madrid is an online platform for citizen engagement, which was created using an open-code program based on Consul. The platform was initially designed by so-called Partido X (Party X), adapted by Podemos through its participatory tool Plaza Podemos (Podemos Square), and then taken up by Ahora Madrid. Ultimately, this initiative has proved to be transferable from social movement collective action repertoires to the policy process. Crucially, Decide Madrid allows any citizen who is registered as a resident to be involved in participatory processes.

Citizen propositions and local consultations

Following the introduction of new guidelines, anyone can suggest concrete policy proposals, measures, and actions through the Decide Madrid platform. If a suggestion obtains support from at least one percent of the electorate (approximately 27,500 votes), it passes to a politically (but not legally) binding consultation. However, the resulting local referendum entails some further legal restrictions, as it requires – at least formally – an authorization from the national government.

In reality, only one multi-consultation was realized in February 2017. It concerned the Gran Via Avenue–Plaza España Square restructuring (which was a top-down proposition made by the city council), the single ticket for metropolitan public transport, the 'Madrid 100% sustainable' proposition, and six other district-scale enquiries. It attracted more than 200,000 participants. While considered successful in terms of participation (largely due to the provision of three channels for voting: ballot box, mail, and digital), it was publicly criticized for the minor relevance and the ambiguity of the issues to be decided and certain deficiencies regarding its organization (El País, 2017). Nevertheless, by overcoming the legal and administrative constraints inscribed in the inherited legislation on local consultations, the local councillor for citizen participation asserted that 'such battles are political' and that they prove that the government has the capacity to put 'everyday decisions into the hands of the people'. Thus, the multi-consultation sought to replicate the prefigurative political practices of the 15-M autonomous collectives, at least in the sense that decision-making procedures were not seen as just a means to an end, but as ends in themselves (Flesher Fominaya, 2020).

However, it must be recalled that 15-M's objective of reforming the procedures of liberal urban democracy by expanding citizen participation in decision-making was as crucial as the goal of transforming the substantive conception of urban democracy by opposing neoliberal urban policies. As both goals are difficult to achieve simultaneously in the short term (Roth et al., 2019, p. 76), conflicts arose among the social movement's collective actors. One activist reported the following:

> This is all very positive, but it is not enough; in reality, this is not participation. If you stand for election with the promise to revert the privatization of urban spaces and then you don't do this, it is secondary if you propose a public consultation about building a sports centre here or there. […] But exactly this has been presented as an important success story. Don't mess it up! The big success is that the electoral mandate was disregarded! What trust can I have in this participation if I had already participated by voting for you, and you were ignoring my vote? Why do you ask me if I prefer a square like this or like that? I already said 'don't privatize, don't give licences for terraces, and don't allow the city to become a brand, a commodity!'
>
> Activist from a popular neighbourhood assembly)

(a) *Participatory budgeting*

Between 2016 and 2019, citizens could propose and vote in open-ended bottom-up processes on specific policy actions across the city and its districts. For instance, in 2017, public investment of €100 million was allocated through this mechanism for 311 proposals. To facilitate well-informed decisions, the government introduced an initiative called a 'decide kit', which was a set of 'marketing recommendations' for successful campaigning. While this initiative can be framed within the autonomous and technopolitical philosophy of 'do it yourself' without intermediaries (Flesher Fominaya, 2020), it triggered strong criticism from neighbourhood movements and civic associations, which reject the apparent logic of commodifying social relations by putting 'individual profits' ahead of practices of deliberation and the satisfaction of social needs. A neighbourhood association representative pointed out the following:

> Imagine that Florentino Pérez [President of Real Madrid] advocated through the platform *Decide Madrid* to expand the business around the Santiago Bernabéu Stadium. How many club members live in the city? – Many. So, the city would serve the interests of Florentino Pérez because of a consultation? This is what we have to face.

(Representative of a neighbourhood association)

In this regard, neighbourhood associations and other formal organizations opposed the individual-centred participatory mechanism of the Decide Madrid platform. For instance, it was claimed that individualized models of participation can weaken over time and that organized collectives and associations are who defend the mechanisms of citizen participation in politically more controversial periods.

However, in response to these assertions, the government fostered collective propositions through on-site participatory activities carried out in so-called Foros Locales de Participación (explained below) and other initiatives. Additionally, facilitators for participatory processes, including participatory budgeting, were allocated to each city district, thus fostering the hybridization of the autonomous and institutional dimensions of urban movements (Martínez, 2016).

(2) *Foros Locales de Participación (Local Forums for Participation)*

In February 2017, local forums for participation (LFPs) were introduced in the 21 districts of the city by the Department of Territorial Coordination. This institutional mechanism was aimed at promoting citizen engagement with local policymaking at the level of neighbourhoods and districts. Unlike the Territorial Board of Associations, which it replaced, the LFPs were conceived to include both individual and collective participation. They included formal associations and informal collectives, such as citizen platforms, and were not limited in their scope or number of participants. In contrast to individual participation, which mainly takes place through the digital platform Decide Madrid, the LFPs rely primarily on collective and on-site forms of participation. A government consultant on this subject explained this position as follows:

> For us, collective forms of citizen participation have an additional interest. On-site and collective participation allows for the establishment and channelling of collective deliberation. For us, the result of collective reflection is appreciated more than individual suggestions. The clash of opinions, the addition of interests and perspectives, adds quality to this debate.

(Consultant, appointed by Ahora Madrid)

Furthermore, the LFPs were also conceived as institutional mechanisms for political mediation between citizen participation in a specific area and the district government.

This participatory mechanism triggered very different reactions from organized collectives in the city. While some groups perceived LFPs as an attempt to control and institutionalize autonomous activities, others were suspicious of the government motivations for strengthening individual participation vis-a-vis associative participation. Following this argumentation, opening participation to individuals:

> it has a clear objective: to diminish the role that collectives have in decision-making processes. In other words, they assume that if only people with time for on-site participation engage, then this participation is biased. So, they consider that participation should be

random, that all types of people should participate, representing all kinds of views. This is the controversy between participatory democracy and representative democracy; so, what we are doing in the name of associations is affirming the value of deliberation.

(Representative of a civic association)

(3) *Public–social co-management of common spaces and services*

A demand of some urban movements was the formal recognition of self-organized social initiatives, such as common spaces, social centres, and urban gardening initiatives. Such bottom-up requests motivated the government to reform the existing regulations concerning citizen participation to facilitate cooperation between the government and civic associations on the co-management of common spaces and services. As one public official noted,

> we understand that it is impossible to build Madrid by excluding those who propose activities for the benefit of everyone [... and ...] transform this into a tool for cooperation. In reality, this is not a public service but a citizen initiative, so we will treat this from a dynamic of public–social cooperation. This is where many opportunities appear for what has been called 'the commons', but we understand it as an area for collaboration between the administration and citizen initiatives. In other words, we do not want to replace public services with non-profit organizations, to change from companies to non-profit organizations. The public–social cooperation must be something different.

(Public official appointed by Ahora Madrid)

Since 2018, a new regulation on public and social cooperation has acknowledged the right of informal and unregistered organizations to become formally involved in public–social co-management activities. While satisfying the demands and aspirations of more autonomous collectives that reject institutionalization, this regulation raised suspicion from formally registered civic associations, who warned about the risks of de-institutionalizing civic engagement:

> [We] understand that social participation requires collective organization, as the only way, if things go wrong, to react and resist attacks from people who are against social participation.

(Representative of a neighbourhood association)

This viewpoint provides some insight into the difference in the conceptualization of participatory processes between social organizations rooted in the institutional left tradition, which defends a representative model of collective political subjects (e.g. citizens, neighbours, workers) with a vertical organizational structure, and autonomous collectives, which are organized as horizontal networks and underpinned by the principles of participatory democracy and autonomy (Flesher Fominaya, 2020).

(4) *Mini-publics and other democratic innovations*

Finally, the individual-centred participatory mechanisms were also accompanied by actions promoting participation through specific forms of deliberation, derived from the experiments of the aforementioned *ParticipaLab*. After two years of digital participation via Decide Madrid, data protection procedures became a prominent factor that limited the scope of deliberative democracy. Consequently, additional democratic innovations were introduced to 'connect the digital platform [Decide Madrid] with an on-site deliberative mechanism' (free culture and digital democracy activist). Accordingly, the first mini-public mechanism, G1000, was implemented in March 2017 (Navarro, 2017). This mechanism involved 1,000 randomly selected citizens discussing and deciding on specific propositions for participatory budgets through the digital platform Decide Madrid. It resulted in the preparation of more than 50 propositions, which were introduced into the 2017 participatory budgeting process.

Another novel mechanism was the Observatory of the City, which was created as a permanent participatory body, enabling forty-nine randomly selected citizens to monitor the policies of the city council (Ganuza & Menéndez, 2020; Nez & Ganuza, 2020). The Observatory also has a mandate to propose policy improvements and citizen consultations. The rationale for this mechanism is twofold:

> [First,] the system of a body by drawing, a face-to-face representative group, providing time to think and reflect, may pick up ideas in a bottom-up mechanism neutrally and in an innocent way, since it bypasses political class and activists, since these people are not involved politically. [Second,] this body doubles the legitimacy of participatory procedures because it passes citizens' proposals directly to public referendum.
>
> (Free culture and digital democracy activist)

Both of the above mechanisms were justified by their inclusiveness, as random selection can be considered the most direct and broad form of participation, avoiding political biases from organizations and associations and acting as a filter against intrusion from professional lobbies. These types of democratic innovations conform to the ideational framework of autonomous politics, which regards the autonomous individual as the only legitimate political actor and 'ordinary citizens' as the corresponding collective actor (Flesher Fominaya, 2020).

Critical consideration of the scope of democratic transformation

The above analysis of the citizen participation policies implemented by Ahora Madrid provides a nuanced account of the interaction between social movements and institutional urban politics. Based on Meyer's theorization of the political impact of protest (Meyer, 2021), it can be argued that, on the municipal level, 15-M succeeded in using elections to influence policy by engaging its own officials and promoting specific policies for urban democracy regeneration. While this outcome can be regarded as an indirect result of mobilization, since it was achieved indirectly via the creation of the Ahora Madrid movement party, we have demonstrated that, like many other movement parties (Della Porta *et al.*, 2017), Ahora Madrid can be considered part of the 15-M movement. Thus, we have traced a series of transferable innovations (McAdam & Tarrow, 2010), including prefigurative decision-making practices and ideational frameworks, from the protest cycle to the electoral stage and further to the policies of the municipal movement government.

Nonetheless, the analysis above demonstrates the continued interaction between Ahora Madrid policy makers and the social movements they came from, revealing a mutual influence that defined both the array of policy options for policy makers and the policy structure for protest mobilization (Meyer, 2003). Since the political culture of

15-M does not offer a neat and coherent alternative model of 'real democracy', the various political movements, traditions and imaginaries that merged synergistically during the protest cycle came into conflict when it came to participatory policy decision-making. Consequently, the conflicting positions of activists and social collectives on democratic innovations align relatively well with the ideational frameworks of collective action that Flesher Fominaya (2020) identifies within 15-M: autonomous politics, technopolitics, and the institutional left. In addition to classic tensions, such as that between horizontal and vertical logics of collective action, the experience of governing caused conflict between movement actors regarding the pace and scope of both substantive and procedural democratic reforms. Our research demonstrates the coexistence of three mutually exclusive and conflicting positions on the design and implementation of participatory mechanisms to regenerate urban democracy:

(1) An individualist, horizontal, disintermediated and digitally oriented perspective (mainly shared by 'free culture' and digital democracy activism);
(2) A collectivist, pro-intermediation – yet not necessarily vertical – approach that supports face-to-face interaction (mainly shared by formalized, more traditional neighbourhood and civic associations); and
(3) A hybrid position that places the electoral programme, and thus substantive purposes of democracy, ahead of procedures for direct participation (mainly shared by activists targeting housing and public space in a strongly contentious manner).

In their attempts to regenerate the public sphere and develop a diametrically alternative model of urban democracy, these positions were often overtly competing, which altered the course of government and ruled out the implementation of a coherent model of civic participation. Consequently, policies changed and were substantially adapted over time. In the first 18 months, democratic innovations were chiefly aligned with ideas stemming from free culture and digital democracy activism and autonomous politics. Hence, the online platform Decide Madrid was the central tool for participatory policy. It was essential for developing socially and politically non-mediated individual participation. In sharp contrast to the clientelist practices of the previous government, Ahora Madrid claimed 'neutrality' in the participatory decision-making processes by incorporating the principles of autonomous politics into its participatory policy. This was particularly obvious in relation to its initial emphasis on inclusive, individual and direct civic engagement (somewhat replicating the 'philosophy' of AGSOL during the protest cycle), which triggered demands from civic and neighbourhood associations for stronger institutional recognition.

> When councillors lack experience and aim to cater to residents individually as witnessed during the first two years [...], they are destroying social movements [...]. This subverts the concept of public policy: An individual defends personal interests, with no criteria for the common good at stake. Neighbourhood associations will never ask a councillor for a particular streetlight next to a house, but about whether streetlights are on or off, if there are enough streetlights or not, if the streets are clean or dirty, and so on. This is the error that Ahora Madrid committed at the beginning. [...] Not every opinion is essential, and not everything matters.

(Representative of a neighbourhood association)

As discussed above, participatory policies expanded to incorporate the involvement of locally rooted social collectives (from the institutional left as well as the autonomous tradition) and experiments favouring deliberation through face-to-face interaction. However, relevant criticisms were raised from most of the less formalized collectives, especially those targeting more radical social transformation, such as popular neighbourhood assemblies stemming directly from the *Indignados* movement, with activists from squatter, anarchist, and anti-capitalist groups. These were showing disregard for, if not disillusion with, the democratic innovations adopted by the city council. In particular, they were demanding that local government play a more transformative role in reversing urban neoliberalization (especially regarding housing policy and the management of public space). For instance, as our interviews demonstrate, activists from the Platform of Mortgage Affected People (PAH) generally shared the view that Ahora Madrid was primarily targeting the freezing of social conflicts. This concern was partially shared by the neighbourhood assemblies, which agreed that 'it seems that the council is not supporting organizations that are protecting citizens from the attacks of the system' (Representative of a neighbourhood association).

The experience of Ahora Madrid prevents us from conceptualising all social movements as homogeneous entities to which success or failures can be attributed (Giugni et al., 1999). The Ahora Madrid' movement party, like the 15-M movement that spawned it, comprised a pluralistic set of groups, organizations and repertoire of actions which shared the goal of transforming urban democracy but differed in the strategies for reaching their aims. Therefore, a given policy change was not necessarily perceived as a success by all the collectives of the movement. To a certain extent, this situation resulted in a 'divorce' between many activists and the local government and eventually led to the splitting of the electoral platform and the loss of power in the 2019 municipal elections. When the new liberal-conservative coalition, supported by the far-right party VOX, assumed power in June 2019, many policies for the regeneration of urban democracy were quickly abandoned. Moreover, the Decide Madrid platform began to be used to launch public consultations aimed at revoking innovative norms and participatory institutions, such as the Municipal Regulation for Public and Social Cooperation (2018), which legally recognized non-formalized and unregistered citizen collectives as political actors. The LFPs introduced in 2017 have also been eliminated.

Consequently, and despite the municipalist government responsiveness to social movements (Martínez & Wissink, 2021), we argue that the coexistence of mutually exclusive and conflicting positions regarding the strategies and policies to transform urban democracy caused the failure of the institutionalization process of Ahora Madrid; that is to say, building stable organizational structures outside or inside government through which to pursue movement goals in a stable and routine fashion (Meyer, 2021, p. 145). This question deserves further theoretical and empirical research to account for the political impact of social movements when marching through the institutions.

Notes

1. Over the course of several years, we attended public events organised by different municipal departments in charge of citizen participation and other civic initiatives (e.g. *ParticipaLab* and *Observatorio de la Participación* [Observatory of Participation in English]). We also engaged in participant observation at dozens of events in different venues across the city, such as *MediaLab Prado*, Cultural Centre of *Casa del Reloj* in Arganzuela district, Cultural Center of *Daoiz y Velarde* in Retiro district, and the City Hall in *Palacio de Cibeles*.
2. The web platform for a collaborative program received 1,240 citizen propositions between March 12 and March 21 of 2015. https://www.ahoramadrid.org/programa_subdomain/index/.

Acknowledgments

The authors thank all informants who kindly collaborated with our fieldwork. We thank the anonymous reviewers whose suggestions helped improve and clarify this manuscript. Likewise, we are grateful to our research project colleagues for their inspiring collaboration in the research design and strategy, and we also acknowledge the helpful assistance of the two UAM's PhD candidates Tania Andreeva and Jacobo Abellán in defining respondent profiles and partially collecting data.

Disclosure statement

No potential conflict of interest was reported by the author(s).

Funding

This work was supported by the Spanish Ministry of Economy and Competitiveness under Grant CSO2015-68314-P.

References

Ahora Madrid. (2015). *Programa Ahora Madrid [Ahora Madrid Electoral Manifesto]*.Retrieved October 24, 2020, from https://ahoramadrid.org//wp-content/uploads/2015/04/AHORAMADRID_Programa_Municipales_2015.pdf

Alexandri, G., & Janoschka, M. (2018). Who loses and who wins in a housing crisis? Lessons from Spain and Greece for a nuanced understanding of dispossession. *Housing Policy Debate, 28*(1), 117–134. https://doi.org/10.1080/10511482.2017.1324891

Blanco, I., Salazar, Y., & Bianchi, I. (2020). Urban governance and political change under a radical left government. The case of Barcelona. *Journal of Urban Affairs, 42*(1), 18–38. https://doi.org/10.1080/07352166.2018.1559648

Bua, A., & Bussu, S. (2021). Between governance-driven democratisation and democracy-driven governance: Explaining changes in participatory governance in the case of Barcelona. *European Journal of Political Research* 60 3 716–737 . . https://doi.org/10.1111/1475-6765.12421

Castañeda, E. (2012). The Indignados of Spain: A precedent to occupy wall street. *Social Movement Studies, 11*(3/4), 309–319. https://doi.org/10.1080/14742837.2012.708830

Castells, M. (1977). *Ciudad, democracia y socialismo* (Siglo XXI Editores).

Castells, M. (2012). *Networks of outrage and hope. Social movements in the internet age.* Polity Press.

Delclós, C. (2015, May 26). *Towards a new municipal agenda in Spain.* Open Democracy. https://www.opendemocracy.net/can-europe-make-it/carlos-delcl%C3%B3s/towards-new-municipal-agenda-in-spain Publisher: openDemocracy Limited

Della Porta, D., Fernández, J., Ouki, H., & Mosca, L. (2017). *Movements parties against austerity.* Polity Press.

Della Porta, D. (2015). *Social movements in times of austerity.* Polity Press.

El País. (2017, February 16). *Madrid vota.* El País. https://elpais.com/elpais/2017/02/15/opinion/1487179241_071770.html

Feenstra, R. A. (2015). Activist and citizens political repertoire in Spain: A reflection based on civil society theory and different logics of political participation. *Journal of Civil Society, 11*(13), 242–258. https://doi.org/10.1080/17448689.2015.1060662

Feenstra, R., Tormey, S., Casero-Ripollés, A., & Keane, J. (2017). *Reconfiguring democracy: The Spanish political laboratory.* Taylor and Francis.

Flesher Fominaya, C. (2014). *Social movements and globalization: How protests, occupations and uprisings are changing the world.* Palgrave McMillan.

Flesher Fominaya, C. (2015). Debunking spontaneity: Spain's 15-M/ Indignados as autonomous movement. *Social Movement Studies, 14*(2), 142–163. https://doi.org/10.1080/14742837.2014.945075

Flesher Fominaya, C. (2020). *Democracy reloaded. Inside Spain's political laboratory from 15-M to Podemos.* Oxford University Press.

Font, J., & García-Espín, P. (2020). From Indignad@s to mayors? Participatory dilemmas in Spanish municipal movements. In C. F. Fominaya & R. A. Feenstra (Eds.), *Routledge handbook of contemporary European social movements. Protest in turbulent times* (pp. 387–401). Routledge.

Font, J. (2017). New participatory policymaking processes: A single concept, different realities. *Recerca, 21,* 131–135. https://doi.org/10.6035/Recerca.2017.21.7

Fuster Morell, M. (2012). The Free Culture and 15M movements in Spain: Composition, social networks and synergies. *Social Movement Studies, 11*(3/4), 386–392. https://doi.org/10.1080/14742837.2012.710323

Ganuza, E., & Menéndez, M. (2020). Did you win? Sortition comes to the politics of Madrid. *Recerca, 25*(1), 95–110. https://doi.org/10.6035/Recerca.2020.25.1.6

Gerbaudo, P. (2017). The indignant citizen: Anti-austerity movements in Southern Europe and the anti-oligarchic reclaiming of citizenship. *Social Movement Studies, 16*(1), 36–50. https://doi.org/10.1080/14742837.2016.1194749

Giugni, M., McAdam, D., & Tilly, C. (1999). *How social movements matter?* University of Minnesota Press.

Hayes, G. (2017). Regimes of austerity. *Social Movement Studies, 16*(1), 21–35. https://doi.org/10.1080/14742837.2016.1252669

Iglesias, A. H., & Barbeito, R. L. (2020). Participatory democracy in local government: An online platform in the city of Madrid. *Croatian and Comparative Public Administration, 20*(2), 241–268 https://doi.org/10.31297/hkju.20.2.3.

Janoschka, M., & Mota, F. (2021). New municipalism in action or urban neoliberalisation reloaded? - An analysis of governance change, stability and path dependence in Madrid (2015-19). *Urban Studies Journal, 58*(13), 2.814–2.830. https://doi.org/10.1177/0042098020925345

Jessop, B. (2019). Authoritarian neoliberalism: Periodization and critique. *South Atlantic Quarterly, 118*(2), 343–361. https://doi.org/10.1215/00382876-7381182

Kitschelt, H. (2006). Movement parties. In R. S. Katz & W. J. Crotty (Eds.), *Handbook of party politics* (pp. 278–291). Sage.

Martín, I. (2015). Podemos y otros modelos de partido-movimiento. *Revista Española de Sociología, 24*, 107–114 https://recyt.fecyt.es/index.php/res/article/view/65425.

Martínez, M. A., & Wissink, B. (2021). Urban movements and municipalist governments in Spain: Alliances, tensions, and achievements. *Social Movement Studies*, 1–18. https://doi.org/10.1080/14742837.2021.1967121 Advance online publication.

Martínez, M. A. (2016). Between autonomy and hybridity: Urban struggles within the 15M movement in Spain. In H. Thorn, M. Meyer, & K. Thorn (Eds.), *Urban uprisings* (pp. 253–281). Palgrave.

McAdam, D., & Tarrow, S. (2010). Ballots and barricades: On the reciprocal relationship between elections and social movements. *Perspectives on Politics, 8*(2), 529–542. https://doi.org/10.1017/S1537592710001234

Meyer, D. S. (2003). *Social movements and public policy: Eggs, chicken, and theory*. UC Irvine Working Papers. https://escholarship.org/uc/item/2m62b74d

Meyer, D. S. (2021). *How social movements (sometimes) matter?* Polity Press.

Navarro, F. (2017). El G1000 de Madrid: Un ejemplo de sorteo y deliberación como complemento de la representación. *Recerca, 21*, 151–157. https://doi.org/10.6035/Recerca.2017.21.9

Nez, H., & Ganuza, E. (2020, November 14). Del 15M a las instituciones. Las políticas participativas de Ahora Madrid (2015-2019). *Encrucijadas Revista Crítica de Ciencias Sociales. 19*, 1–19/a1901 https://recyt.fecyt.es/index.php/encrucijadas/article/view/80208. .

Ordóñez, V., Feenstra, R. A., & Franks, B. (2018). Spanish anarchist engagements in electoralism: From street to party politics. *Social Movement Studies, 17*(1), 85–98. https://doi.org/10.1080/14742837.2017.1381593

Perrugoría, I., & Tejerina, B. (2013). Politics of the encounter: Cognition, emotions, and networks in the Spanish 15M. *Current Sociology, 61*(4), 424–442. https://doi.org/10.1177/0011392113479743

Romanos, E., & Sádaba, I. (2016). From the street to institutions through the app: Digitally enabled political outcomes of the Spanish Indignados movement. *Revista Internacional de Sociología, 74* (4), e048, 1–13. https://doi.org/10.3989/ris.2016.74.4.048

Roth, L., Monterde, A., & Calleja López, A. (2019). *Ciudades Democráticas. La revuelta municipalista en el ciclo post-15M*. Icaria.

Rubio-Pueyo, V. (2017). *Municipalism in Spain. From Barcelona to Madrid, and beyond*. Rosa Luxemburg Foundation.

Russell, B. (2019). Beyond the local trap: New municipalism and the rise of the fearless cities. *Antipode, 51*(3), 989–1010. https://doi.org/10.1111/anti.12520

Thompson, M. (2021). What's so new about new municipalism? *Progress in Human Geography* 45 2 317–342 . https://doi.org/10.1177/0309132520909480

Tormey, S. (2015). *The end of representative politics*. Polity.

Walliser, A. (2008). Participación y regeneración Urbana. El movimiento asociativo y las instituciones locales 1979-1999. In V. Pérez & P. Sánchez (Eds.), *Memoria ciudadana y movimiento vecinal. Madrid 1968-2008* (pp. 263–282). Catarata.

Caring democracy now: neighborhood support networks in the wake of the 15-M

Carlos Diz, Brais Estévez and Raquel Martínez-Buján

ABSTRACT
In 2011 the *Indignados* traced a line of flight from austerity policies. They invented unprecedented spaces for participation, re-imagined Spanish democracy and turned their attention to forms of life as spaces for political transformation. Their practices enacted a collective sensitivity that challenged the regime of impotence blocking their lives. The global financial crisis was denying them a future, and their ability to think and act together. Ten years later, while the COVID-19 pandemic interrupted the world's normal course, self-organizing neighbours updated the *Indignados'* sensibility and methods. This article analyses the neighborhood support networks created by the Mutual Aid Groups (GAM) in A Coruña, Spain, during the lockdown in March 2020. As the government urged people to stay at home and obey the public health directives, the GAM took care of vulnerable life and democracy, threatened today by new authoritarian drives. From the standpoint of the ethics of care and an interest in experimental social movements, we discuss the power of a caring democracy, which sustains life and renews the democratic turn of the 15-M.

Introduction

The Mutual Aid Groups (known by its Galician acronym as GAM) arose in A Coruña on 13 March 2020 during the state of emergency declared by the Spanish government in the COVID-19 pandemic. They started by creating a digital infrastructure for neighbours to meet during the lockdown. This made it possible for an alliance of activists and ordinary citizens to break out of the role of spectators that the government had assigned them in the lockdown. People involved in the GAM affirmed and shared the equal intelligences and capacities that politicians and experts had denied them. They took on questions that they weren't supposed to meddle with, managing to circulate, act and care in a city under lockdown.

To quote their website, they are 'a self-managed response initiative seeking to mobilize solidarity to help the most vulnerable of our neighbours' (Grupos de Apoio Mutuo, 2020). This idea shows that, for them, COVID-19 is more than a simple pandemic restricted to the biomedical and epidemiological fields; rather it is a 'syndemic'

(Horton, 2020) where the illness interacts with economic and social inequality, precarity and vulnerability, and for which there is no single, specialized solution, but multiple forms of action and responsibility.

In this article we analyse some practices tried out by the GAM during the pandemic catastrophe, with two issues in mind: democracy and care. Firstly, we see this process of neighbourhood support as an experimental and litigious movement through which people can learn and act with others amid uncertainty. This is reminiscent of the idea of 'getting a hold on' deployed by Stengers and Pignarre (2011) in their analysis of capitalism as sorcery. In their words, neoliberalism operates as a spell that captures our attention and restricts our ability to think, making us impotent and torpedoing the democratic decision-making processes. Thus, the way to face the spells of capitalism does not have to do with mere denunciation, but with 'getting a hold' by creating spaces for thought and action that turn a specific problem into both a situation of struggle and an opportunity to learn with others. In this sense, 'getting a hold' would be like a counter-sorcery that allows us to relearn the art of paying attention to the world.

In the pandemic, these self-organizing neighbours succeeded in breaching government orders to stay home. Far from resigning themselves to obeying or criticizing the lockdown, they got a hold on the situation to actively respond to the emergency. These types of situations which leave no choice but resignation or impotent denunciation, were coined by Stengers and Pignarre (2011) as 'infernal alternatives' (p. 23). According to them, we understand that politics emerge as a vital and transforming activity, when the infernal alternatives are abandoned in favour of a 'hold' that allows us to take charge of reality. In this way, we do not understand politics as a mere moral judgment of what happens; rather, politics has to do with inventing, together with others, something that is not given in advance.

In our view, the GAM echoes the 'democratic turn' embodied by the 15-M, which sprung up in 2011 in the wake of the global financial crisis (Flesher Fominaya, 2020). The *Indignados* traced a line of flight from the crisis and demanded radical change in Spanish democracy, doing 'politics without representatives' (Tormey, 2015). The 15-M not only protested austerity policies but also enacted an idea of democracy, understood as the 'power of anyone', contrary to the logic of the delegation of liberal democracies. This is redolent of Rancière's (1999) notion of democracy as the paradoxical power of those who do not count: the count of the unaccounted for.

Also, following Puig de la Bellacasa (2017), we argue that the GAM problematize democracy as a 'matter of care'. In a dialogue with the distinction between 'matter of fact' and 'matter of concern' (Latour, 2004), de la Bellacasa affirms that, beyond treating things as mere questions of fact (objective and incontrovertible facts) or questions of interest (issues that concern us), we can promote a caring relationship with them: 'paying attention to undervalued and neglected issues [...] becoming affected within them, and transforming their potential to affect others' (Puig de la Bellacasa, 2017, pp. 57–64).

Experimenting with relationships of care among neighbours and putting vulnerability and the interdependence of lives at the core of their actions (Butler, 2009), the GAM managed to sustain bodies that were isolated and intimidated by the pandemic (with their marks of class, race, sex, age, and capacity), while attending to neighbourhoods, infrastructures and the city itself. In doing so, they also took care to unveil the relational infrastructure through which the Rancièrian idea of democracy as 'the power of anyone' may be enacted. For this reason, we see care not only in its phenomenological dimension but also as a collective and speculative process (Wilkie et al., 2017). Paraphrasing Barad (2007), we argue that caring actions can be a kind of 'material engagement with the world' (p. 49) that allow us to collectively explore other horizons of the possible. It is in this field of experimentation and socio-material mediation that we can rethink our relationship with the world in catastrophic times (Stengers, 2015). This caring politicisation of the pandemic sustains the life of democracy as an object in danger while, at the same time, it allows us to imagine the power of a caring democracy. Following Tronto (2013), we consider that the aforementioned idea affords an apt conceptual framework for reimagining a care-centered democracy, one that is capable of detecting the needs of all its members and of distributing responsibilities from the standpoint of ethical, political, and relational commitment in a world subjected to uncertainty.

Before continuing we should outline the political geography of the GAM. They emerged in Galicia, a region often seen as peripheral to the south of Europe, and specifically in A Coruña, a medium-sized city on the Atlantic seaboard. As a collective response to the COVID-19 crisis, the GAM share repertoires with similar movements in Spain and worldwide (Kavada, 2020; Pleyers, 2020). These movements refuse politics as a representational device that hijacks our capacity for cooperation. They also enact politics as an egalitarian space in which those who had been reduced to incapable beings take on complex issues by sharing their capacities. Self-organising neighbours who burst forth during the pandemic with supportive and caring actions where no government expected their participation, led to the modification of the normal account of identifications and occupations in a harmonious and consensual community. It is in this dissensual gesture where *demos*, as understood by Rancière (1999), resonates: those with no entitlement to intervene in the pandemic, neighbours condemned to having no active part, identified with the community as a whole and emerged as key actors.

While events in large cities tend to monopolize the literature of social movements, in this paper we highlight the action of the GAM in the field of political experimentation forged in Galicia over the last decade. Despite the importance of what we call the Galician ecosystem of citizen innovation, the media, academia, and political spokespersons have relegated it to a subordinate role, disregarding its actions in favour of the impressive agendas of cities like Madrid and Barcelona. In this text, we see the GAM as a care-related revision of this barely visible field of invention.

The article is structured as follows. First, we outline the methodological aspects and immediately after we situate the GAM in the wake of the democratic experimentation of the 15-M. Second, from the standpoint of the feminist ethics of care, we investigate the practices of these groups and analyse the emergence of a community brought together by vulnerability. Third, we examine the way in which neighbours' mutual aid practices entail the incorporation of an affective politics of life. Lastly, we outline our idea of a caring democracy as the situated materialisation of the slogan 'Real Democracy Now'.

Doing (Digital) ethnography in the pandemic

From May to December 2020, we decided to investigate the care practices that the GAM were deploying in A Coruña. Due to the restrictions imposed by the government, we were forced to do research with very limited possibilities of physical encounters. This prompted us to question how we could approach the study object to be interacted with at a distance. All three of us were familiar with ethnographic methods, understood as encountering and collaboration devices (including long-term commitment), rather than as simple data-gathering in the study of social movements, urban issues, and community care networks (Diz, 2018; Estévez, 2019; Martínez-Buján et al., 2021). We were stricken by doubts about how to proceed. The digital infrastructure introduced by the GAM in social networks embodied technologically mediated politics of encounter that inspired us to do research.

This pressing context turned our work into 'rapid response' research (Ferrándiz, 2013). First, we sought to identify and discuss the mutual support practices that were emerging in the city. Second, we aimed to unveil the tensions between the governmental management of the pandemic and the neighborhood support networks. To do this, we used digital ethnography (Pink et al., 2015) where most encounters took place from a distance with the use of videoconferencing and digital messaging applications. These technologies represent the specific material expression of the GAM, although they are not the focus of our analysis. Our ethnographic gaze focused on the care practices resulting from the imaginative forms of social interaction deployed by the GAM, between the screen and the street.

Despite the restrictions, we attended public workshops where women from the GAM presented their experiences. We participated in Telegram groups and followed interactions on their website, Twitter and Facebook. However, we spent most of the time talking with the people involved in the GAM, on free software videoconferencing platforms. For this purpose, we chose the semi-structured interview technique. Our sample consisted of fifteen people: ten women, most of them white Galicians. They ranged in age from twenty-five to seventy-five, with a higher percentage belonging to the thirty-forty age group. Our selection criteria were in keeping with the heterogeneity of the GAM: people with and without experience in activism and institutional politics; people involved in the 15-M and others who were not; young people and seniors; men and women. We made our first contacts through activists with whom we had previously collaborated. From there, through a snowball strategy, we established contact with strangers, comprising a diverse sampling.

Only one of the interviews was conducted by telephone and at the request of the elderly interviewee. This process is not comparable to face-to-face encounters, but we emphasize the duration and the emotional importance of the interviews. Instead of simple exchanges of data, they proved to be a space of care and healing, for them and for us, in a context where people longed to speak and to be heard. We elaborated a script structured into several thematic blocks, with questions referring to the GAM and their practices of mutual support, and inquiries about democracy, care during the pandemic and the relationship between the GAM, the 15-M and social movements.

Democratic experimentation in the wake of the 15-M

Marla, a graphic designer in her forties who defined herself as a 'volunteer', described her feelings towards the shock caused by the March 2020 lockdown: 'We looked out at the street from our windows and saw the most vulnerable people'. A new landscape in a situation of exception: 'A disturbing silence in the city' (Marla, public workshop registered by authors, 16 November 2020). The GAM were a hold-on able to listen to vulnerability, render visibility to what was invisible and mobilize mutual aid in the face of legal regulations that obliged people to stay home. However, this silence also had another dimension reminiscent of the past. The protests in the streets that had previously brought people together, roused by the 15-M and temporarily shut down by COVID-19, had for some time been resonating as silence in the city.

The GAM emerged in a twofold sense: as an emergency, faced with the sensitive web of life in a city full of needs and demands; and as the emergence of care practices that were previously hidden. As the pandemic revealed inequalities, the GAM rebelled against them reclaiming new relational worlds to come. On 13 March, before the Spanish government imposed measures to deal with the lockdown, a group of volunteers, activists, social organisations, and makers set up a campaign and a website, Flatten the Curve (Frena la curva, n.d.). In their words, this was 'a cooperative device able to weave together affections between different actors', and 'an aggregator of wills, maximising the possibilities of collective intelligence' (Oliván, 2020). Bypassing bureaucratic slowness, they rapidly created interactive maps, making solidarity visible and channelling it, bringing neighbours' initiatives into connection with each other. This creative imaging, a hybrid assemblage of urban and digital elements, spread through the city's neighbourhoods. In the words of Dalia, an activist in her thirties, involved in the institutional turn of the *Indignados*, and one of the instigators of the GAM, they sprang up around this 'ecosystem of citizen innovation, heir to the 15-M' (Dalia, interview by authors, 21 December 2020). Although their origins were in the 'municipalist' projects, linked to what, in the wake of the 15-M, was called the 'new politics' (Díaz-Parra et al., 2017), they were joined by a heterogeneous alliance of locals, activists and volunteers.

In A Coruña, *Marea Atlántica*, a self-proclaimed 'movement-party' or 'instrumental party', that is, a mixed political form, somewhere between a movement and a party, born in the image and likeness of the democratic radicalisation rehearsed in the 15-M camps (Fernández de Rota, 2020), had led the city council from 2015 to 2019. In the years before, turbulence had filled the streets. The *Indignados*' political practices, a kind of sensibility defined by some authors as 'the politics of experimentation' (Corsín-Jiménez & Estalella, 2013), encountered a strong echo in the city. The interweaving of different practices and subjects was the keynote from 2011 to 2014, marking a departure from more identity-based activism (Della Porta & Diani, 2011). 15-M had garnered wide popular sympathy. Its inclusive language had the ability to interpellate anyone, politicizing 'ordinary citizens', beyond activists and experts (Flesher Fominaya, 2020). It is in this sense that Fernández-Savater (2017) defined it as a 'society in movement' rather than a social movement; that is, a 'political climate' in which communitarian ways of imagining life in common became possible.

These experiments began in the social media and digital culture (Postill, 2014) and quickly took shape as the 'A Coruña camp', interacting with the city and exploring the importance of the infrastructures in the maintenance of life: rest spaces, kitchens, nurseries, and so on brought about the re-enactment of life in common. The camp gave way to neighbourhood assemblies, where the *vecino* (neighbour), the assembly and the *barrio* (neighbourhood) became keystones of the political imagination: the 15-M traced an affective, close-knit geography where doing politics meant becoming neighbours (Corsín-Jiménez & Estalella, 2013). The term *vecino* did not draw on a pre-existing identity. Becoming a 'neighbour' in the 15-M involved a double operation of de-identification and political subjectivation (see, Rancière, 1999). While the *vecinos* de-naturalized state-assigned identities (mere statistics, victims of the crisis), they also created a space and a mode of subjectivity where anyone could be included.

The assemblies cared for neighbours and their more-than-human entanglements when addressing neighbourhood issues together. In A Coruña, the 15-M encouraged spaces where people could explore life in common (social centres, cooperatives, community gardens, feminist magazines) and strengthened groups like *Stop Desahucios*, whose mobilisations against evictions, as well as in other Spanish cities, also provided mutual aid and emotional care (Romanos, 2014). The movement used pre-existing infrastructures such as social centres, revitalized the assemblies and renewed the currency of the *vecino*, a figure key both to the citizens' movements of the Spanish transition to democracy (Castells, 1983) and to the subsequent emergence of the GAM.

The 15-M acted as a seedbed in which collective expression flourished, experimenting with self-organization in a kind of existential trade-unionism. The clearest example of this was the inclusive and non-corporatist *mareas* (Lobera, 2019), forms of sectorial self-organization responding to privatisation and austerity policies (white *marea* of health, green of education, and so forth), and defending the social rights embodied in a deteriorating welfare state (e.g., universal healthcare). *Mareas* had appeared during the 2008 financial crisis which, in Spain, coincided with a crisis of representation and government legitimacy bringing liberal democracy and the state under strong criticism (Della Porta, 2015). In this context, the *Indignados*' propositional critique sought to challenge the so-called 'Culture of the Transition', enshrined in the transition from dictatorship to democracy and perceived by 15-M as hierarchical, individualistic and depoliticising, typical of the 'old politics' carried out only by traditional parties, experts and intellectuals (Moreno-Caballud, 2015).

On the contrary, the practices of democratic experimentation of the 15-M tried out horizontal and caring gestures, gradually drawing closer to feminism, even when feminist proposals initially encountered rejection in the camps. To overcome this, the Spanish feminists pedagogically focused their discourse on the material links between patriarchy and neoliberal policies, establishing another form of politics in which the subject could not be understood outside a framework of vulnerabilities, collective empowerment and care (Gámez Fuentes, 2015). In doing so, the 15-M enacted democracy not as a vertical, government issue of politicians and experts but as the distributed and unfinished practice of organizing life in common.

The effects of this experimentation had consequences in A Coruña's electoral politics. When the protests died down in 2014, the 15-M took an 'electoral turn' (Díaz-Parra et al., 2017). *Marea Atlántica*, inspired by the citizens' *mareas* and adding the non-identifying adjective 'Atlantic', as a subjectivation that defined an open 'us' (Rancière, 1999) which potentially addressed anyone, won the mayorship in 2015.

Three of Galicia's main cities were governed by the 'movements-parties'. This emergence of parties stemmed from the crisis of traditional parties, the facilities afforded by new digital technologies and the perceived limitation of 'street politics' (Tormey & Feenstra, 2015), and attempted to articulate 'a politics that resonates rather than represents' (p. 602). This political innovation, however, had already begun in 2012. According to Pablo Iglesias, former Vice-President of Spain: 'the first electoral form taken by the 15-M wasn't Podemos' (Europa Press, 2016). Iglesias was a consultant for the Galician Alternative Left coalition, where aesthetics and signifiers later used by Podemos were first tested in 2012.

Part of the success of *Marea Atlántica* stemmed from its skill in embodying this collective sensibility in its rhetoric and the social media. Once in the city council government, the names of its councillorships echoed the 15-M: 'Regeneration', 'Diversity', 'Care', 'Participation and Democratic Innovation'. While many activists devoted themselves to the municipal project, autonomists stayed in the social centres and the struggle against evictions. Others transited both areas, but the noise in the streets had died down. The Spanish government, in the hands of the right from late 2011 to 2018, repressed the movements with penal and administrative reforms that increased sanctions and wore them down. Repression and institutionalisation, two typical effects of protest cycles (Tarrow, 1998), dampened and displaced the power of the 15-M from 2015 to 2019. The *Marea Atlántica* council promoted participatory politics and networks of social innovation that formed the backdrop to the appearance of the GAM. However, in addition to the ruthless aggressiveness of the city's elites, *Marea Atlántica* made its own mistakes. Self-referentiality, isolation and a violent eviction from a squatted social centre, alienated the local government from its electoral bases leading to the defeat in 2019 of the municipal candidature in A Coruña.

In March 2020, the GAM emerged in the midst of a double silence: in the street, deserted due to the pandemic, and in a city that had not seen an encountering political initiative for some time. In 2011 people previously unaccounted for had confronted the politics of expropriating the commons (Hardt & Negri, 2011), through dissenting operations of collective intelligence that induced new forms of political subjectivity and rearticulated the common: what Rancière (1999) calls the 'redistribution of the sensible'. This enabled people to experiment, beyond conventional channels, with ways of living in common. COVID-19 brought home the feeling of losing the world and reinvigorated the distinction made by Esposito (2008) between 'politics over life' and a 'politics of life'. In his words, 'no politics exists other than that *of* bodies, conducted *on* bodies, *through* bodies' (p. 84). That is, there is no site from which to explain the world apart from life and bodies; and this also applies to politically managing the pandemic. Faced with the pandemic catastrophe, the GAM opted to reframe it as a chance to think and act in common, reclaiming the strategies of encountering and experimentation that seemed to have been exhausted during the 2015–2019 electoral cycle. From the standpoint of politics of life, the GAM reconnected with the drive to re-imagine democracy, putting care at the core of their practices and also caring for democracy. We explain this in greater depth in the following sections.

A community woven together by care

Xela, 75 years old, retired and locked down, sewed cloth facemasks and sanitary headgear until the early hours. She is not the usual profile found in collective action literature. In an intergenerational gesture that brought together analogue and digital forms of action, her daughter encouraged her to participate in the GAM. She learned to sew in *Cose na Casa* (Sew at Home), a GAM working group which, along with those for Local Commerce Support, Housing Rights, Community Counselling, Food Emergencies and Bicycle Logistics (distributing food and health materials), spread across the city. In the lockdown, *Cose na Casa* produced 7,138 facemasks and 952 caps. At first, they had a single mask model, but the wide demand on WhatsApp and Telegram groups led them to design variations, including children's models (Figure 1). Xela was not a professional seamstress, but she decided to act: 'I can't sit still watching TV. Old people have experience, and that counts!'. The media and politicians portrayed older people counting their dead or framing them as victims. Xela and other elders, often encouraged by their friends, neighbours and relatives, joined the GAM to 'do something' (Xela, *Cose na Casa* volunteer, interview by authors, 12 December 2020).

Figure 1. GAM masks for children with immune disorders. Source: Susana Crespo

Lina, a photographer in her fifties with experience in volunteering with NGOs, explained how they took elastic bands from their children's and grandchildren's school folders to make masks. There was not enough material. Long social services waiting lists spurred on the GAM's response. The nurses' cry for help reached the GAM from the public hospitals. At home, neighbours began recycling cloth, thread, quilts, and old cotton sheets to make masks and surgical caps. They found offcuts of material in local shops and through donations. They took in hospital sheets that they turned into masks. Soon they organized a circuit distributing material throughout the city, transported by the GAM logistical support group (known as Bicycle Logistics), who also took food to families. Instead of money, *Cose na Casa* accepted payment in food, which was then passed on to the Food Emergencies group; this is how the groups worked: in a connected and interdependent way. In the main hospital, staff collected food to 'pay' for their caps. Lina felt that they were caring for the carers: 'it was a way of taking care *with* them', describing the experience as 'aid between local neighbours, a feedback loop, a chain' (Lina, *Cose na Casa* volunteer, interview by authors, 8 December 2020).

The pandemic revealed deep inequalities. In old people's homes and hospitals, austerity policies had left staff and resources scarce and gave rise to the necropolitical daily death count. Economic paralysis caused a huge employment crisis, added to the precarity of the flexible, outsourced, and submerged economy. Mobility was brought to a halt, but drivers, health workers and food providers still had to get to work. COVID-19 put the web of life at risk in a more-than-a-biological sense. The GAM set themselves in motion, committed to the practice of care, that is, the protection, maintenance and endurance of our world (Fisher & Tronto, 1990) when many families could not carry on. Families, especially grandparents, were the main support during the 2008 crisis, but now saw their lives in danger. The distribution by the GAM of food, medicine, nappies and bottles of butane gas, and their support for housing needs, revealed across-the-board but unevenly distributed vulnerability. As Lina said in our interview, 'the needs varied by neighbourhood', and were more acute in impoverished and densely populated areas (A Agra do Orzán, Os Mallos, Montealto, Sagrada Familia), far from the city centre and inhabited by the elderly, migrants and working people. It was in these districts that the GAM, the only mutual aid network in the city, had the largest number of participants offering and demanding support.

Instead of being caught up in the pandemic spectacle with which the government and the media restricted the agency of the people, the GAM drew attention to a world that was already there, among people and things, composed of an infinite number of capacities, knowledges, experiences, and forms of care that were already sustaining lives. This echoed feminist ethical principles of care, such as the assumption of interdependence as a fundamental condition in sustaining the existence of human and nonhuman beings (Puig de la Bellacasa, 2017).

While the feminist ethics was not initially present in the 15-M (Cruells & Ezquerra, 2015), its current popularity in Spanish activism can be seen as a victory for the *Indignados*, which gradually (not without conflict) incorporated the feminist agenda and its caring practices, built around ideas such as diversity, inclusion, precariousness, reproduction, vulnerability, intersectionality or affection, and which have made Spanish feminism today a much more transversal and popular movement than it was a decade ago (Jiménez-Esquinas & Diz, 2021). In A Coruña, women's participation in the GAM was greater than in any other recent movement (Figures 2–3). Here are some data on the composition of the groups:

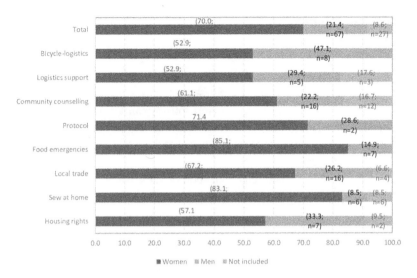

Figure 2. Participation in working groups according to field of action and sex. Source: GAM

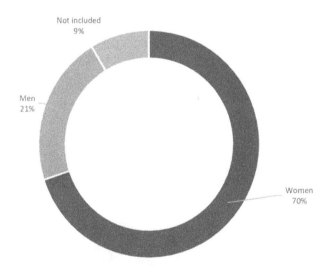

Figure 3. Participation in working groups by sex. Source: GAM

These data, not collected exhaustively by the GAM, due to problems with quantification in the social networks and the emergency situation during that period, reflect the lower number of total participants. Even so, women represented 70% of the people involved. Those providing support were mainly women, but this was differentiated: basic care, food and sewing activities were mainly in the hands of women, while more technological issues (digital mapping, social networks, or even bicycle delivery) were carried out more by men. At the other end of the chain, those receiving support were also mainly women, who took on the burden of supporting their families; working-class and middle-class women, impoverished by the successive crises, and others who never thought they would find themselves in such vulnerable circumstances. Bibiana, a feminist and anti-capitalist activist in her forties, trained in psychology and working in the service sector, said that 'poverty has a woman's face, more precisely that of a migrant woman' (Bibiana, GAM activist, public workshop registered by authors, 16 November 2020).

But apart from turning towards neighbourhood demands, as an exercise of the rematerialization of politics and life, the GAM, like the 15-M, mobilized a cognitive dimension to resignify the crisis (Pleyers, 2020). The pandemic provoked a chain reaction of solidarity. While the government was portraying the pandemic as a war (Presidencia del Gobierno, 2020), the GAM pooled their vulnerability and sewed facemasks. Those branded as incapable organized themselves by circumventing the state of alarm. In a mocking tone, some claimed to be 'dealing clandestinely' with masks, escaping the scrutiny of the police and frightened neighbours who didn't like them going out on the street (Figure 4). Others claimed to be 'skipping' the state of alarm to support the most vulnerable, disobeying the government. When they were reprimanded, they showed the bag of food or health supplies that seemed to justify their urban wanderings. Defying lockdown or collaborating from their homes, they showed the official spokespersons that their forms of organization (the technicalities, decisions, and expert orders) were as insufficient as they were authoritarian. In the pandemic, neither democratic despotism nor modern scientific practice seemed to work properly. The former ignored the possibility that people capable of thinking and acting together could make decisions; the latter emitted truths without taking seriously the concerns and knowledges of those who are also capable of experimenting with caring for the world, despite not having been invited to participate in modern assemblies.

Figure 4. 'We are neighbours, not cops'. Source: GAM.

The lack of facemasks, when uncertainty about contagion was at its highest, caused anxiety. The government and the WHO claimed a monopoly of knowledge and made public recommendations whose source seemed to be this same uncertainty. On 6 April 2020 the WHO published a guide only recommending facemasks for suspected cases, health workers and carers of infected people (World Health Organization, 2020). The organization considered that masks provided a 'false sense of security' and that their generalized use could hinder more effective measures such as hand-washing and social distancing. The report also warned of the risks of cloth masks, as there was no scientific evidence for their effectiveness. Faced with these inconsistencies, the GAM turned a socio-technical issue into a matter of care (see, Puig de la Bellacasa, 2017). While the government asserted its technocratic power (imposing rules whose justification no one knew) or showed its authoritarian face (bringing army officers to press conferences), GAM enabled neighbours to become engaged in a process of socio-material invention echoing Puig de la Bellacasa's (2017, p. 42) threefold vision of care: 'an affective state, a material vital doing, and an ethico-political obligation'. This required immediate attention to the growing vulnerability, which in turn required practices such as active listening, mask-making, or collecting and distributing money and food. It also engendered a specific type of relationship, distinct from that of welfarism: an ethical sociability enabling the defence of the community and multiplying its potential beyond the paralyzing context of the pandemic catastrophe.

The lockdown awakened the sense of radical interdependence discerned by feminist theory analysing capitalism as underpinned by reproduction and invisible care (Federici, 2014). Within this framework the GAM invited us to imagine new communitarian ways of existing as vulnerable beings in an uncertain world. Currently this is a key issue for social movements. Indeed, Butler (2009) distinguishes 'precariousness', a universal existential condition of vulnerability, from 'precarity', a politically-induced condition. Precarity is an assignation, distinguishing groups and individuals and stemming from the performative effects of power, which can either paralyze people or spur them to action. The existential conception of precariousness linked with a political notion of precarity heightened by the lockdown can help us rethink the ethics of political interdependence and mutual protection. The ambivalence of the concept allows for its reappropriation in a non-binary way. The GAM accepted precariousness and communalized it. Both inside and outside, they allied their vulnerable bodies (mixing precarity and precariousness) and stitched together a community to face the virus. Bibiana summed it up this way: 'We're precarious people helping precarious people' (Public workshop registered by authors, 16 November 2020). Although asymmetrically (the unemployed, the migrant mother, the self-employed youth, the activist, the evicted and so forth), these precarious positions came together in their precariousness to resignify the pandemic and care for others.

Indeed, ten years before the pandemic the 15-M had already spread the ethics of care. Even before the 2008 crisis, social movements had already originated concepts and practices paving the way for the central importance care has now acquired in Spanish activism. In response to passive welfare and neoliberalism, autonomous movements set up Social Rights Offices and from 2008 they have propagated, through the self-organization of domestic workers, a demand that took on new visibility due to COVID-19: 'Toward a social reorganization of care' (Casas-Cortes, 2019). Uxía, an architect in her thirties, reinvented as a social mediator and a participant in the GAM Housing Rights group, claimed that this reorganization meant 'a collectivization of care giving value to unproductive work' (Uxía, interview by authors, 11 November 2020). In fact, the notion of the 'crisis of care' was coined by feminist authors linked to social movements to problematize the tension between capital, employment, human reproduction, and the limits of the latter's political organisation (Orozco, 2006).

As the nightmarish situation in old people's homes and public hospitals revealed, austerity and shrinking state-based support mean that the state and the market provide assistance but not care. For this reason, over a decade ago Spanish feminist groups conceived a play on words: 'Care-tizenship', switching the vowels in *ciudadanía* (citizenship) to give *cuidadanía* (from *cuidar*, to care for; Casas-Cortes, 2019). This 'care-tizenship' suggests an allied community, reimagines democracy beyond the excluding limits of citizenship and reorganizes relationships for caring politics: not centred on the nation or individual rights, but on collective care for life. This is what the GAM did. In the next section, we discuss their politics through two concepts that afford further insights into the relationship between care and democracy: mutual aid and the neighborhood support networks.

Mutual aid in catastrophic times: an affective politics of life

The anarchist idea of mutual aid stresses that cooperation is just as decisive a factor in natural selection and in the preservation of life as competition (Grubacic & Graeber, 2020). In the lockdown, social movements mapped out international 'caring geographies' based on cooperation, reciprocity, and mutual aid, sustaining collective life, and expanding care beyond family and friends (Springer, 2020). The anarchist origin of the concept was advocated by Xaime, who created the first GAM Telegram groups in A Coruña. He is an activist in his forties, a participant in social movements but also in *Marea Atlántica*. For him it was not a contradiction, but rather a way of avoiding disengaging from common issues under the moral umbrella of antagonism. Xaime and one of his *compañeiros* had chosen the term 'to give it a non-welfare assistance focus and separate it from the idea of volunteering' (Xaime, GAM activist, interview by authors, 17 December 2020).

The GAM challenged the hierarchy of expert knowledge represented by the state and the WHO. The groups went into action, exchanging knowledge and learning, since the repertoire of action is learned in practice, not through rhetoric (Tilly, 1993). Many participants did not know each other but joined individually through social media and by word of mouth. Others had militated together in the feminist movement, *Stop Desahucios* and the 15-M. Some had never participated in politics, while others had mobilized in the municipal process of the *Marea Atlántica*. In the face of catastrophic times, they experimented with a visceral affective politics whose starting point was collective pain, nervousness, and fear. They turned this into mutual aid and emotional care, that should be interpreted in terms of the affective turn in social movements (Flam & King, 2005).

In contrast to Xaime's rhetorical distinctions, the GAM went beyond their initial conceptualization in what he and Dalia called the 'ecosystem' of the *Marea Atlántica*, seen as the 'heir to the 15-M'. Instead, participants saw themselves as 'mere neighbours', 'activists' or 'volunteers', on their own terms. There was enormous heterogeneity. On the one hand there were 'the regulars', old school activists who described the GAM as prefigurative 'direct action' aimed at social change (Grubacic & Graeber, 2020). Some of them were still holding a grudge against the *Marea Atlántica*, due to the eviction of the squatter *A Insumisa* during their term in government. Indeed, not all activists in the city joined the GAM: some because they were afraid or lacked time, others because they wanted nothing to do with people outside of activism and, in some cases, close to institutional politics. On the other hand, there were 'volunteers', driven more by compassion than passion, situated in the conjuncture of collective trauma and 'humanitarian reason' (Fassin, 2012). In the words of Sabela, a therapist in her forties who works as an occasional freelancer, and who joined the GAM to provide psychological support, 'the GAM are a meeting point for different types of people' (Sabela, Community Counselling volunteer, interview by authors, 7 December 2020). Diverse profiles, sometimes even antagonistic, which nevertheless ally in a context of pain. These impure alliances resonate with the allied communities emerging in the face of disasters in which new collaborations and hopes may arise (Solnit, 2010).

In A Coruña, organizing the community network enabled these people to become neighbours in the pandemic. Being a neighbour meant shedding their particular identities, taking an interest in others and caring for them through the GAM.

Neighborhood support networks

In the context of the pandemic, the starting point of care was to see oneself as vulnerable and interdependent, politicising the anguish. It was urgent to communicate with people and determine their needs, which was not easy: anyone could be infected and the city was full of mistrust. Thus, a digital meeting infrastructure was created using WhatsApp and Telegram groups. As in the 15-M, the 'logics of aggregation' of social media quickly spread through the community, bringing together individuals with diverse interests (Juris, 2012). Faced with paralyzing official statements, this caring use of technology enabled a 'disintermediation' with regard to government (Pressman & Choi-Fitzpatrick, 2020). This infrastructure favoured leaderless self-organization among people with varying degrees of expertise. In contrast to movements unfolding in the public sphere, the GAM had to reinvent their repertoire. Not only was the city as a whole in lockdown. The very thrown-togetherness of bodies could be life-threatening; hence, each encounter was an uncertainty.

Many actions (sewing, counselling, digital mapping) took place behind closed doors, at home. During the lockdown the intensity of communications was unprecedented. Some older people, like Xela, found the incessant stream of messages distressing, preferring more analogue communication: 'They made me very nervous because they were all talking at once' (Xela, *Cose na Casa* volunteer, interview by authors, 12 December 2020). Julia, a teacher and an experienced activist in the mental health field, who joined the GAM after they helped her with her shopping when she fell ill and was quarantined, acknowledges that it was difficult to handle so much information, and explained it this way: 'The public square and the social centre were now the phone! We organized another street on Telegram; it was a mixture of the spaces that had disappeared' (Figure 5). For her, this context of urgency made it necessary to put ideological purism aside, even though discussions about the role of certain political parties in the GAM, or about the government's management of the pandemic, sometimes appeared in the chat groups. Julia and others claimed that, unlike during their years of activism, the central concern was not so much in discourse as in embodied practice. As she said, despite the tensions caused by their heterogeneity, 'we had little time for debates and assemblies' (Julia, Food Emergencies activist, interview by authors, 17 November 2020). Apart from the overcoded politics focused on identity and representation, the GAM's care for life through mutual aid referred more to affective politics, like what Harney and Moten (2013) call 'hapticality': 'the capacity to feel through others, for others to feel through you, for you to feel them feeling you' (p. 98).

Figure 5. Working on a food emergency case remotely from home. Source: Óscar Górriz.

This logic of action spurred numerous practices, inside and outside people's homes. Therapists offered what they called a 'friendly ear' on the phone to accompany vulnerable others in their solitude. Listening became a caring gesture, also when confidentially recorded people's needs. Tupperware containers of food were distributed. Resistance funds were set up in shops. Bicycles went round the city with masks. The Housing GAM mobilized to stop evictions and provide shelter, for example, for a refugee couple in flight from anti-LGBTIQ violence in their country. This group also rehearsed a rent strike. On the eve of May Day, they circulated on Twitter and Telegram the hashtag #HuelgaAlquileres, along with this message: 'Many of our neighbours will have to choose between eating and paying rent. Will we continue to put rents above people's lives? If we don't get paid, we don't pay' (GAM Twitter, 30 April 2020). This list of practices is incomplete, but it illustrates a deep affection. While the city hall was not able to rise to the occasion, the GAM were agile and efficient. The PSOE (Socialist party) which ruled the city council attacked GAM as a *chiringuito*, that is, a profitable and propagandistic extension of the *Marea Atlántica* (Otero, 2020). They did not seem (or did not wish) to understand neighbours' self-organized practices, which went beyond the limits and forms of democratic institutions.

In our interviews, mutual aid was often described as a chain. Gloria, a woman in her thirties who defined herself as a GAM volunteer despite her activist experience in autonomous movements, described this idea with great sensitivity: 'It's like a chain. I'm one link and you're another', she said, thinking poetically through images: 'it's like skin: it protects you and it's your link with the other. [...] Holding out your hands, which bring things and also give them; a very fine balance between sustaining and being sustained, where you don't know who is who' (Gloria, Bicycle Logistics volunteer, interview by authors, 15 December 2020). This connects with Butler's (2009) idea that one's life is always in the hands of the other person, since 'precariousness implies living socially' (p. 14). This hapticality and the ethics of commitment, define the democratic politics of the GAM.

The pandemic worked as a collective affect bringing everyone together in the same atmosphere, although not harmoniously. These neighborhood support networks recalled iconic images from Galicia's recent history. The volunteers of the *Marea Blanca*, for example, who, faced with government inaction after the 2002 Prestige oil spill, cleaned up the disastrously polluted coast with their own hands. Or the human chains of local residents, carrying buckets of water, defending themselves from the 2017 forest fires. Such moments of vulnerability had created alliances among locals and strangers, weaving a collective response to shared problems. During the lockdown, these chains re-emerged to take on 'emergency work' (Lina, *Cose na Casa* volunteer, interview by authors, 8 December 2020). The GAM care chains made visible a whole web of factors hitherto unknown or ignored by many: situations of absolute precarity and practices of social reproduction and care, paid and unpaid, upholding life that was previously hidden in the shadows. The GAM revealed a new map of the city. However, to make this sensitive web visible, women had to put themselves in the front line. This is where the paradox lies. While they took on a leading role, their participation, according to sex, was symptomatic of the unequal distribution of care in our society and in social movements.

Conclusions: caring democracy now

The 15-M posed questions about the forms of life of the unaccounted-for and explored the enactment of an alternative world potentially open to anyone. This world did not completely succeed, but the experimentation that endeavoured to create it brought subjective and institutional transformations that shook the Spanish democratic consensus. The COVID-19 pandemic generated an idea of the end of the world in which both life itself and the life of democracy appear to be in jeopardy. We argue that the concept of caring democracy (Tronto, 2013), that we propose should be reassembled with the idea of the 'power of anyone' (Rancière, 1999), may help us think about sustaining lives that are hard to lead and about implied forms of life in common through which democracy can be reimagined. The way of caring about and for anyone that emerges from the GAM is an ethical and political engagement set apart from welfarism. Indeed, the GAM do not deny it either, but rather propose radical democratization through collective engagement practices and entanglements of socio-material intervention.

The pandemic was also a political issue and the GAM reordered it from collaborative dynamics. By means of mutual aid, these groups opened up a space hierarchized by the government, with its authoritarian discourses of war and expertise. They managed to introduce care where there was only fear, mistrust and obedience. The GAM tackled the growing vulnerability from the standpoint of multiple alliances. They approached democracy as a condition of possibility to address the problems of our time through more egalitarian compositions. We consider that this kind of collective experimentation, similar to that of the *Indignados* and the 'municipalist' turn, contains important elements that will allow us to rethink social movements in catastrophic times. Paradoxically, in the pandemic, physical distancing gave way to relational and proximity politics based on the encounter, which was outlawed by the lockdown. These dissensual gestures were not entirely new. Ten years after the 15-M, the GAM took on the challenge of an affective politics of life and continued with that democratic impulse.

Disclosure statement

No potential conflict of interest was reported by the author(s).

References

Barad, K. (2007). *Meeting the universe halfway: Quantum physics and the entanglement of matter and meaning*. Duke University Press.
Butler, J. (2009). *Frames of war: When is life grievable?* Verso.

Casas-Cortes, M. (2019). *Care-tizenship*: Precarity, social movements, and the deleting/re-writing of citizenship. *Citizenship Studies, 23*(1), 19–42. https://doi.org/10.1080/13621025.2018.1556248

Castells, M. (1983). *The city and the grassroots: A cross-cultural theory of urban social movements*. University of California Press.

Corsín-Jiménez, A., & Estalella, A. (2013). The atmospheric person: Value, experiment, and "making neighbors" in Madrid's popular assemblies. *HAU, 3*(2), 119–139. https://doi.org/10.14318/hau3.2.008

Cruells, M., & Ezquerra, S. (2015). Procesos de voluntad democratizadora: La expresión feminista en el 15-M. *An International Journal for Critical Geographies, 14*(1), 42–60. https://www.acme-journal.org/index.php/acme/article/view/1133.

Della Porta, D., & Diani, M. (2011). *Los movimientos sociales*. CIS.

Della Porta, D. (2015). *Social movements in times of austerity: Bringing capitalism back into protest analysis*. John Wiley & Sons.

Díaz-Parra, I., Roca, B., and Martín-Díaz E. 2017. Indignados, municipalism and Podemos. In B. Roca, Eds. *Challenging austerity. Radical left and social movements in the South of Europe*, (pp. 70–89). Routledge.

Diz, C. (2018). Tácticas del cuerpo: Activismo y resistencia en la ciudad en crisis. *Disparidades. Revista de Antropología, 73*(1), 127–152 doi:10.3989/rdtp.2018.01.005.

Esposito, R. (2008). *Bíos: Biopolitics and philosophy*. University of Minnesota Press.

Estévez, B. (2019). Reassembling lesseps square, rethinking Barcelona: A more-than-human approach. *International Journal of Urban and Regional Research, 43*(6), 1123–1147. https://doi.org/10.1111/1468-2427.12767

Europa Press (2016, September 20). *La primera traducción electoral del 15M no fue Podemos*. Eldiario.es. https://www.eldiario.es/politica/iglesias-podemos-age-manuel-beiras_1_3819967.html

Fassin, D. (2012). *Humanitarian reason*. University of California Press.

Federici, S. (2014). *Caliban and the witch: Women, the body, and primitive accumulation*. Autonomedia.

Fernández de Rota, A. (2020). ¿Qué es la democracia? Sobre su concepto, práctica, aporías y exceso, con un estudio de caso del movimiento de los Indignados. *Antropología Experimental, 20*(20), 93–118. https://doi.org/10.17561/rae.v20.08

Fernández-Savater, A. (2017). La política de los despolitizados. In R. Cuenca, W. Gadea, & D. Allen-Perkins (Eds.), *Hacia una (re)conceptualización de la democracia contemporánea* (pp. 161.172). Fénix Editora.

Ferrándiz, F. (2013). Rapid response ethnographies in turbulent times: Researching mass grave exhumations in contemporary Spain. *Anthropology Today, 29*(6), 18–22 doi:10.1111/1467-8322.12073.

Fisher, B., & Tronto, J. (1990). Toward a feminist theory of caring. In E. Abel & M. Nelson (Eds.), *Circles of care* (pp. 35–61). NYC: University of New York Press.

Flam, H., & King, D. (Eds.). (2005). *Emotions and social movements*. Routledge.

Flesher Fominaya, C. (2020). *Democracy reloaded: Inside Spain's political laboratory from 15M to Podemos*. Oxford University Press.

Frena la curva. (n.d.). *Actua.frenalacurva*. https://actua.frenalacurva.net/

Gámez Fuentes, M. (2015). Feminisms and the 15M movement in Spain: Between frames of recognition and contexts of action. *Social Movement Studies, 14*(3), 359–365. https://doi.org/10.1080/14742837.2014.994492

Grubacic, A., & Graeber, D. (2020). Introduction to mutual aid Bonzo, N. In *Mutual Aid: An Illuminated Factor of Evolution* (pp. 1–8). PM Press/Kairos.

Grupos de Apoio Mutuo, GAM (2020). https://gamcoruna.org/

Hardt, M., & Negri, A. (2011). *Commonwealth*. Harvard University Press.

Harney, S., & Moten, F. (2013). *The undercommons: Fugitive planning & black study*. Minor Compositions.

Horton, R. (2020). Offline: COVID-19 is not a pandemic. *Lancet, 396*(10255), 874. https://doi.org/10.1016/S0140-6736(20)32000-6

Jiménez-Esquinas, G., & Diz, C. (2021). Féminisme espagnol. Que reste-t-il du mouvement des Indignés? *La Revue Nouvelle, 4*(4), 54–61. https://doi.org/10.3917/rn.214.0054

Juris, J. (2012). Reflections on #occupy everywhere. Social media, public space, and emerging logics of aggregation. *American Ethnologist, 39*(2), 259–279. https://doi.org/10.1111/j.1548-1425.2012.01362.x

Kavada, A. (2020, June 12). *Creating a hyperlocal infrastructure of care: COVID-19 mutual aid groups. Open Democracy.* https://www.opendemocracy.net/en/openmovements/creating-hyperlocal-infrastructure-care-covid-19-mutual-aid-groups/

Latour, B. (2004). Why has critique run out of steam? From matters of fact to matters of concern. *Critical Inquiry, 30*(2), 225–248. https://doi.org/10.1086/421123

Lobera, J. (2019). Anti-austerity movements in Europe. In C. Flesher Fominaya & R. Feenstra (Eds.), *Routledge Handbook of Contemporary European social movements* (pp. 267–283). Routledge.

Martínez-Buján, R., Taboadela, O., & Del Moral, L. (2021). Experiencias colectivas de cuidados durante la infancia: Dinámicas, debates y tensiones. *Revista Española de Sociología, 30*(2), a31. https://doi.org/10.22325/fes/res.2021.31

Moreno-Caballud, L. (2015). *Cultures of anyone: Studies on cultural democratization in the spanish neoliberal crisis.* Liverpool University Press.

Oliván, R. (2020, September 9). *Frena la curva.* https://raulolivan.com/2020/09/09/frena-la-curva-innovacion-abierta-y-cooperacion-anfibia/?fbclid=IwAR3XPB7xbPXahQ_7RZzkL1ZyYFzqs2AECzZfL6PXOk9AYNSca4ijx77kID

Orozco, A. P. (2006). Amenaza tormenta: La crisis de los cuidados y la reorganización del sistema económico. *Revista de Economía Crítica, 5,* 7–37 http://revistaeconomiacritica.org/index.php/rec/article/view/388.

Otero, M. (2020, June 6). *Pulso vecinal en María Pita. La Opinión A Coruña.* https://www.laopinioncoruna.es/coruna/2020/06/06/pulso-vecinal-maria-pita-23514058.html

Pink, S., Horst, H., Postill, J., Hjorth, L., & Lewis, T. (2015). *Digital ethnography: principles and practice.* SAGE.

Pleyers, G. (2020). The Pandemic is a battlefield. Social movements in the COVID-19 lockdown. *Journal of Civil Society* 16,(4),1–18 doi:10.1080/17448689.2020.1794398

Postill, J. (2014). Democracy in an age of viral Reality: A media Epidemiography of Spain's Indignados Movement. *Ethnography, 15*(1), 51–69. https://doi.org/10.1177/1466138113502513

Presidencia del Gobierno (2020, April 4). *Comparecencia del presidente del Gobierno sobre nuevas medidas de la COVID19.* Lamoncloa. https://www.lamoncloa.gob.es/presidente/Paginas/EnlaceTranscripciones2020/04042020_covid19.aspx

Pressman, J., & Choi-Fitzpatrick, A. (2020). Covid19 and protest repertoires in the United States. *Social Movement Studies,* 20(6),1–8 doi:10.1080/14742837.2020.1860743

Puig de la Bellacasa, M. (2017). *Matters of care: Speculative ethics in more than human worlds.* University of Minnesota Press.

Rancière, J. (1999). *Disagreement: Politics and philosophy.* University of Minnesota Press.

Romanos, E. (2014). Evictions, petitions and escraches: Contentious housing in austerity Spain. *Social Movement Studies, 13*(2), 296–302. https://doi.org/10.1080/14742837.2013.830567

Solnit, R. (2010). *A paradise built in hell: The extraordinary communities that arise in disaster.* Penguin Books.

Springer, S. (2020). Caring geographies: The COVID-19 interregnum and a return to mutual aid. *Dialogues in Human Geography, 10*(2), 112–115. https://doi.org/10.1177/2043820620931277

Stengers, I., & Pignarre, P. (2011). *Capitalist sorcery: Breaking the spell.* Palgrave.

Stengers, I. (2015). *In catastrophic times: Resisting the coming barbarism.* Open Humanities Press.

Tarrow, S. (1998). *Power in movement: Social movements, collective action and politics.* Cambridge University Press.

Tilly, C. (1993). Contentious repertoires in Great Britain, 1758-1834. *Social Science History*, *17*(2), 253–280 doi:10.2307/1171282

Tormey, S., & Feenstra, R. (2015). Reinventing the political party in Spain: The case of 15M and the Spanish mobilisations. *Policy Studies*, *36*(6), 590–606. https://doi.org/10.1080/01442872.2015.1073243

Tormey, S. (2015). *The end of representative politics*. Polity.

Tronto, J. (2013). *Caring democracy: Markets, equality, and justice*. NYU Press.

Wilkie, A., Rosengarten, M., & Savransky, M. (2017). *Speculative techniques*. Routledge.

World Health Organization (2020, April 6). *Advice on the use of masks in the context of COVID-19*. Iris. https://apps.who.int/iris/handle/10665/331693

The rise of a new media ecosystem: exploring 15M's educommunicative legacy for radical democracy

Ángel Barbas and Emiliano Treré

ABSTRACT
This article explores the influence that the educommunicative dimension of the 15M Movement has had on the creation and consolidation of a new ecosystem of independent media. To this end, we rely on a document analysis of the movement's minutes and manifestos and on the review of the editorial principles and educational activities of a sample of independent media. We also draw on ten in-depth interviews with key journalists and activists who actively participated in the 15M. We argue that the movement's media activism had a clear educommunicative orientation that strengthened pre-existing media activism, opening windows of opportunity for media innovation. This contributed to the rise of a new media ecosystem of independent media characterised by three key elements: (1) synergies and mutual support; (2) the key role of the community of subscribers and users; and (3) an educational agency with a public service orientation. Finally, we illustrate that this new media ecosystem displays a clear educommunicative orientation. This orientation is rooted in the imaginary and practices of the 15M and is based on the revitalised civic role of journalism and on the value of information for radical democracy. This article advances social movement studies by engaging a dialogue between an educommunicative perspective and a media ecology lens. It articulates the relevance of media as educational agents and explores the impact of a social movement in the creation and shaping of a new media ecosystem.

Introduction

The 15M – or *The indignados* – Movement was a cross-cutting social movement that emerged in Spain as a response to the consequences of the 2008 economic crisis (Flesher Fominaya, 2020). It protested against what was perceived as an obsolete political system that catered more to the interests of banks and financial corporations, than to the problems of citizens.

The first manifesto of the 15M, published on 7 March 2011, raised awareness around the economic and political situation in Spain and urged citizens to be actively involved in what they called an 'ethical revolution'.[1] In this first manifesto, not only a series of demands on specific issues – such as public health, housing policies and labor rights –

were made public, but a symbolic imaginary oriented towards the construction of a more open and participatory democracy was expressed (Candón-Mena et al., 2018). After the 15 May demonstrations, this imaginary was further developed. In particular, the movement gave special importance to the role of communication and education processes in raising the awareness of citizens about their role as political actors, the promotion of democratic values and the expansion of spaces for participation in the public sphere: communication and education were, for *the Indignados*, the means through which a utopia of radical democracy could be reached.

While the communicative dimension of the 15M has been studied from different perspectives (Castells, 2012; Micó & Casero-Ripollés, 2014; Postill, 2014), the relationship between communication and education processes in the Spanish movement has received less attention. There are works that mention the relevance of learning in relation to prefigurative politics and deliberative democracy practices (Hernández et al., 2013; Razquin, 2017; Romanos, 2013) and a few studies have addressed this aspect from the paradigm of educommunication (Barbas, 2020).

This article digs deeper into this relationship, exploring the influence that the educommunicative dimension of the 15M Movement has had on the creation and consolidation of a new media ecosystem constituted by several so-called independent media. We refer to the media that emerged after the 15M's outbreak and that altered the media ecosystem of political communication in Spain (Flesher Fominaya & Gillan, 2017).

We link the educommunicative orientation of the 15M with the principles and practices of independent media. We argue that the 15M's media activism strengthened pre-existing media activism and its educommunicative dimension, and established the conditions of possibility for media innovation. We illustrate that the new independent media have coalesced into a media ecosystem sustained on a social contract between the media and its users, based on the value of information committed to social justice and democracy. Ultimately, we demonstrate that this new media ecosystem has a clear educommunicative orientation that is rooted in the imaginary and practices of the 15M for radical democracy.

The structure of the article consists of the following sections. We start outlining an interdisciplinary theoretical framework comprised of three research streams. Firstly, we connect the symbolic-cultural perspective of collective behaviour theories with knowledge production and learning in social movements. We point out that a dialogue between these currents and the tradition of educommunication has not been established yet. Secondly, we look at the paradigm of educommunication and its conception of the media as educational agents and means of learning. Thirdly, we introduce the media ecology approach and blend it with the educommunication paradigm showing that every media ecosystem is always an ecosystem of knowledge and learning.

We then outline our methodology that combines the analysis of movement's documents with ten in-depth interviews with journalists and activists who contributed to the establishment of the independent media. Subsequently, we explore the influence of the educommunicative dimension of the 15M on the creation and consolidation of a new ecosystem of independent media. We illustrate our findings along three areas of analysis: (1) the educommunicative dimension of the 15M; (2)

the influence of the movement on the strengthening of media activism and on the pre-existing educommunicative dimension; and (3) the key traits of this new media ecosystem, its educommunicative orientation and its implications for radical democracy. Finally, we reflect on the contributions of our article and sketch future avenues for inquiry.

Theoretically, this article brings three innovative elements to the study of social movements, communication and democracy: (a) it brings into dialogue an educommunicative perspective with social movement studies highlighting the relevance of the media as educational agents and means of learning; (b) it blends the educommunicative perspective with the media ecology approach to explore the impact of a social movement in the shaping of a new ecosystem of independent media; (c) it illustrates that this new media ecosystem has a clear educommunicative orientation. This orientation is rooted in the imaginary and practices of the 15M and is based on a revitalized civic role of journalism at the service of social justice and democracy. Hence, our findings also contribute to broader debates about the relationships between civil society, the media and deliberative democracy.

Social movements, knowledge production and learning processes

Social movements operate as pedagogical-political actors insofar as their pursuit of cultural transformation involves learning processes aimed at raising awareness and empowering citizens (Della Porta & Diani, 2020). In order to ground this pedagogical-political perspective we connect theories of collective behaviour with both theories of knowledge production and learning in social movements.

In relation to the research currents in the field of social movement studies, we rely on the symbolic-cultural perspective of collective behaviour. This current focuses on the study of the processes, repertoire of actions and forms through which social movements generate a specific symbolic production, alternative to the dominant one, or in response to that symbolic production with which they seek to confront their ideas, demands or socio-cultural models (Gusfield, 1994). To carry out such production, social movements create their own media. These may generate changes in how people view the world, contributing to broader cultural transformations. In this sense, social movements use the media as pedagogical tools at the service of social change (Barbas & Postill, 2017).

From this perspective, contentious collective action has a cultural character but also a cognitive character (Holford, 1995). This allows us to connect the symbolic-cultural approach of theories of collective behaviour with works that address the production of knowledge of social movements and with the social movement learning current (Hall et al., 2012).

Some works explore the ways in which social movements create and transmit knowledge, as well as its variety and typology (Casas-Cortés et al., 2008; Chesters, 2012). Social movements are, in this sense, laboratories of knowledge production (Della Porta & Pavan, 2017) or 'epistemic communities' (Eyerman & Jamison, 1991). This approach has also been developed in works by currents closer to theories of collective behaviour

(Laraña, 1996) and in recent contributions that comprehensively address the study of the 15M understood as a laboratory of political and democratic innovation (Feenstra et al., 2017; Flesher Fominaya, 2020).

Closer to Pedagogy, we find works more based on educational epistemologies, where explicit reference is made to the tradition of popular education understood as a social movement (Cox, 2014; Cox & Flesher Fominaya, 2009). These works incorporate an important part of the literature on social movement learning, illuminating a dialogue between both streams of research.

Social movement learning is a pedagogical research current which draws mainly on the tradition of popular and adult education, but that has been greatly influenced by new social movements studies (Finger, 1989; Welton, 1993). It recognizes social movements as rich learning environments. In recent years, important efforts have also been made to systematize this current of research and its encounters with other disciplines (Kuk & Tarlau, 2020; Niesz et al., 2018). In this regard, although we can find connections between scholars of social movement learning and scholars of social movement studies, who point out the centrality of the media for social change, there is no evidence of dialogue between these research currents and educommunication.

The educommunication paradigm

Educommunication emerged during the second half of the 1960s within the Latin American School of Communication, as part of the intellectual response to developmentalist policies driven by international institutions[2] in the context of the struggles of social movements against inequalities, poverty and illiteracy.

Its philosophy and practice are nourished by the work of Paulo Freire in the field of popular education (Freire, 1965, 1970); as well as the contributions of other authors dedicated to finding ways to articulate communication and education as a theoretical-practical tool for social transformation (Díaz Bordenave, 1976; Kaplún, 1985; Prieto Castillo, 1979). Communication and education began to be seen as constitutive parts of the same training process with a strong socio-political component aimed at promoting awareness, empowerment and emancipation of the most disadvantaged populations.

Although there is no academic consensus when it comes to defining ucommunication (Buitrago et al., 2017; Cohen-Montoya, 2021; Huergo, 2000), we rely on its epistemological development and its transdisciplinary nature to define it as a field of study focused on the relationships established between communicative and educational processes in a comprehensive, dynamic and interdependent manner. We conceive educommunication as a unified conceptual tool for theoretical reflection and praxis. While this general conceptualization may have different practical concretions, we see educommunication as a paradigm which studies the communicative dimension of education and the educative dimension of communication. Within this framework, another strand of educommunication focuses on media literacy (Tyner, 2010), that is the educational initiatives focused on teaching and learning how to use the media and ICT. Media literacy aims to provide skills and knowledge to foster participation and civic engagement by using the media.

We understand educommunication as a form of socio-critical pedagogy that conceives the media as both educational agents and means and tools for learning how to participate in social and political processes. Hence, educommunication is engaged in empowering citizens by using the media and in promoting long-term cultural and social transformations. The epistemology of educommunication provides a paradigmatic positioning for the analysis and implementation of communication-education dynamics, developed by social movements, as part of their repertoire of actions aimed at expanding political participation spaces and develop practices of radical democracy.

The media ecology approach

Media and social movements scholars have increasingly started to rely on media ecology framework to make sense of the uses of communication technologies in protests, and more generally in processes aimed at social change and political transformation. The media ecology approach aims to disentangle the 'communicative complexity' of social movements by focusing on how activists engage holistically and critically with a wide ecology of media technologies to organize, mobilize, influence public opinion and pursue radical change (Foust & Hoyt, 2018; Treré, 2019). Inspired by the media ecology tradition that conceives the media as complex environments, the strength of this approach lies in its holistic gaze that does not privilege any specific technology, but instead investigate how activists, in their movement-related practices, make sense of, navigate and merge newer and older media formats, physical and digital spaces, internal and external forms of communication, as well as alternative and corporate social media. Even if within media ecology studies of protest movements, the educational dimension has been usually neglected, educommunication and media ecology share the critique of – and the necessity to overcome – the instrumental role of the media within collective action. They both focus on the role of the media and technologies as active agents that are able to (re)shape various dimensions and dynamics of social movements.

In this paper, we bring together these two conceptual lenses to foreground the importance of looking at the communicative complexity of social movements, in particular to the role of the media as means and tools for learning and socio-political transformation. Every media is an educational agent. Therefore, every media ecosystem is always also an ecosystem of knowledges and learning, that is an educational media ecosystem.

Methods

This article aims to explore the influence that the educommunicative dimension of the 15M has had on the creation and consolidation of a new media ecosystem constituted by several so-called independent media. To do this, we blend document analysis with in-depth interviews. The document analysis has been divided into two parts. The first part had three main objectives: (1) to identify discursive aspects in the minutes and manifestos of the 15M related to communication, education, citizen participation and democracy; (2) to identify projects and media created by the 15M; and (3) to identify training projects carried out by the movement.

Table 1. Websites analyzed.

Name and website	Description	Documents
#Acampadasol https://madrid.tomalaplaza.net/	Website of the tent city of 'Puerta del Sol' in Madrid.	Manifestos and minutes of assemblies.
#Tomalosbarrios https://madrid.tomalosbarrios.net/	Website of the 15 M's grassroots groups from Madrid neighbourhoods.	Minutes of assemblies.
15 Mpedia https://15mpedia.org/	Free encyclopaedia about 15 M and social movements.	Manifestos, minutes of assemblies, lists of issues, topics, media directories.

Table 2. Training projects.

Name and website	Description	Training
Radio Guerrilla https://www.radioguerrilla.org/	Project created in 2014 to teach grassroots collectives and activists how to create their own radio stations.	Skills to create and develop online radio stations.
Asamblea Carabanchel https://asambleacarabanchel.org/	15M's grassroot group from Carabanchel neighbourhood (Madrid), created in 2012 to empower local residents and defend their social rights.	Activist use of social media; how to speak in public; assembly-based movement organizing practices; social rights (labour, housing, participation).
El Binario http://ww.elbinario.net/	Project created in 2013 by 15M's hackers to disseminate information about free culture, provide communication services to social movements and teach computing skills.	Computer and data security, free software, digital creation, free culture, social rights.

Documents prepared by the movement at different times were reviewed (see, Table 1). We also relied on ethnographic research carried out during the years 2014 and 2015 on the educational communication of the 15M, where 23 communication projects developed by the movement were detected (Barbas & Postill, 2017), and a list of alternative media hosted in the *15Mpedia* project site.

We then reviewed the training projects carried out by three collectives that originated from the movement (see, Table 2).

The second part of the document analysis consisted in selecting a sample of independent media from the 'Independent media platform' (Table 3). Their selection was guided by the following criteria: (a) the media should have emerged after the 15M; (b) they should cover all types of information (not specialised); and (c) they should include training projects among their activities. The selected media were *La Marea, El Salto* and *Ctxt*. We carried out a review of their editorial principles and training activities.

The ten in-depth interviews aimed at studying the perceptions of both journalists from the selected media and journalists who actively participated in the 15M on the educommunicative influence of the movement on the creation and consolidation of independent media. The questions focused on three fundamental topics: (1) the mutual influences between the 15M, media activism as well as independent journalism; (2) their public service orientation, that is, to what extent they position themselves and act as a service of public utility that helps to know and understand the world outside of partisan or economic interests; and (3) their educational agency, that is, the pedagogical intentionality of their journalistic action and its contribution to an informed and critical

Table 3. Media analysed.

Name, year, website	Editorial principles	Media presence	Training activities	Subscribers/ Tw followers (Nov 2021)
La Marea, 2012 https://www.lamarea.com/	Freedom, equality, secularism, defence of welfare state, sovereignty of the people, fair economy, democratic regeneration, republicanism, democratic memory, free culture, decent work and housing, respect for the environment.	Print and digital edition, YouTube, Twitter, Facebook, Instagram, Telegram.	Gender-sensitive journalism; Human rights approach journalism; Consumption as a political act; Climate crisis.	4.000 / 246.520
El Salto, 2017 https://www.elsaltodiario.com/	Independence, internal democracy, horizontal structure and collective ownership, quality and journalistic rigour.	Print and digital edition (national plus 8 local editions), YouTube, Radio, Twitter, Facebook, Instagram, TikTok, Telegram, Mastodon.	Health journalism; Critical and anti-racist journalism; Migrations and journalism; Economics and journalism; Production of podcast.	8.100 / 184.565
Ctxt, 2015 https://ctxt.es/	Slow, analytical and honest journalism; first-hand information, collected on the ground, well written, edited and verified; providing political and economic context; anticipating the major issues on the agenda; stimulating culture and creation; promoting the debate of ideas; being a public service that helps citizens to construct their own criteria and to act responsibly and coherently.	Print and digital edition, YouTube, Twitter, Facebook, Instagram, Telegram.	Cultural studies; LGTB realities; Critical art; Climate crisis; Journalism in context.	12.328 / 200.776

Table 4. Informants data.

Name	Biographical note	Current labour	Interview date
Patricia Simón	Co-founder and Deputy Director of *Periodismo Humano*. Award from Spanish Association of Professional Women of the Media 2013.	Reporter of *La Marea*.	10/01/2021
Pablo Elorduy	Journalist of *Diagonal* and co-founder of *El Salto*.	Editor and Coordinator of the political section of *El Salto*.	15/01/2021
Clara Jiménez	Journalist of *La Sexta* TV. Co-founder of *Maldita.es*. Madrid's Press Association Award (2021).	Project Manager of *Maldita.es*	18/01/2021
Pablo Hernández	Journalist of *La Sexta*, *CNN+*, *Cuatro* and *Localia* TV. Editor of *EFE* and *ABC*.	Research coordinator of *Maldita.es*	18/01/2021
Tomás Muñoz	Journalist of *SER* radio station and *Diagonal* and *El Salto*.	Communication advisor for Unidas Podemos, City Hall of Alicante.	22/01/2021
Vanesa Jiménez	Journalist of *El Mundo* and *El País*.	Deputy Director of *Ctxt*.	28/01/2021
Javier Gallego	Journalist of *SER*, *M80* and *Radio 3*; and *TVE* and *La Sexta* TV. Ondas Award 2012.	Director and host of *Carne Cruda* radio show.	29/01/2021
Magda Bandera	Journalist of *La Vanguardia*, *El Periódico* and *Público*. Co-founder of *La Marea*.	Director of *La Marea*.	30/01/2021
Javier Bauluz	Photojournalist. Co-founder and Director of *Periodismo Humano*. Pulitzer Prize (1995).	Freelance photojournalist.	30/01/2021
Mª Ángeles Fernández	Freelance journalist. Joan Gomis Journalism Award (2020).	Head of editorial area of *Pikara* magazine.	05/02/2021

citizenship. Purposive sampling was combined with snowball or referral sampling, which helped to meet new informants (Gentles et al., 2015). The interviews were conducted in Spanish and subsequently translated into English by the authors of this article. Their duration ranged from sixty to ninety minutes. The final selection of the sample of informants and their related information are illustrated in Table 4.

Transcribed interviews and documents were inputted and analysed with Nvivo following the principles of content analysis and thematic coding (Flick, 2018).

Findings have been structured following three categories of analysis that have been elaborated inductively from a dialogue between the aim of the research, the conceptual framework and the data collected. These are: (1) the educommunicative dimension of the 15M; (2) the influence of the 15M on the strengthening of media activism and of its pre-existing educommunicative dimension; and (3) the creation and consolidation of a new media ecosystem. These categories are explained and developed in the following section.

Findings

We present the findings structured according to the above-mentioned categories of analysis. We show that the movement had a clear educational intentionality that was largely channeled and developed through the media. Nevertheless, we state that the alliances between activism and independent journalism were already created before the emergence of the 15M. Moreover, we hold that the educommunicative dimension was inherent in the action of social movements and in the activist media, even if the 15M opened windows of opportunity for media innovation strengthening this dimension. Finally, we illustrate the existence of a new media ecosystem whose traits reveal the educommunicative legacy of the 15M.

The educommunicative dimension of the 15M

The 15M had a clear educommunicative orientation. Relying on the previous definition of educommunication, we appreciate that this orientation was expressed from the creation and appropriation of media as means and objects of learning. This was a key tool for the movement within its struggle to build a radical democracy. In the following lines, we disentangle these aspects.

The movement's founding manifesto which was disseminated on 20 May 2011 from the tent-city of *Puerta del Sol* in Madrid, already included concepts and ideas such as 'participatory democracy', 'direct democracy' and 'popular access to the media, which must be ethical and truthful'[3]; likewise, platforms as *Democracia Real ¡Ya! (Real democracy, now!)* included several claimings referring to 'citizen freedoms and participatory democracy'[4] and a list drawn up by the *15Mpedia* project show that education, direct democracy and citizen participation were the most frequent proposals made by several 15M collectives.[5] Therefore, from the outset, alongside demands for a more inclusive and participatory democracy, there was a demand for education and criticism of the mainstream media.

The communicational dimension of the 15M became evident with the creation of the movement's own media and communication projects. As various authors have pointed out (Barranquero & Meda, 2015; Candón, 2014), one of the defining characteristics of the

15M was the importance given to communication; for that reason, the 15M was defined as a communicational movement (Barranquero, 2014). In the words of Tomás Muñoz, journalist at *Diagonal* and *El Salto* and 15M activist: 'from the first moment it was clear to us that taking care of communication was strategic'.

The frenetic and fruitful activity of the movement in the creation of a wide range of media and experimental communication projects, which made it possible to generate what Feenstra and Casero-Ripollés (2012) have defined as a hybrid information environment. This aspect represents an extraordinary change in relation to the hegemony of the mainstream media in Spain, and it exemplifies the cultural nature of the movement (Candón, 2014; Laraña & Díez, 2012).

We find a relationship between the communicational and educational dimension of the 15M, insofar as some of its communication projects possessed a pedagogical intentionality oriented to change people's minds to generate socio-cultural transformations at a broader level (Laraña & Díez, 2012; Perugorría & Tejerina, 2013). In other words, some of these projects – e.g. *Audiovisol, Tomalatele* or *Ágora Sol Radio* – were created not only to spread information bypassing the filter of the mainstream media, but also to promote citizen education around economic, political, and social issues. In these cases, educational communication processes were developed, since media operated as means and tools of learning, in alignment with the epistemology of educommunication (Kaplún, 1985; Prieto Castillo, 1998).

Likewise, other researchers have underlined the pedagogical nature of the 15M in two ways. On the one hand, as a generator of informal education dynamics through the creation of spaces for participation where deliberative democratic processes were put into practice (Hernández et al., 2013; Razquin, 2017; Romanos, 2013). In other words, the construction of participatory democracy implied learning to participate and putting participatory processes into practice, in such a way that participation was both a tool and an objective in itself, as it is understood from popular education (Gil-Jaurena et al., 2021) and from educommunication (Gozálvez-Pérez & Contreras-Pulido, 2014). As Pablo Elorduy points out, the 15M generated processes of citizen literacy in terms of political discussion and what in Spanish is known as *prácticas asamblearias (assembly-based movement organizing practices)*; something that Javier Gallego defines as 'a political university in the squares'. For Patricia Simón, the interaction between people from different backgrounds led to a multidisciplinary dialogue that influenced the way in which journalism related to public opinion. On the other hand, as an educational agent promoting more formalised education initiatives, that can be categorized as 'pedagogical sovereignty' (Barbas & Postill, 2017). Many of those educational initiatives were oriented towards media literacy, insofar as the construction of participatory democracy required learning to participate and this implied, in turn, having specific knowledge and media skills to be able to engage also through the media and ICT. Therefore, as the movement developed processes of educational communication through media content production to educate, also carried out more formalized training initiatives which aimed teaching key media skills to people through the use of the media and ICT. In such cases, the media worked as both means and objects of learning *in themselves*, establishing a connection to media education studies (Buckingham, 2013; Tyner, 2010).

Table 2 shows key examples of the 15M's training initiatives, some of them aimed specifically at media literacy, such as: creation and development of online radio stations; activist uses of social media and digital devices; dissemination of demands and calls; coordination of actions; denouncement of police abuse; digital creation techniques; data security protocols, etc. During the movement's peak period (2011–2015) these types of training projects were very common. In line with the social movement learning approach, activists deploy a wide range of learning resources (Kuk & Tarlau, 2020; Niesz et al., 2018). Nevertheless, this approach has neglected learning developed through media practices. This signals the importance of the educommunication paradigm and the necessary dialogue with social movement studies.

The strengthening of the pre-existing educommunicative dimension of media activism

Since late 2010 and early 2011, students joined housing rights activists and the free culture movement in the organisation of protests against the political system. This system was seen as incapable of responding to the huge increase of unemployment and inequality. Moreover, the frequent cases of political corruption were also undermining citizens' trust in the institutions. These groups shared hopelessness towards representative democratic system, together with the need to raise people's awareness and promote forms of direct action.

Whereas mainstream media were not focusing on civil society's responses to the economic, social and political crisis in Spain prior the 15M's outbreak, independent media from Madrid, such as the newspaper *Diagonal* and the radio show *Carne Cruda*, did report on the citizens' mobilizations that would lead to the demonstrations on 15 May. On 4 May 2011, *Diagonal* published a news item reporting on the protest actions that would give rise to the 15 M Movement. The headline read: *El 15 de mayo la indignación tiene un plan* (*On 15 May, indignation has a plan*). *Carne Cruda* also reported on the social protests that were taking place in Spain, clearly positioning itself as an advocate of the people most affected by the crisis and calling for mobilisations. On 31 January 2011, they disseminated an editorial entitled *¿Qué hace falta para que nos encendamos?* (*What does it take to get us fired up?*) and on 11 May they interviewed the authors of the book *¡Reacciona! (React!)* to address the 15 May's demonstrations.

Diagonal was a newspaper created in Madrid that began to take shape in 2003 in the context of the alter-globalization movement and the demonstrations against the Iraq war (López & Roig, 2004). It was a reference for the social movements of the time and its forms of organization based on self-management and horizontality served as a model for some of the independent media that would emerge years later. *Diagonal* wove a dense network of relationships with activism and played a key role in journalists' training as Patricia Simón and Tomás Muñoz explained in the interviews. Many of these journalists later contributed to the emergence and growth of the 15M (Mª Ángeles Fernández); in a way, *Diagonal* became 'the media of the movement, especially during the first weeks' (Tomás Muñoz).

Carne Cruda is a radio show that was born in 2009 with a clear activism orientation. Its creator and director, journalist Javier Gallego, points out that it is a show inspired by the spirit of activist and counter-cultural media. He refers to media as *Diagonal* newspaper and community-based and pirate radio stations (Javier Gallego). It was broadcasted on mainstream radio stations until 2014, when it began to be aired on the Internet funded through the contributions of its subscribers in collaboration with *elDiario.es*, one of the most important independent media to emerge from the outbreak of the 15M.

These two examples show that a connection between independent-activist media and the seeds of the 15M was already strong from the beginning. Likewise, the creative power that emanated from the 15M influenced the creation and characteristics of the independent media that emerged from then. From the point of view of Javier Gallego and Tomás Muñoz, the 15M permeated everything, including old and new media. Similarly, Clara Jiménez and Pablo Hernández point out the powerful influence that the 15M had on the creation of *Maldita.es*. Magda Bandera nuances this influence, remarking that activist and independent media already existed before the 15M and refers to the significance of community-based radio stations and newspapers such as the aforementioned *Diagonal* (2005), but also others as *L'Avanç* (1999) and *La Directa* (2006).

Indeed, activist and independent media already existed before the 15M. In addition, as Tomás Muñoz remarks, the groups who organised the protests that would trigger the outbreak of the movement already had a long experience in activist communication due to their involvement in some flagship media projects of Spanish activism – *Nodo50*, *Sindominio* and *Diagonal*, among others – which usually organized workshops and training on media activism and counter-information (Tomás Muñoz). As studies of social movement learning have shown, activists often create and engage in learning environments (Welton, 1993). Thus, there were many people interested in deploying the possibilities of communication, including the creation of their own media as pedagogical tools (Mª Ángeles Fernández). This shows that the educommunicative dimension was already part of the activist media strategies prior to the 15M, even though such media practices had not been examined through educommunication so far.

It is important to consider this aspect in the context of the economic crisis to understand that the increase in activism and the creation of new independent media are two derivations of the same phenomenon, that is: the 15M as 'a transversal social movement' (Javier Gallego) that strengthened the pre-existing educommunicative dimension of media activism and influenced the creation of an independent media ecosystem – as we will see in the next section. In this sense, the 15M opened windows of opportunity for media innovation: 'the 15M promoted changes, it created vias, generated possibilities' (Javier Bauluz).

A new media ecosystem

The 15M emerged in the context of the 2008 global economic crisis, that hit the journalism sector hard. The drop in sales of the print newspapers and the decrease in advertising revenues damaged newsrooms. A significant number of journalists were forced to work under precarious conditions, or had to leave the field of journalism and look for jobs in other sectors. As Vanesa Jiménez clarifies, this also had an effect on the lack of freedom of journalists and on the loss of influence and credibility of the mainstream media. In this context, digital media such as *FronteraD* (2009), *Periodismo Humano* (2010), *Pikara* (2010) and *Cuarto Poder* (2010) emerged, attracting a significant number of readers due to their open content and coverage of topics that were not usually addressed by mainstream media (human rights, feminism, social movements, etc.).

As Javier Bauluz and Patricia Simón point out, 'there was a need for people to read and listen to journalism that was different from traditional journalism, with a different approach' (Javier Bauluz). In addition, this approach was linked to an ethical commitment that implied 'putting information at the service of the social interest' (Patricia Simón). This phenomenon has been analyzed in several studies (Peña-Ascacíbar & Álvarez-Peralta, 2021; Rubio, 2014; Tuñez et al., 2010) and defined as the crisis and regeneration of journalism (Rius Baró, 2018).

As the following excerpts from our interviews illustrate, most of our informants agree in pointing out a change in the media paradigm engendered by the economic, social and political crisis and a loss of legitimacy of the mainstream media: 'People were not being listened to, society had many things to say that were not being transmitted in the media' (Clara Jiménez); 'during that period the number of people who demanded another way of doing journalism increased' (Magda Bandera); 'many people stopped consuming the information produced by the mainstream media' (Tomás Muñoz).

Another important event is represented by the wave of redundancies carried out during 2012 by some of the most important media in Spain, which despite leaving several hundred journalists unemployed, also represented an opportunity for innovation and collective creation. As Pablo Elorduy and Mª Ángeles Fernández point out, this was a key aspect for the formation of a new independent media. More specifically, it allowed many journalists to get in touch with people with whom they did not usually share spaces for political participation, generating a creative force that was reflected in multiple initiatives including new media.

Between 2012 and 2018, media such as *elDiario.es, La Marea, Ctxt, Alternativas Económicas, El Salto* or *InfoLibre* emerged. Some of them in the context of the wave of the 15M protest in Spain and others not directly connected to the protests but influenced by them. Even if these media have particular origins and specific traits, they are all the result of the same economic, political and social earthquake that was channelled and expressed by the 15M. To a large extent, these media adopted some of the demands of the 15M. They knew how to interpret the claims of a significant part of citizens regarding the role of media within society. These media are committed to independence and to the empowerment of journalists, as well as the flourishing of their community of readers and subscribers. Through their critical approach, they have reclaimed the dignity of a journalism that is centred on public service. These media have created different business models, each with their own internal policies and funding strategies. Yet, as we will see below, we can identify some common traits among them, which leads us to consider them as a new media ecosystem with an educommunicative orientation that is rooted in the imaginary and practices of the 15M for radical democracy. Our research complements other studies that have already theorized about media ecologies and the *Indignados* (Feenstra & Casero-Ripollés, 2012; Flesher Fominaya & Gillan, 2017; Treré, 2018). More specifically, it further ground Flesher Fominaya and Gillan's (2017, p. 391) reflections on the ways the movement not only appropriated a multifaceted ecosystem of technologies,

> [...] but provided a support base and impetus for the development of various critical media initiatives that attempted to put into practice alternative media business models [... .]. While some such initiatives existed prior to 15-M [...], the supply of and demand for independent critical media increased in a virtuous circle, with mobilization enabling the emergence of independent critical 'mass' media, thus altering the media ecology of political communication in Spain.

Next, we shed light on the common elements that define this media ecosystem, namely: the existence of synergies and mutual support; the fundamental role of the community of subscribers and users; an educational agency with a public service orientation.

Synergies and mutual support

Many of the independent media that have emerged in recent years have been creating synergies and collaborations among themselves. This collaboration became more solid on 2 April 2020, when seventeen media joined together to call on the government to protect plurality and quality of information.[6] A few months later, on 8 September, sixteen of these media created the *Plataforma de Medios Independientes (Independent media platform)*.[7] It was created to advocate the interests and sustainability of independent media and as a tool for collaboration and mutual support. So far, the platform has not had a structured organisation with tasks and specific functions. However, in November 2021 they started to carry out new actions including joint manifestos, creation of common content and alliances to shape their own media agenda. While these newer actions fall outside the scope of this article, they represent key developments that will need to receive academic attention in the future. Vanesa Jiménez establishes a similarity between the imaginary of the 15M and the imaginary of this platform. The aim of this platform is to serve as a tool for mutual support, as a means of making collective demands and develop concrete projects: 'although we are very different, we have many things in common and we need each other' (Magda Bandera).

All of them share the need to practice a journalism at the service of society and not at the service of economic or partisan interests. Despite the difficulties derived from being small media and the self-imposed restrictions of their funding policies – which guarantee their autonomy and credibility–, many of these media are supported by an important community of subscribers and users whose role has been key to create and consolidate a media ecosystem in itself.

The community of subscribers and users

Independent media are largely financed by fees paid by their subscribers. This has a fundamental importance not only for the economic sustainability of the projects, but also for the added value that they bring. The process of crisis, citizens' reactions and innovations, which we file under the umbrella of the '15M Movement', fostered the generation of a specific kind of critical user with a clear civic engagement who contributes by paying subscription fees and/or acting as a node of information transmission, and who Javier Gallego defines as 'an activist of the independent media'.

In this sense, Pablo Elorduy, Vanesa Jiménez and Mª Ángeles Fernández consider that the 15M created a mass of critical and committed people, who currently maintain their commitment through the support they give to independent media. In a way, we could say that, just as in the era of mainstream media hegemony readers established an emotional and ideological link with traditional newspapers, critical users have also established an emotional and ideological link with the independent media. Also, it is important to underline that independent media share subscribers and users, so that the media ecosystem that has been created is characterised by a contract of trust between media and users based on a compromise between a way of doing journalism and a way of constructing society: 'Our future lies in continuing to cultivate a relationship of trust and commitment with our readers, remaining faithful to our ethical principles and caring for information as a public service' (Magda Bandera).

Educational agency and public service orientation

Our informants agree that the kind of journalism they do, based on a public service orientation, was already there, before the 15M, because it constitutes the essence of journalism. In their opinion, the independent media are rescuing and dignifying a way of doing journalism based on civic engagement. Indeed, in our review of the editorial principles, we found clear references to this public service orientation and civic engagement (see, Table 3), an aspect that was corroborated in the interviews.

For Vanesa Jiménez, these media have recovered an old idea of journalism: 'it is a journalism of analysis and context; a journalism that has a critical component, that permanently questions and seeks answers'. According to the deputy director of *Ctxt*, 'it is also a journalism that is very respectful of the readers, because it assumes that they are intelligent, educated, with a critical thought'. It is a journalism 'committed to the people, to the citizens' right to freedom of information and expression'. For this journalist, all this is – plain and simple – 'doing journalism', without tags.

Javier Bauluz, Magda Bandera and Patricia Simón also expressed similar arguments. The winner of the Pulitzer Prize stresses the value of public service journalism, since information should be at the service of citizens and not at the service of economic or partisan groups. This remark is part of a climate of opinion that has spread among Spaniards since the 2008 crisis, especially in the wake of the protests of the Indignados. According to such view, mainstream media work at the service of economic and partisan interests and not at the service of citizens' needs. This was another trigger for the emergence of new journalistic projects in the context of the media paradigm change that we mention above. For the director of *La Marea*, 'all media should be public service media. Working from the idea of public service journalism simply means being journalists, doing journalism with honesty and rigour'. This is an idea with which the co-founder of *Periodismo Humano* and reporter for *La Marea* also agrees, when she underlines the value of journalism 'as a pillar of public ethics'. This way of understanding journalism is in line with the demands of the 15M in relation to the importance of the media in protecting and strengthening democratic values.

This public service orientation, revitalised by the key role played by the community of users, has a pedagogical intentionality insofar as independent media journalists aim not only to produce rigorous information, but also to contribute cross-cutting issues with a treatment that goes beyond the immediate or the stereotyped and polarised representation of reality. Eventually, they contribute to develop critical thinking among citizens. Patricia Simón points out that this topic is often present in the debates that take place in the editorial staff of *La Marea*. As Pablo Elorduy underlines, independent media have a purpose of 'long-term pedagogy'; that is, it aims to contribute issues and approaches constructed as tools for the understanding of social complexity, planting seeds and fertilising the ground for major social transformations. Ultimately, independent media reclaim the essence of journalism in order to contribute to the improvement of our democratic system, and that is why they see themselves as pedagogical tools at the service of our society as a whole.

In short, the journalism of independent media is in alignment with the educommunicative approach that considers the media as educational agents and means and tools of learning, an approach that the 15M also deployed through its media production and its pedagogical sovereignty.

Furthermore, several media have enriched its educomunicative dimension by including training as part of their social action. It aims to provide knowledge on the topics we have already mentioned in Table 3 and to which we must add the activity developed by *Maldita.es* on media literacy to fight against fake news and disinformation. In this way, some independent media have turned into educational environments, putting into practice their pedagogical sovereignty with a high level of formality. Thus, they reinforce their civic engagement, weave alliances with civil society, and provide knowledge and tools that allow them to continue working for a fairer and more democratic society.

Concluding remarks

This article established a strong connection between the educommunicative dimension of the 15M and the new ecosystem of independent media. It demonstrated that the Spanish movement focused much of its activity on the creation of spaces for participation and the fostering of citizen awareness and engagement. As part of the same socio-political action strategy, several communication projects were created, and educational initiatives were launched. Therefore, based on the paradigm of educommunication, we show that the 15M had a clear educommunicative orientation.

Furthermore, we demonstrated the influence of the 15M on the strengthening of media activism and of the pre-existing educommunicative dimension, foregrounding the important role played by journalists and communication activists in the imaginary and actions undertaken by the movement. We observed that the creation of the independent media that emerged from 2012 onwards is one of the responses that both society in general and critical journalists in particular gave to the 2008 Spanish's economic, social and political crisis. We do not establish a cause-effect relationship between the 15M and the creation of independent media, but rather we highlight a strengthening of the educommunicative dimension of pre-existing media activism enhanced by a social phenomenon – the 15 M Movement – that opened windows of opportunity for media innovation; windows of opportunity from which the independent media emerged.

This article demonstrates that independent media have formed a new media ecosystem characterised by three key elements: (1) synergies and mutual support; (2) the fundamental role of the community of subscribers and users; and (3) an educational agency with a public service orientation. Regarding the first element, we highlight the creation of the *Plataforma de Medios Independientes* (*Independent media platform*) as a long-term strategy to carry out joint projects and collective campaigns, and to weave alliances with civil society. Regarding the second, we underline the existence of an important shared community of critical subscribers and users, whose role is key both for the economic sustainability of the media and for their capacity to impact on society. Independent media and their subscribers have established an agreement of trust based on the value of information committed to social justice and democracy. Finally, the educational agency of the independent media is underpinned by a pedagogical dimension insofar as they aim not only to inform, but also to educate and provide tools for understanding the world and for social transformation. This pedagogical dimension is embodied in the choice and news treatment of topics and, in some cases, also in training initiatives provided by the media themselves in coherence with their journalistic ethics and civic engagement. In this way, independent media put their public service orientation into practice.

For these reasons, we consider that this new media ecosystem has a clear educommunicative orientation rooted in the imaginary and practices of the 15M and based on a revitalised civic engagement with journalism and the value of information for democracy.

Even if communication and social movement studies have incorporated interdisciplinary contributions that include tools close to social pedagogy, educommunication has been so far partially ignored. Educommunication paradigm opens up avenues of research that will allow for a deeper understanding of the key role of social movements and independent media as educational agents. At the same time, its combination with a media ecology approach has allowed us to foreground the prominence of the educational dimension within a new ecosystem, an aspect that was previously understudied. This combination has also contributed to expand the horizons of media ecology research and social movement studies. Our findings demonstrate that social movements are linked to the generation of independent critical media ecosystems with an educommunicative orientation for radical democracy.

Notes

1. The first manifesto was published firstly in a Facebook group's page, but it may be read from here: https://bit.ly/3GJMadK
2. Such as the United States Agency for International Development (USAID), Food and Agriculture Organization of the United Nations (FAO) and the World Bank, among others.
3. The first manifesto from the tent-city of Puerta del Sol: https://bit.ly/3ma6tcF
4. Claimings of the platform *Democracia Real ¡Ya!*: https://bit.ly/31Vu7Tr
5. List of the most frequent proposals made by several 15M collectives: https://bit.ly/3yyo1nB
6. The seventeen media outlets came together following the news that the government was studying measures to support the media in the midst of the pandemic crisis. The independent media thus published a manifesto for fear of not being included in these government measures. See: Ctxt (02/04/2020): https://bit.ly/3m9PPKl

7. The *Independent media platform* includes the following media: La Marea, El Salto, Ctxt, Carne Cruda, Público, Alternativas Económicas, Pikara, Mongolia, Crític, Nueva Tribuna, Praza, Nortes, Cataluyna Plural, Cuarto Poder and Luzes.

Disclosure statement

No potential conflict of interest was reported by the author(s).

ORCID

Ángel Barbas http://orcid.org/0000-0001-7803-3265
Emiliano Treré http://orcid.org/0000-0002-2496-4571

References

Barbas, A. (2020). Educommunication for social change: Contributions to the construction of a theory of activist media practices. In H. C. Stephansen & E. Treré (Eds.), *Citizen media and practice: Currents, connections, challenges* (pp. 73–88). Routledge.

Barbas, A., & Postill, J. (2017). Communication activism as a school of politics: Lessons from Spain's Indignados movement. *Journal of Communication*, 6(5), 646–664. https://doi.org/10.1111/jcom.12321

Barranquero, A. (2014). Comunicación, cambio social y ONG en España. Pistas para profundizar en la cultura de la cooperación desde los nuevos movimientos comunicacionales. El caso del 15M. *COMMONS*, 3(1), 6–28. https://doi.org/10.25267/COMMONS.2014.v3.i1.01

Barranquero, A., & Meda, M. (2015). Los medios comunitarios y alternativos en el ciclo de protestas ciudadanas desde el 15M. *Athenea Digital*, 15(1), 139–170. https://doi.org/10.5565/rev/athenea.1385

Buckingham, D. (2013). *Media Education: Literacy, learning and contemporary culture*. Polity.

Buitrago, A., García, A., & Gutiérrez, A. (2017). Perspectiva histórica y claves actuales de la diversidad terminológica aplicada a la educación mediática. *EDMETIC*, 6(2), 81–104. https://doi.org/10.21071/edmetic.v6i2.7002

Candón, J. (2014). Comunicación, internet y democracia deliberativa en el 15M. In A. Calleja-López, A. Monterde, E. Serrano, & J. Toret, (Eds.), *15MP2P. Una mirada transdisciplinar del 15M* (pp. 107–119). http://dx.doi.org/10.7238/in3.2014.1

Candón-Mena, J., Montero-Sánchez, D., & Calle-Collado, A. (2018). Discourses and practices of radical democracy. The 15M movement as a space of mobilization. *Partecipazione e conflitto, 11*(2), 571–598. http://siba-ese.unisalento.it/index.php/paco/article/view/19557

Casas-Cortés, M. I., Osterweil, M., & Powell, D. E. (2008). Blurring Boundaries: Recognizing knowledge-practices in the study of social movements. *Anthropological Quarterly, 81*(1), 17–58. https://doi.org/10.1353/anq.2008.0006

Castells, M. (2012). *Redes de indignación y esperanza*. Alianza.

Chesters, G. (2012). Social movements and the ethics of knowledge production. *Social Movement Studies, 11*(2), 145–160. https://doi.org/10.1080/14742837.2012.664894

Cohen-Montoya, A. (2021). *Educomunicación. 20 diálogos teórico-prácticos*. Neret.

Cox, L. (2014). Movements making knowledge: A new wave of inspiration for sociology? *Sociology, 48*(5), 954–971. https://doi.org/10.1177/0038038514539063

Cox, L., & Flesher Fominaya, C. (2009). Movement knowledge: What do we know, how do we create knowledge and what do we do with it? *Interface, 1*(1), 1–20. http://mural.maynoothuniversity.ie/1534/

Della Porta, D., & Diani, M. (2020). *Social movements: An introduction*. John Wiley & Sons.

Della Porta, D., & Pavan, E. (2017). Repertoires of knowledge practices: Social movements in times of crisis. *Qualitative Research in Organizations and Management, 12*(4), 297–314. https://doi.org/10.1108/QROM-01-2017-1483

Díaz Bordenave, J. (1976). La comunicación social como instrumento de desarrollo de comunidades rurales y urbanas. *Chasqui: Revista Latinoamericana de Comunicación, 15*, 9–35. https://dialnet.unirioja.es/servlet/articulo?codigo=5792005

Eyerman, R., & Jamison, A. (1991). *Social movements: A cognitive approach*. Pennsylvania State University Press.

Feenstra, R., & Casero-Ripollés, A. (2012). Nuevas formas de producción de noticias en el entorno digital y cambios en el periodismo: El caso del 15-M. *Revista Comunicación y Hombre, 8*, 129–140. https://bit.ly/3jnyWcb

Feenstra, R. A., Tormey, S., Casero-Ripollés, A., & Keane, J. (2017). *Refiguring democracy: The Spanish political laboratory*. Routledge.

Finger, M. (1989). New social movements and their implications for adult education. *Adult Education Quarterly, 40*(1), 15–22. https://doi.org/10.1177/074171368904000102

Flesher Fominaya, C. (2020). *Democracy reloaded: Inside Spain's political laboratory from 15-M to podemos*. Oxford University Press.

Flesher Fominaya, C., & Gillan, K. (2017). Navigating the technology-media-movements complex. *Social Movement Studies, 16*(4), 383–402. https://doi.org/10.1080/14742837.2017.1338943

Flick, U. (2018). *An introduction to qualitative research*. Sage.

Foust, C. R., & Hoyt, K. D. (2018). Social movement 2.0: Integrating and assessing scholarship on social media and movement. *Review of Communication, 18*(1), 37–55. https://doi.org/10.1080/15358593.2017.1411970

Freire, P. (1965). *La educación como práctica de la libertad*. Tierra Nueva.

Freire, P. (1970). *Pedagogía del oprimido*. Tierra Nueva.

Gentles, S. J., Charles, C., Ploeg, J., & McKibbon, K. A. (2015). Sampling in qualitative research: Insights from an overview of the methods literature. *The Qualitative Report, 20*(11), 1772–1789. https://nsuworks.nova.edu/tqr/vol20/iss11/5

Gil-Jaurena, I., Goig-Martínez, R. M., & Barbas-Coslado, A. (2021). *Animación e intervención sociocultural. Intervención educativa en contextos sociales*. UNED.

Gozálvez-Pérez, V., & Contreras-Pulido, P. (2014). Empowering media citizenship through educommunication. *Comunicar, 42*(42), 129–136. https://doi.org/10.3916/C42-2014-12

Gusfield, J. (1994). La reflexividad de los movimientos sociales: Una revisión de las teorías sobre la sociedad de masas y el comportamiento colectivo. In E. Laraña & J. Gusfield (Eds.), *Los nuevos movimientos sociales. De la ideología a la identidad* (pp. 93–117). CIS.

Hall, B. L., Clover, D. E., Crowther, J., & Scandrett, E. (2012). *Learning and education for a better world: The role of social movements Leiden.* Sense Publishers.

Hernández, E., Robles, M. C., & Martínez, J. B. (2013). Jóvenes interactivos y culturas cívicas: Sentido educativo, mediático y político del 15M. *Comunicar, XX*(40), 59–67. https://doi.org/10.3916/C40-2013-02-06

Holford, J. (1995). Why social movements matter Adult education theory, cognitive praxis, and the creation of knowledge. *Adult Education Quarterly, 45*(2), 95–111. https://doi.org/10.1177/0741713695045002003

Huergo, J. A. (2000). Comunicación/educación: Itinerarios transversales. In C. E. Valderrama (Ed.), *Comunicación-Educación. Coordenadas, abordajes y travesías* (pp. 3–25). Siglo del Hombre Editores.

Kaplún, M. (1985). *El comunicador popular.* CIESPAL/CESAP.

Kuk, H., & Tarlau, R. (2020). The confluence of popular education and social movement studies into social movement learning: A systematic literature review. *International Journal of Lifelong Education, 39*(5–6), 591–604. https://doi.org/10.1080/02601370.2020.1845833

Laraña, E. (1996). La actualidad de los clásicos y las teorías del comportamiento colectivo. *Reis: Revista española de investigaciones sociológicas, 74*(74), 15–44. https://doi.org/10.2307/40183884

Laraña, E., & Díez, R. (2012). Las raíces del Movimiento 15-M. Orden social e indignación moral. *Revista Española del Tercer Sector, 20,* 105–144. https://bit.ly/38j7Otx

López, S., & Roig, G. (7 May 2004). *Del tam-tam al doble click. Una historia conceptual de la contrainformación.* Nodo50. https://info.nodo50.org/IMG/pdf/historia_contrainformacion.pdf

Micó, J., & Casero-Ripollés, A. (2014). Political activism online: Organization and media relations in the case of 15M in Spain. *Information, Communication & Society, 17*(7), 858–871. https://doi.org/10.1080/1369118X.2013.830634

Niesz, T., Korora, A. M., Walkuski, C. B., & Foot, R. E. (2018). Social movements and educational research: Toward a united field of scholarship. *Teachers College Record, 120*(3), 1–41. https://doi.org/10.1177/016146811812000305

Peña-Ascacíbar, G., & Álvarez-Peralta, M. (2021). Emergencia, innovación y consolidación de nuevos modelos para el periodismo digital: Estudio de los casos de El Confidencial, elDiario.es e infoLibre. *Estudios sobre el Mensaje Periodístico, 27*(2), 593–606. https://doi.org/10.5209/esmp.71245

Perugorría, I., & Tejerina, B. (2013). Politics of the encounter: Cognition, emotions, and networks in the Spanish 15M. *Current Sociology, 61*(4), 424–442. https://doi.org/10.1177/0011392113479743

Postill, J. (2014). Democracy in the age of viral reality: A media epidemiography of Spain's indignados movement. *Ethnography, 15*(1), 51–69. https://doi.org/10.1177/1466138113502513

Prieto Castillo, D. (1979). *Discurso autoritario y comunicación alternativa.* Edicol.

Prieto Castillo, D. (1998). Comunicación educativa en el contexto latinoamericano. *Psychosocial Intervention, 7*(3), 329–345. https://bit.ly/3uv4Wm1

Razquin, A. (2017). *Didáctica ciudadana: La vida política en las plazas, etnografía del movimiento 15M.* Universidad de Granada.

Rius Baró, J. C. (2018). *La regeneración del periodismo: El modelo de eldiario. es (2012-2017).* Universitat Autònoma de Barcelona.

Romanos, E. (2013). Collective learning processes within social movements. Some insights into the Spanish 15-M/Indignados movement. In C. Flesher Fominaya & L. Cox (Eds.), *Understanding European movements: New social movements, global justice struggles, anti-austerity protest* (pp. 203–219). Routledge.

Rubio, A. V. (2014). La aparición de InfoLibre y eldiario. es para la defensa de un periodismo más democrático y participativo. *Historia y comunicación social, 19,* 491–500. http://dx.doi.org/10.5209/rev_HICS.2014.v19.44979

Treré, E. (2018). The sublime of digital activism: Hybrid media ecologies and the new grammar of protest. *Journalism and Communication Monographs, 20*(2), 137–148. https://doi.org/10.1177/1522637918770435

Treré, E. (2019). *Hybrid media activism: Ecologies, imaginaries, algorithms.* Routledge.

Tuñez, M., Martínez, Y., & Abejón, P. (2010). Nuevos entornos, nuevas demandas, nuevos periodistas. *Estudios sobre el mensaje periodístico, 16,* 79–94. https://bit.ly/3E3aQ11

Tyner, K. (ed.). (2010). *Media literacy. New agendas in communication.* Routledge.

Welton, M. (1993). Social revolutionary learning: The new social movements as learning sites. *Adult Education Quarterly, 43*(3), 152–164. https://doi.org/10.1177/0741713693043003002

The mobilising memory of the 15-M movement: recollections and sediments in Spanish protest culture

Manuel Jiménez-Sánchez ⓘ and Patricia García-Espín ⓘ

ABSTRACT
The 15-M movement, which emerged in 2011 amidst the Great Recession in Spain, has achieved the status of transformative protest event. Social movement research using this concept has mostly focused on meso-level legacies: event memories shape later organisational dynamics within social movements and among activists. Collective memories can, however, transcend the activists' milieu, acting as a sediment in the political culture of broader social sectors. Along this line of inquiry, this article examines the memory of the 15-M movement among ordinary demonstrators in two recent mobilisations (International Women's Day and the pensioners' protests). Based on forty-four in-depth interviews, we show not only a widespread recollection of 15-M eight years later, but also that memories include mobilising components, influencing the perceptions of protest as an efficacious political tool, or extending protest repertoires that are now considered familiar and legitimate. Recollections of 15-M are also associated with changes in the critical understanding of the political system and the advancement of a new political subject, which envisages an active role in politics for ordinary citizens. Significantly, these mobilising memories are discernible even among those who did not participate at the time, showing that cultural legacies may have transcended the first-instance protagonists. In short, protest action, subjects, critical mentalities and repertoires gained an enduring legitimacy, which is consistent with the extension of alternative horizontal logics of politics and more active understandings of citizenship.

Introduction

McAdam and Sewell coined the concept of transformative events to define 'concentrated moments of political and cultural creativity when the logic of historical development is reconfigured by human action but by no means abolished' (McAdam & Sewell, 2001, p. 102). This concept can be traced back to Sewell's conception of events as drivers of historical change (Sewell, 1996b, p. 262). In contrast to ordinary situations, he describes transformative events as 'a ramified sequence of occurrences that is recognized as notable by contemporaries, and that result in a durable transformation of structures' (Sewell, 1996a, p. 844).

Following this approach, the literature on the cultural outcomes of movements has increasingly explored connections between significant past protest events and subsequent dynamics of popular contestation (Amenta & Polletta, 2019; Daphi & Zamponi, 2019). Some researchers have converged with studies of collective memory focused on how shared ideas about the past provide a framework for interpreting and acting in the present (Schudson, 1997). The way in which protest events are remembered provides an avenue for investigating their cultural legacies (Kubal & Becerra, 2014).

Most of these studies have dealt with 'memories in movements' (Daphi & Zamponi, 2019; Doerr, 2014), examining the legacies of past protests in movements' organisational trends and collective identities. Global Justice campaigns at the turn of the 21st century, for example, have been regarded as a milestone in the evolution of activism in various countries (Daphi, 2017; Della Porta, 2018; Vicari, 2015; Wood et al., 2017). For instance, focusing on Italian activists' memories of the 2001 anti-G8 summit in Genoa, Daphi (2017) traced subsequent processes of collective identification in that social movement sector.

Other studies have focused on the memory of those events as an object of appropriation and construction by activists themselves (as agents of memory). Vicari (2015) explored the interpretative processes of the police's violent crush of the anti-G8 summit in Genoa, showing how, through the framing of activists, the event became iconic, favouring subsequent dynamic of coordination between groups. More recently, other works have analysed the strategic revision of memories about transitions to democracy during anti-austerity mobilisations in Southern Europe (Baumgarten, 2017; Della Porta et al., 2018; Kornetis, 2019).

Less attention has been paid, however, to protests as transformative events for larger sectors of the public beyond the narrow milieu of activists. Within the limited corpus, Griffin and Bollen studied recollections of the Civil Rights Movement among the US public revealing connections to sensitivity to racial inequalities, and to the perception that they can be ameliorated through action (Griffin & Bollen, 2009, p. 601). Their study signals the relevance of focusing on ordinary people as 'memory-users' and the attitudinal implications of their remembrances of significant past protests.

Tracing cultural legacies beyond movements' core milieus is especially appropriate in the current context, where protests can attain high levels of visibility and public resonance (Jiménez-Sánchez, et al. 2022). Conceivably, from the outset, memories of protests are not just bound to movement activists, but also concern those who experienced events as attentive publics.

This perspective is particularly appropriate for studying the cultural legacies of the anti-austerity mobilisations triggered by the Great Recession.[1] Those protests clearly surpassed the relatively small circle of activists and turned out to be 'spectacular events' (Berezin, 2017), experienced by large audiences. This was particularly true for the Spanish 15-M movement (dubbed simply '15-M'). 15-M brought great numbers of people out onto the streets and gained extraordinary visibility. In 2011, nearly every citizen (90%) had heard about it, and more than one third strongly supported the protests.[2] Interestingly, by the end of the decade, still a large majority (78%) remembered the movement (Jiménez-Sánchez et al., 20192019 May, 14). Therefore, it seems particularly worth inquiring into the content of these recollections to explore the movement's cultural legacies.

15-M was successful in pushing its critique of the Spanish political system and its democratic flaws. Its narrative, emphasising the political component of the economic crisis, became particularly salient in public discourse (Zamponi & Bosi, 2016), and resonated strongly with Spaniards (Muro & Vidal, 2017) and political elites (Coller et al., 2020). The demand for 'real democracy' at the heart of the mobilisations meant not only fixing elements that were not working (corruption, responsiveness, and accountability), but also sought to deepen or reload democracy (Flesher Fominaya, 2017, 2020). One central discourse challenged the 'myth of the consensual Transition' (Della Porta et al., 2018; Kornetis, 2019), which offered a restricted electoral view of popular participation, proposing alternative, citizen-based, and anti-oligarchic democratic practices (Gerbaudo, 2017). Functioning as pre-figurative politics, the movement put into effect deliberative democratic procedures through protest campouts in public squares and hundreds of citizens' assemblies (Flesher Fominaya, 2015). Similarly, the framing of public mobilisation as a legitimate tool to gain a stronger voice called into question previous notions of protests as useless, inappropriate, or linked to partisan instrumentalisation (Fishman, 2019). Overall, through these practices and contentious repertoires, the 15-M movement expanded a horizontal logic of political action, alternative to the dominant vertical conception of politics (Feenstra, 2015).

This paper asks to what extent, once that moment of visibility and salience is over, those political visions and contentious practices advanced by 15-M have left a mark on protest culture in Spain. Has 15-M become a transformative event, which is not only widely remembered, but whose collective memory reflects a vision of the political system and protesting that serves as a guide in subsequent popular contestation? The research strategy applied analyses the collective memory of 15-M among a group of current ordinary protesters, focusing on the extent to which that memory gives meaning to their contentious activity in the present.

When the tide recedes: 15-M legacies in protest culture

To leave a sediment (and be transformative) beyond activists, events must involve wide-scale disruption. They must be unexpected and able to capture the attention of broad sectors of the public (McAdam & Sewell, 2001; Sewell, 1996b). Disruptive events experienced by a small group of people can have transformative effects, but their scope will be limited (to activist circles). A highly visible event which attracts massive attention without that disruptive element can reinforce previous cultural patterns, hardly changing them.

Anti-austerity protests, particularly in Spain, fulfil both criteria – disruption and visibility – to become transformative events (Della Porta, 2018, p. 4). Certainly, they were concentrated moments of political and cultural creativity (McAdam and Sewell, 2001), in which 'politics burst its bounds to invade all of life' (Zolberg, 1972, p. 183) and were recognised as notable by contemporaries. The extent to which they have given rise to durable transformations is, however, a research question that is emerging now, as time goes by.

Della Porta (2018) proposed analysing these anti-austerity protests as a sequence of three phases: cracking, vibration, and sedimentation. The cracking refers to the initial triggering event that brings about the sudden disturbance of normality, paving the way to question dominant understandings and practices. In our case, it was initiated by the demonstrations on 15 May 2011, which occurred across many Spanish cities and, more decisively, in the subsequent *Acampadas* (campouts) organised in public squares, lasting several weeks (Feenstra, 2015; Flesher Fominaya, 2020). Like many current processes of mass protestation, the 15-M movement operated as a hybrid media event (Vaccari et al., 2015), whereby interaction between traditional and social media enlarged its audience and strengthened its capacity to generate active publics, broadening its scope and disruptive potential.

The vibration process refers to the spread of protests when those disruptive elements replicate. In the 15-M movement, this occurred in the numerous citizens' assemblies held in neighbourhoods and towns after the *Acampadas*, as well as in the subsequent anti-austerity mobilisations ranging from the *Yayoflautas*[3] to the *Mareas*, and the *Stop-Desahucios* movement. This is how 15-M transcended that initial date, evolving as a polyphonic process of popular contestation, extending its spatial and temporal impact. The vibration phase was the broadest protest experience since the political Transition (Portos, 2021). It hugely increased citizens' opportunities to be exposed, either as participants or as curious bystanders, to the movement's alternative political visions and contentious performances that, under normal circumstances, are limited to activists' milieus (Flesher Fominaya, 2015).

The event was a huge political laboratory of democratic practices (Feenstra et al., 2017). Assemblies held in public spaces open to everyone, for instance, became widespread (and highly visible), acting as pre-figurative politics and reinforcing the citizen-based image of the movement. Similarly, confrontational protest repertoires performed by ordinary citizens (such as symbolic occupations of bank branches, for example, *escraches*, or resistance to evictions) also gained extraordinary visibility, expanding the protest repertoire familiar to the public. Hence, the movement could have entailed a political learning experience (and attitudinal change) for a wide range of citizens, even for those not directly involved in the mobilisations. Likewise, media exposure to these mobilisations could also have a demonstrative effect, favouring vicarious learning.

Subsequently, when the tide of mobilisation recedes, transformative effects are consolidated in a sedimentation phase. Della Porta (2018) proposes two sites of sedimentation deposits: institutional legacies (affecting the properties of the political system) and movement memories (which affect organisational practices, strategies, and identities within social movements). Our research is set within this sedimentation phase but focuses on a different site: memories of the broader, more heterogeneous, social sector of ordinary (non-activist) protesters at present, to explore 15-M legacies.

As mentioned, the movement implied a highly visible critique of prevailing democratic practices (Fishman, 2019). At the same time, it promoted (and put in motion) alternative political understandings. Likewise, these alternative understandings implied a more prominent role for citizens (not limited to voting) together with a re-legitimation of protest as a genuine tool to communicate demands, and a useful instrument to make one's voice heard. Our research asks what, if anything, has remained of these visions and practices in the protest culture of current ordinary demonstrators. The research strategy applied analyses their 15-M collective memory and, particularly, those recollections we describe as 'mobilising memories', exploring the extent to which they use that memory as a guide that gives meaning to their present contentious action.

Mobilising memories as a heuristic to explore protest legacies

Collective memories are shared ideas about the past, providing an attitudinal framework for interpreting the present and guiding behaviour (Kubal & Becerra, 2014). Memories are the product of previous experiences. In this paper, they are understood as a (intended or unintended) cultural outcome of protest events. These memories can operate as socialisation mechanisms, affecting people who did not experience the event directly, preventing forgetfulness and prolonging its transformative capacity.

The analysis of event memories provides an empirical path to examine the cultural legacies of past protests. Extant empirical research shows that the way actors remember contentious events shapes their contemporary attitudes and behaviours (Andrews et al., 2016; Armstrong & Crage, 2006; Daher, 2013; Griffin & Bollen, 2009; Lee, 2012). In our case, we begin with the idea that 15-M recollection can be connected to changes in protest understandings and behaviours (protest culture). We build our empirical analysis around the concept of mobilising memories, understood as a set of representations and discourses about a past protest event containing perceptions about the role of citizens and their possibilities for participation. The concept mobilising memories stresses the motivational and guidance for action function of memories. Mobilising memories may provide attitudinal stimulus, motivation, or justification for one's own political action (or inaction) in the present, grasping what is appropriate or inappropriate for oneself or with respect to others. We understand mobilising memories as vehicles of meaning that motivate and justify protest action, offering a path to explore the connection of past events with current protest behaviour and views.

Following this reasoning, we posit that transformative events may engender mobilising memories among broader publics, beyond core activists. We explore 15-M mobilising memories among current (2018–2019) ordinary protestors, a research strategy described below.

Methods, data, and analysis

Survey data suggest that, almost a decade later, 15-M is still widely remembered among Spaniards, notably among the ideological left (Jiménez-Sánchez et al., 2019). However, these data say little about the nature of these memories and their mobilising effects. To search for such 15-M sediments, we deployed a qualitative strategy based on focused interviews (Merton, 1987) with ordinary demonstrators in two major mobilisations in 2018: the International Women's Day protest and the pensioners' mobilisations.

The Women's Day marches have recently become massive events: in 2018, around 21% of the adult population claimed to have participated in diverse actions (Campillo, 2019). The pensioners' movement also became widely known in 2018, when thousands marched to demand decent public pensions (Jiménez-Sánchez et al., 2021). Both protests represent a new mobilisation peak several years after 15-M, and share an impressive mobilisation capacity, bringing to the streets broad social sectors including new and occasional participants. Both can be rooted in the same (progressive) contentious tradition as 15-M, providing a favourable context to analyse the presence of 15-M mobilising memories beyond circles of activists: if no traces of such memories are found among this sector of current ordinary demonstrators, they would hardly be present elsewhere.

We conducted forty-four interviews in November 2018-January 2019. Twenty interviewees were recruited among demonstrators in the Women's Day marches (hereafter WM), and twenty-four were demonstrators in the Pensioners' mobilisations (PM). Purposeful sampling ensured a diversity of profiles (Patton, 1990).[4] For some interviewees (9), the 2018 demonstrations were the first they ever attended. The majority (26) had occasionally attended past demonstrations such as labour strikes, anti-war protests in 2003, marches against terrorism, or, more recently, anti-austerity calls. Another group of interviewees (9) engaged more frequently in protest activities; they can be considered regular protestors, but they were not social movement activists immersed in the organisation of protest activities. The final sample included 23 women and 21 men. Women made up the majority of WM interviewees (16 vs. 4 men) while men were the majority among pensioners (17 vs. 7 women). The latter were aged between 60–88 years old, while the WM participants were aged 18–55. To ensure contextual diversity, interviews were conducted in Seville, Madrid, and Bilbao.

To build a rigorous sample of ordinary protestors, we followed a two-step selection strategy. First, a series of messages were disseminated through social media inviting participants in either of the two mobilisations to collaborate in the investigation. Those interested were required to complete a short online form with basic demographic and socio-political information. In a short period of time, a dataset including more than 1,000 candidates was available. In a second step, potential interviewees were selected from that pool and contacted by phone to confirm adequacy and availability to set up an interview.[5]

During the selection process, interviewees were informed that the purpose was to chat about their experiences in the WM or pensioners' protests.[6] The interview script also addressed their previous history of protest participation, and questions regarding the 15-M movement were carefully introduced in the last part of the interviews. First, their memories of 15-M were addressed and, later, the personal or contextual effects of these were explored. This strategy was useful to capture the interaction between past and present (McLeod & Thomson, 2009), and particularly to explore how their 15-M memories were associated with current protest perceptions.

We carefully tried to avoid response induction or social desirability through interview dynamics. Interviews followed a non-directive approach, combining unstructured and semi-structured questions. Therefore, to introduce the topic, interviewers proposed a memory exercise to reflect on the initial years of the economic crisis (2011). Six interviewees mentioned 15-M spontaneously. The rest were asked about their recollection of the protests during those years, and eight mentioned 15-M in this way. If still not mentioned, they were directly asked ('and do you remember 15-M?'). In nine cases, despite not appearing spontaneously, interviewees showed an intense recollection of the movement. Similarly, interviewers' guidance was kept to a minimum when addressing the consequences of 15-M. If it did not emerge naturally, the issue was introduced through an unstructured vague question (e.g.: 'As time passes, do you think those mobilisations had any effect?').

Interviews lasted an average of ninety minutes and were transcribed. For their analysis, we followed an inductive strategy based on a coding process using ATLAS. ti 9 software. Firstly, excerpts containing any of the three issues of interest were identified: personal exposure to the movement, 15-M recollections, and perception of the movement's effects. The first types of quotations were analysed as attributes of the interviewees (personal experience, exposure to 15-M, and intensity of recall). The third code was used to identify categories of mobilising memories. We combined two coding phases (Blair, 2015): an initial process of open coding (Strauss & Corbin, 1990) which was applied to a subset of 20 interviews, enabling us to build a manageable set of categories, and a second phase in which all interviews were coded, fragmented, and classified.

Table 1 shows the classification of interviewees according to how they experienced the 15-M movement, and the intensity of their recollection. Twelve had direct experience, meaning they attended demonstrations, assemblies, etc. In twenty cases, 15-M was experienced in a mediated way through mass media (this can also refer to an asynchronous experience, for example, when they were too young but were exposed to it several years later). The remaining twelve interviewees did not experience the movement: they either had not heard about it (four cases) or did not pay much attention to the event and were not exposed to it later.

Intensity of recollections refers to the degree of detail expressed in their 15-M memories: eleven interviewees reflected very weak or non-existent recollections (four out of these ten were not able to recognise the movement), ten interviewees had rather disperse recollections, while the remaining twenty-three displayed intense and detailed recall. The latter group includes those who gave a detailed account, regardless of whether they mentioned 15-M spontaneously or not.

As shown in Table 1, the intensity of 15-M recollection is clearly associated with how the event was experienced.[7] Those who participated directly show intense recollection, but, also, a majority of onlookers and even one interviewee who experienced the movement years later reflect a similarly intense recall. This opens the door to expect mobilising memories among interviewees who did not engage directly, as we discuss in the following section.

Table 1. Classification of interviewees according to 15-M experience and intensity of recollection (1).

			Intensity of recollection			
			Weak (nonexistent)	Disperse	Intense	Total
15-M Experience	Weak	No exposure	4			4
		Weak exposure	5	3		8
	Mediated	Years later	2	3	1	6
		Attentive onlooker		4	10	14
	Direct	Less intense			4	4
		More intense			8	8
	Total		11	10	23	44

(1) Number of interviewees
A detailed list of interviewees is provided in Table A1 in the Appendix.
Source: Authors' own

Findings: mobilising memories as a legacy of the 15-M movement

We understand mobilising memories (hereafter MM) as a set of representations and discourses about a protest event containing perceptions of the role of citizens and their participation possibilities, which operate as attitudinal and behavioural guides in the present. In this paper, we are interested in MM affecting citizens' ideas and practices of protest. We analyse how interviewees connect their recollection of 15-M with changes in their understandings of protest. From the analysis of interviews, four categories of MM emerged. Two reflected (new) understandings about protest and the other two reflected changes in the perception of the political system and the role of citizens as participants (protestors).

A common discourse (coded in 31 out of 44 interviews) links the 15-M movement with a new understanding of protest as an effective political instrument (*protest efficacy*). Less frequently, we identified memories that connect 15-M with learning of organisational and protest repertoires (23 interviewees), attributed to the interviewee or a social group. Furthermore, quite generalised (coded in 31 interviews), there are narratives that evidence a revived political consciousness regarding the shortfalls of the socio-political system and the need for reform (*new consciousness*). This implies a transformation that the interviewee claims to have experienced personally or which is attributed to society as a whole (e.g.: 'people opened their eyes'). A final MM (coded in 22 interviews) connects 15-M with recognition of an active political subject characterised by public commitment (*discovery of a new active political subject*).

Figure 1 shows the distribution of these four MM among the interviewees, according to the intensity of their recollection. The more intense the recollections, the more abundant the number of MM. We hardly find any traces of them among interviewees

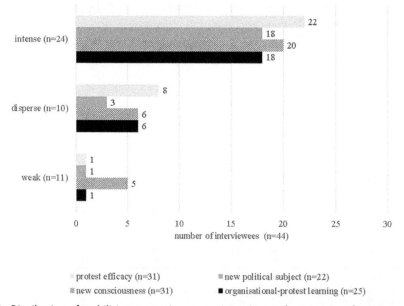

Figure 1. :Distribution of mobilising memories among interviewees by intensity of 15-M recollection. Source: authors' own

with a weak recollection of 15-M. These interviewees tend to view any protest as futile, and, only when asked directly, some pointed to an increase in people's political consciousness after 15-M (coded in 5 out of 11 interviews). In the group with intense recollections, discourses associating 15-M with changes in their political understanding emerged naturally and were more frequent and varied. Overall, MM about the emergence of a new political subject and a new consciousness (expressed as a personal effect) distinguish the narratives of this group. In the following sections, we describe the four mobilising memories.

Protest becomes efficacious

Most interviewees' recollections suggest that the 15-M mobilisations persuaded them that demonstrating is efficacious. The worthiness of popular protest is connected here to changes in the party system and the renewal of political elites. There are also references to policy change, but less frequent or less developed (e.g., laws on mortgages, bank regulations). For example, Samuel, an undergrad student, connects his (intense) 15-M recollection to the creation of new parties, '*Podemos* emerged from it. The mobilisations are at its origins. Other parties also grew out of that'. Similarly, other interviewees refer to that renewal of the political elite. According to Alejandro, a pensioner who went to one demonstration in 2011 to 'have a look around', retaining an intense recollection, the main consequence of 15-M was that *Podemos* emerged and traditional leaders were challenged. In his words, 'their beret began to tremble' [*les tembló la boina*]. For him, protests triggered evident changes in the representative regime, highlighting the incorporation of new visions and agents not present before.

Similar discourses are also frequent among interviewees with a disperse recollection of the movement. For example, Itziar, a pensioner with no previous protest experience, who saw the 15-M protests on TV, said that the mobilisations were crucial so that 'new leaders won votes. [. . .]. Also, there were changes in the ideas put forward by the *Partido Popular*, weren't there? With all these mobilisations, and with new parties winning votes, some things changed'. Similarly, Mateo, a university-educated man in his eighties, did not pay much attention to the movement but still points out its efficaciousness: 'It seems that *Podemos* originated there, though it took some years'. Mateo is one of the few cases (3) of interviewees who were ideologically more conservative and unfavourable to *Podemos*, but still, he reflected on the efficaciousness of the protest to provoke changes in the political system.

The recognition of these outcomes led many interviewees to view street protests as a crucial tool for citizens to be heard by, otherwise unresponsive, elites. More importantly, this sense of usefulness (or external political efficacy) is, in most cases, regarded as a stimulus or justification for their subsequent engagement in protests. As Guillermo, a participant in the PM, argues, 'Thanks to 15-M, pensioners also took to the streets. It became clear that, unless you mobilise, nobody hears you'.

This mobilising memory is also discernible among young interviewees who did not experience 15-M directly. Samuel, mentioned above, who was only fourteen in 2011, considered that the movement, which he experienced as an attentive onlooker (watching TV and participating in conversations with his parents and teachers), awakened his political engagement. Other young interviewees with disperse recollections include the perception of protest efficacy in their motives for later political activation. Abigail, a WM participant in her thirties, said that the main legacy was a change in the perception of protests, which encouraged later movements.

> 'I think the fact that you can demonstrate in the streets, and it's not seen as bad behaviour anymore. You have nothing to lose if you've already lost everything... We have learnt that if you demonstrate, you'll get something at least'

In short, 15-M is often associated with a memory of protest efficacy. This improved reputation of protest as a political tool has operated later as a motivational mechanism for some interviewees when deciding to engage in protests in 2018. This mobilising memory is not only present among those who have an intense remembrance; it is in fact quite generalised among protesters with a disperse recollection of 15-M, such as Abigail or Itziar. And, as we can gather from Abigail's quote above, along with effectiveness, the collective memory of 15-M also concerns the way of thinking about the legitimacy of protest.

Organisational and protest learning

Together with a revised understanding of the efficacy of protest, discourses about 15-M suggest that it provided a learning experience concerning protest forms and their legitimacy. In half of the interviews (23), memories of 15-M are associated with encountering certain contentious practices, while reflecting on their appropriateness.

Many of our interviewees became familiar with the protest repertoire popularised by 15-M. For example, when seeing, often for the first time, citizen's assemblies in public spaces (as during the *Acampadas* or pacific sit-ins in public squares), they reflected about assembly-based forms of organisation; they came to discuss new forms of protest such as *escraches* (protests staged against politicians in public places or at their homes), pacific resistance to evictions, or campouts in public squares. These recollections, in turn, become a resource for interviewees' decisions to take part, or for their assessment of subsequent protest events

For those with a vivid recollection of 15-M, these mobilising memories are acute. New tools acquired are transferred to present movements, as these two pensioners, regular protestors who also attended some 15-M events, explain:

> Olivia: They met in the squares, in the streets; we [the pensioners' movement] still do that. We go there, set up a sign, and anyone who wants to, can come.

***

> Jacobo: I think that these [forms of protest] were valid back then and are now. [In the PM], we are thinking about changing strategy and have been discussing perhaps occupying some public offices.

There are also traces of this learning among attentive onlookers with intense recollections. Carlota, a pensioner who did not participate in 15-M but claims to have become more active afterwards, explains that she became familiar with assembly-based techniques during that period, 'They [15-M protesters] promoted a habit, a way of doing things'. Now she is participating in the local assemblies of a pensioners' group. Similarly,

Rosa, a participant in the WM in her thirties, argues that 'Assemblies ... they are still around. They were understood as useful in that moment, and they are useful right now to mobilise for other reasons'. Rosa supports the idea that there were organisational and protest formulas (assembly-based models, non-partisan organisation, and rallies in public squares), popularised by 15-M, which have endured as legitimate forms of participation.

The narratives of those with a more disperse recollection also reflect this type of protest learning. For example, six interviewees recalled repertoires of action that, for them, were newer and more controversial such as squatting, campouts, and *escraches*. Confrontational actions, because they were discussed so extensively by mass media, gained enormous visibility, and entered these observers' everyday discussions, so they are remembered with a certain degree of detail. Sara (WM), who was seventeen in 2011, now argues,

> They were critiqued because 'Ooph, you're taking over the square, the streets are not yours, you're annoying me'. But a demonstration needs to be visible, it must be noticed. So, I think that they [15-M protesters] found the formula' [...]. Since then, it's like there is a procedure to change things.

Benjamín, a pensioner who seems to have reflected about the 15-M protests during his experience in the PM, also says that the 'Pensioners copied those actions to start their mobilisation'.

In short, attending 15-M protests or, more often, watching other citizens protesting might have convinced some interviewees that new contentious forms of participation could be legitimate. This learning was connected to their current vision of protest action, and seems to be especially powerful among those with intense recollections, but is similarly discernible among interviewees with a more disperse memory. Hence, the transference of practices usually observed in activists' milieus has also occurred within this broader sector of occasional demonstrators.

Breaking the wall: a new political consciousness

Another set of memories about the 15-M movement suggests that it inspired a new consciousness about the social order and the political system. As discussed above, 15-M protesters framed existing problems such as political corruption or social injustices as connected to flaws in the democratic system. Interviewees describe this new awareness similarly to the way Berezin (2017) depicts spectacular events: as the denaturalisation of dominant political views, a 'breaking down of the wall', showing realities that were previously veiled or considered immutable. Particularly, 31 interviewees refer to this process both as an increased personal or collective awareness.

Discourses in the first person (15-M associated with new personal awareness) are more frequent among those with intense recollections: for many of them, the protests confirmed their existing but somehow dormant awareness of political and social injustices. Mariana is a retired nurse who experienced the movement as an attentive onlooker:

> It was a terrible period. The mortgages, there were many people who couldn't afford their home; all those pensioners who lost their retirement savings, massive corruption [...] And they, 15-M protesters, opened your eyes and said to you, 'We can fight this'.

She had always been sensitive to these issues, but the mobilisations stirred a sense of urgency she had not felt before 15-M, which led her afterwards to adopt an active position 'to fight'. Similarly, Sebastián, a retired schoolteacher, says that the movement 'Woke me up. "This is so good," I thought. It was like May 1968 in France. I felt a great sense of expectation'. He started to believe that change was possible. Joseph was 15 years old when the 15-M movement emerged, and he could not attend any protests, neither did his relatives. His (intense) recollection was formed by watching TV images and through the casual conversations of his parents. For him, the 15-M movement was a kind of revelation of the 'true' reality:

> It made the situation visible. I was a kid, but I remember that image, I remember people helping other families who had been strangers before that. The police or the firemen refusing to evict people. You became conscious when you saw it.

Those events triggered a powerful sensation, an increased awareness that transformed his teenage passivity into political curiosity and attention. He connects this critical consciousness with subsequent participation in protests. Similarly, Amelia, a young woman who had only heard about the 15-M movement, also thinks that 'People in their twenties became conscious of their situation in those days and they have continued to mobilise [referring to the WM]'.

A similar pattern of awareness-raising is seen among interviewees with disperse or even weak recollections. Manuel, practically a novice protester in the pensioners' movement, said that he did not pay much attention to 15-M because he had two jobs and 'was not in that mood', but he now thinks that he and many fellow pensioners underwent a process of awareness-raising: 'Many people became conscious of what was happening [...]They led us to recover that determination, they reawakened that spirit, to do what we are doing now [current PM protests]'. Sara, a young participant in the WM also thinks that 'They made you open your eyes', and Elvira (WM), who was 11 in 2011 and shows limited exposure and a weak 15-M recollection, suggests 'That was when people became aware of this crazy way of living".

The memory of 15-M as awakening citizens' critical consciousness is identified with interviewees who experienced it in more direct ways and have an intense memory, but is also discernible among those who experienced the protests in more mediated ways and who display weaker memories. For some of them, 15-M reaffirmed their awareness of the country's political and economic flaws, raising their levels of concern, and increasing their motivation and sense of urgency. For others, it was enlightening, contributing to their readiness to mobilise years later.

The discovery of an active political subject

Close to the idea of a new political consciousness, we have identified a set of discourses that connect remembrances of the 15-M movement with the discovery of an active political subject, constituted by civically engaged and contentious citizens. Such a popular subject enacts (makes reality) an energetic citizenship, capable of acting collectively to ensure its rights. The recognition of this subject contributes to the view that, likewise, one can alter the state of affairs.

Half the interviewees (22) pointed to this discovery, though it was proportionally more frequent among people with an intense memory. They describe this discovery as a relief or a kind of reconciliation with (some of) their fellow citizens, as long as these people stood in contrast to the dominant representation of Spaniards as nonchalant or resigned. Their mobilisations proved that wide-ranging sectors of citizens were acting collectively for change. For pensioners like Olivia, this (new) dynamic (and empowered) political subject was mainly represented by youth, 'I saw that people, especially young people, were changing, were starting to become active. I got goose bumps when I saw that'. For others, the 2011 mobilisations revealed a patchwork of critical publics fighting against political and economic injustices, stressing different profiles (pro-democratic, deprived, young, or old people) as the main strands of this energetic body. The testimony of Eulogio, a committed PM participant, illustrates how this new understanding of an active political subject is delimited, 'It was the union of all generations. [...]. Old people, younger ones, middle-aged, those on social benefits, people who didn't need them. [...]. A bit of everything'.

Admiration for the 15-M protesters motivated them in their later shift towards protestation, as role models. This is clear in the interviews of pensioners who recognise that the previous wave of protests preceded their own mobilisation, tracing a sense of common history, a connection with that earlier political subject, sharing a similar fight for justice. As Carlota describes,

> It [the 15-M movement] left a sediment. I can't say how many people [...]. But there was a sediment. Now, many people are quick [to mobilise] [...]. If you look at the Women's Marches, for example, they don't happen by chance. They come from previous movements [...] Until that moment [2011] you were only expected to vote [...]the 15-M movement proposed something different: 'Politics should be an everyday occurrence out in the streets involving everyone'.

Like other interviewees, she connects an identification with 15-M protesters with a change in her attitude towards protests, providing a source of personal motivation for further engagement: 'It changed me. Before 2008, I had not even thought that someone like me could engage actively in politics as I do now'. Nowadays, she attends both the WM and the PM. Similarly, Camelia, an attentive onlooker, who was only seventeen in 2011, unreservedly states that:

> The fact that you see so many people who are active or people who share your own ideas, and they take on an active role ... well, you see yourself [doing the same]. [...]. It encourages or drives you to take a step forward.

Interviewees with a disperse 15-M recollection also point to the discovery of an engaged subject, previously hidden for them, though this effect had a more moderate impact on them than it did on interviewees with stronger recollections. Isabel, a pensioner who caught a little of the TV coverage, reports that she was happy to see people were finally mobilising, 'It was wonderful, it was necessary to protest, I always say that it's young people who must lead, they have the impetus'. Gracia, a WM participant, also states that 'When you see people mobilising, you feel encouraged to do the same'.

Overall, current ordinary demonstrators retain a positive, even idealised, image of 15-M protesters. Furthermore, their narratives suggest that the discovery of an active political subject still inspires recognition. This memory is associated with two relevant mobilising conditions. Firstly, it counter-balanced the previous dominant perception of citizens' passivity, exemplifying that citizen-led contestation was possible. Secondly, this had a demonstrative effect, stimulating their later engagement. Camelia, for example, who did not participate in any 15-M event but retained an intense recollection, illustrates the prolonged mobilising consequences of such memories.

Conclusion

The 15-M movement could certainly fall within the category of transformative protest events. It was highly disruptive and visible, winning widespread public support (Jiménez-Sánchez et al.). 15-M was very successful in pushing its critique of the Spanish political system, proposing alternative anti-oligarchic (citizen-based) practices. It mobilised huge numbers of citizens and popularised contentious practices beyond the milieu of the social movement. In this work, we have investigated what, if anything, of those visions and practices remains years after. To trace those legacies (or transformative outcomes) in protest culture, we analysed the presence of 'mobilising memories' (memories of past protests that guide contentious activity in the present) among a group of current ordinary protestors. Some attended 15-M demonstrations, while a majority watched them on TV or heard about these events (later) through the conversations of family or acquaintances.

Findings indicate that 15-M recollections are associated with emerging feelings of protest efficacy, breaking away from previous widespread discourses of protest as spurious and useless. This collective memory also reflects the extension of extra-institutional participatory practices that are generally recognised as valid and valuable. Interviewees also suggest an attitudinal sediment in their attitudes comprising a denaturalisation of the functioning of the socio-political system. Finally, memories of the event portray ordinary citizens as politically capable of (and responsible for) bringing about changes (active political subject). Overall, through these mobilising memories, 15-M is connected to a more critical, empowered, and contentious citizenship, and these findings are congruent with other studies that associate anti-austerity protests with the extension of contentious repertoires to the general public (Flesher Fominaya, 2020), with greater acceptance (Cristancho et al., 2019), and with the growth of critical citizenship (Valentim, 2021).

Consequently, it can be argued that 15-M contributed to the establishment of a more contentious, critical, and active conception of democratic citizenship, despite the negative framing of protest that institutions and the main party agents had deployed for years, after the transition to Democracy in the 1970s (Fishman, 2019). As this study confirms, protest action and the deliberative activity associated with it have gained an extraordinary legitimacy as tools of political participation (Feenstra et al., 2017). This can be also interpreted as a new 'democratic sensibility' (Tormey, 2015) in which the direct participation of ordinary people is given a more central position.

Findings also indicate that these mobilising memories are not similarly present among all interviewees. They are more noticeable and wide-ranging among those with intense recollections of 15-M. Importantly, among this group, we find those who experienced the 15-M protests as attentive onlookers and even some who were too young or were not biographically available to experience them at that time. This shows that the political culture legacies of the event may have transcended its first-instance protagonists (interviewees who attended demonstrations). The identification of mobilising memories among those who learnt about the 15-M movement later (those who were not present or were not attentive onlookers during the events themselves), suggests the role of memories as prolonged socialising mechanisms.

Mobilising memoires are less discernible among those with disperse recollections. Furthermore, in spite of the precautions taken, in some cases, the dynamic of the conversation during the interview might have induced certain responses. However, similarities between their discourses and those generated more spontaneously, for example, about protest efficacy, suggest an analogous collective memory, albeit with less intense mobilising consequences. We consider these empirical findings to be a valuable contribution to existing research about the effects of protest events on political culture beyond the core activists. Overall, this research endorses the broad transformative capacity of spectacular protest events such as 15-M.

The research also shows the analytical strength of the proposed concept of mobilising memory, as a pathway to connect the remembrance of past events with their legacies in protest culture. Mobilising memories can act as vehicles of collective meanings that help to justify, motivate, and shape contentious activities in the present. In this sense, our findings are in line with previous research showing that the way actors remember contentious events shapes their contemporary attitudes and behaviour.

However, our work is not without limitations, and the interpretation of the results must consider at least three precautions. Firstly, memories of the past are constructed from the present (they do not reflect the events and their effects exactly as they happened). However, mobilising memories can be understood as features of the current protest culture rooted in the past, insofar as they guide and motivate action (or inaction) in the present. Although our findings are congruent with the hypothesis that 15-M impacted Spain's protest culture (becoming a transformative event beyond the core activists of social movements), in this paper, we cannot establish an unequivocal relationship between 15-M and such attitudinal changes. It could be that the current experience of mobilisation (the present) influences both attitudes towards protest and a review of their 15-M remembrances. This is especially conceivable in our sample of demonstrators (in women's and pensioners' mobilisations) which can be placed in the same contentious tradition. This seems to be at work, for instance, in some interviewees who ignored 15-M when it was happening, but value it now positively and even regret not having participated then.

This reminds us of the changing nature of collective memories and draws our attention to a second precaution: memories are fragile cultural products under permanent construction, continuously threatened by oblivion. Although our investigation is set almost a decade after the 15-M movement, future research will have to confirm the temporal endurance of its memory and mobilising consequences. Finally, it is important to be aware that collective memories are plural: their meanings and significance may differ between social groups. Our results draw on a progressive and politically active social sector, which are prone to sympathize with the 15-M movement. Although we might think that it delimits a very broad sector, it is hardly representative of all Spanish citizens. The few cases among our interviewees with less affinity towards 15-M suggest the need for future studies to examine recollections and mobilising (or demobilising) memories among conservative or apathetic sectors that do not hold such positive memories of the 15-M events.

Notes

1. The Great Recession was the acute economic crisis experienced worldwide starting in 2009, whose effects were felt for several years. In Spain, the economic crisis and the austerity measures adopted led to an unprecedented wave of protests between 2011 and 2013 and to a deep political crisis (see, Portos, 2021).
2. In 2011, the scope of the audience for the 15-M movement was much broader than that of the anti-globalisation mobilisations the previous decade, which barely exceeded 50% knowledge (CIS, study number 2574). In addition, among those who knew about the 15-M movement, three out of four sympathised with the protests (compared to scarcely 50% among those who had heard of the anti-globalisation movement in 2004).
3. *Yayoflautas* are groups of senior activists involved in 15-M and anti-austerity mobilisations. They are connected to the *Marea Pensionista* and the pensioners' mobilisations in 2018 (Jiménez-Sánchez et al., 2021).
4. Profiles of interviewees are detailed in the Table A1 in the Appendix.
5. The initial aim was to conduct a total of forty interviews. A theoretical sample was defined to ensure a similar number of interviews per event (WM and PM), the three territories selected, gender and education (with and without university degree). Suitable candidates were initially contacted on the bases of the date they filled out the online form, giving priority to candidates with low protest experience.
6. Interviews were conducted in accordance with an ethical protocol approved by the Ethical Research Committee of the Autonomous Government of Andalusia (code 1581-N-18). Prior to the interviews, participants were provided with an information sheet and signed a consent document.
7. No clear pattern emerges between recollection intensity and education: more detailed memories do not necessarily correspond to higher educational levels (whereas they are connected with exposure to 15-M). Nor are differences detected in relation to the event (WM or PM), gender, or age

Acknowledgments

We thanks to anonymous reviewers of Social Movement Studies for their valuable feedback on previous versions of this manuscript.

Disclosure statement

No potential conflict of interest was reported by the author(s).

Funding

This work was supported by the Ministerio de Ciencia, Innovaci?n y Universidades [CSO2017-84861-P].

ORCID

Manuel Jiménez-Sánchez http://orcid.org/0000-0001-5479-8511
Patricia García-Espín http://orcid.org/0000-0001-7984-5716

References

Amenta, E., & Polletta, F. (2019). The Cultural Impacts of Social Movements. *Annual Review of Sociology*, *45*(1), 279–299. https://doi.org/10.1146/annurev-soc-073018-022342

Andrews, K. T., Beyerlein, K., & Tucker Farnum, T. (2016). The Legitimacy of Protest: Explaining White Southerners' Attitudes Toward the Civil Rights Movement. *Social Forces*, *94*(3), 1021–1044. https://doi.org/10.1093/SF/SOV097

Armstrong, E. A., & Crage, S. M. (2006). Movements and memory: The making of the Stonewall myth. *American Sociological Review*, *71*(5), 724–751. https://doi.org/10.1177/000312240607100502

Baumgarten, B. (2017). The children of the Carnation Revolution? Connections between Portugal's anti-austerity movement and the revolutionary period 1974/1975. *Social Movement Studies*, *16*(1), 51–63. https://doi.org/10.1080/14742837.2016.1239195

Berezin, M. (2017). Events as templates of possibility: An analytic typology of political facts. In J. C. Alexander, R. N. Jacobs, & P. Smith (Eds.), *The Oxford Handbook of Cultural Sociology* (pp. 613–635). Oxford Handbook Online. https://doi.org/10.1093/oxfordhb/9780195377767.013.23

Blair, E. (2015). A reflexive exploration of two qualitative data coding techniques. *Journal of Methods and Measurement in the Social Sciences*, *6*(1), 14–29. https://doi.org/10.2458/v6i1.18772

Campillo, I. (2019). 'If we stop, the world stops': The 2018 feminist strike in Spain. *Social Movement Studies*, *18*(2), 252–258. https://doi.org/10.1080/14742837.2018.1556092

Coller, X., Jiménez-Sánchez, M., & Portillo-Pérez, M. (2020). It Is Not Just the Economy. How Spanish Established Political Elites Understand the (Political) Crisis and Its Effects. In A. Freire, M. Barragán, X. Coller, M. Lisi, & E. Tsatsanis (Eds.), *Political Representation in Southern Europe and Latin America* (pp. 85–101). Routledge. https://doi.org/10.4324/9780429400414-5

Cristancho, C., Uba, K., & Zamponi, L. (2019). Discarding protests? Relating crisis experience to approval of protests among activists and bystanders. *Acta Politica*, *54*(3), 430–457. https://doi.org/10.1057/s41269-017-0061-1

Daher, L. M. (2013). From memory to legacies. Cultural outcomes, successes, and failures of the feminist movement in Sicily. *International Review of Sociology*, *23*(2), 438–460. https://doi.org/10.1080/03906701.2013.804290

Daphi, P. (2017). "Imagine the streets": The spatial dimension of protests' transformative effects and its role in building movement identity. *Political Geography*, *56*, 34–43. https://doi.org/10.1016/j.polgeo.2016.10.003.

Daphi, P., & Zamponi, L. (2019). Exploring the movement-memory nexus: Insights and ways forward. *Mobilization*, *24*(4), 399–417. https://doi.org/10.17813/1086-671X-24-4-399

Della Porta, D. (2018). Protests as critical junctures: Some reflections towards a momentous approach to social movements. *Social Movement Studies*, *19*(5–6), 556–575. https://doi.org/10.1080/14742837.2018.1555458

Della Porta, D., Andretta, M., Fernandes, T., Romanos, E., & Vogiatzoglou, M. (2018). *Legacies and memories in movements: Justice and democracy in Southern Europe*. Oxford University Press. https://doi.org/10.1093/oso/9780190860936.001.0001

Doerr, N. (2014). Memory and Culture in Social Movements. In B. Baumgarten, P. Daphi, & P. Ullrich (Eds.), *Conceptualizing Culture in Social Movement Research* (pp. 206–226). Palgrave Macmillan. https://doi.org/10.1057/9781137385796_10

Feenstra, R. A. (2015). Activist and Citizen Political Repertoire in Spain: A Reflection Based on Civil Society Theory and Different Logics of Political Participation. *Journal of Civil Society, 11* (3), 242–258. https://doi.org/10.1080/17448689.2015.1060662

Feenstra, R. A., Tormey, S., Casero-Ripollés, A., & Keane, J. (2017). *Refiguring Democracy: The Spanish Political Laboratory*. Routledge. https://doi.org/10.4324/9781315160733

Fishman, R. M. (2019). *Democratic Practice*. Oxford University Press. https://doi.org/10.1093/oso/9780190912871.001.0001

Flesher Fominaya, C. (2015). Debunking Spontaneity: Spain's 15-M/Indignados as Autonomous Movement. *Social Movement Studies, 14*(2), 142–163 doi:https://doi.org/10.1080/14742837.2014.945075.

Flesher Fominaya, C. (2017). European anti-austerity and pro-democracy protests in the wake of the global financial crisis. *Social Movement Studies, 16*(1), 1–20. https://doi.org/10.1080/14742837.2016.1256193

Flesher Fominaya, C. (2020). *Democracy Reloaded*. Oxford University Press. https://doi.org/10.1093/oso/9780190099961.001.0001

Gerbaudo, P. (2017). The indignant citizen: Anti-austerity movements in Southern Europe and the anti-oligarchic reclaiming of citizenship. *Social Movement Studies, 16*(1), 36–50. https://doi.org/10.1080/14742837.2016.1194749

Griffin, L. J., & Bollen, K. A. (2009). What do these memories do? Civil rights remembrance and racial attitudes. *American Sociological Review, 74*(4), 594–614. https://doi.org/10.1177/000312240907400405

Jiménez-Sánchez, M., Fraile, M., & Lobera, J. (2019, May 14). El 15M sigue despertando simpatías, ocho años después. Piedras de Papel Blog. https://www.eldiario.es/piedrasdepapel/sigue-despertando-simpatias-anos-despues_132_1551646.html

Jiménez-Sánchez, M., Fraile, M., Lobera, J. 2022 Testing public reactions to mass protest hybrid media events: a rolling cross-sectional study of International Women's Day in Spain. *Public Opinion Quarterly*.

Jiménez-Sánchez, M., Pérez, R. Á., & Nuez, G. B. (2021). The mobilization of pensioners in Spain as a process of construction and learning of a new collective identity. *Empiria, 52*, 97–124. https://doi.org/10.5944/EMPIRIA.52.2021.31366

Kornetis, K. (2019). Projections onto the past: Memories of democratization in Spain, Greece, and Portugal during the great recession. *Mobilization, 24*(4), 511–524. https://doi.org/10.17813/1086-671X-24-4-512

Kubal, T., & Becerra, R. (2014). Social Movements and Collective Memory. *Sociology Compass, 8* (6), 865–875. https://doi.org/10.1111/soc4.12166

Lee, F. L. F. (2012). Generational Differences in the Impact of Historical Events: The Tiananmen Square Incident in Contemporary Hong Kong Public Opinion. *International Journal of Public Opinion Research, 24*(2), 141–162. https://doi.org/10.1093/ijpor/edr042

McAdam, D., & Sewell, W. H. J. (2001). It's about time: Temporality in the study of social movements and revolutions. In R. R. Aminzade, J. A. Goldstone, D. McAdam, E. J. Perry, W. H. Sewell Jr, S. Tarrow, & C. Tilley (Eds.), *Silence and Voice in the Study of Contentious Politics* (pp. 89–125). Cambridge University Press. https://doi.org/10.1017/CBO9780511815331.005

McLeod, J., & Thomson, R. (2009). *Researching Social Change: Qualitative approaches*. SAGE Publications Ltd.

Merton, R. K. (1987). The Focussed Interview and Focus Groups: Continuities and Discontinuities. *The Public Opinion Quarterly, 51* (4), 550–566. https://doi.org/10.1086/269057.

Muro, D., & Vidal, G. (2017). Political mistrust in Southern Europe since the Great Recession. *Mediterranean Politics, 22*(2), 197–217. https://doi.org/10.1080/13629395.2016.1168962

Patton, M. Q. (1990). *Qualitative evaluation and research methods* (2nd ed.). Sage.
Portos, M. (2021). *Grievances and Public Protests: Political Mobilisation in Spain in the Age of Austerity*. Palgrave Macmillan. https://doi.org/10.1007/978-3-030-53405-9
Schudson, M. (1997). Lives, laws, and language: Commemorative versus non-commemorative forms of effective public memory. *Communication Review*, 2(1), 3–17 doi:https://doi.org/10.1080/10714429709368547.
Sewell, W. H. J. (1996a). Historical events as transformations of structures: Inventing revolution at the Bastille. *Theory and Society*, 25(6), 841–881. https://doi.org/10.1007/BF00159818
Sewell, W. H. J. (1996b). Three Temporalities: Toward an Eventful Sociology. In M. J. McDonald (Ed.), *The Historic Turn in the Human Sciences* (pp. 81–123). University of Michigan Press.
Strauss, A. L., & Corbin, J. M. (1990). *Basics of qualitative research : Grounded theory procedures and techniques*. Sage Publications.
Tormey, S. (2015). Democracy will never be the same again: 21st Century Protest and the Transformation of Politics. *RECERCA. Revista de pensament i anàlisi*, (17), 107–128 doi: http://dx.doi.org/10.6035/Recerca.2015.17.6.
Vaccari, C., Chadwick, A., & O'Loughlin, B. (2015). Dual Screening the Political: Media Events, Social Media, and Citizen Engagement. *Journal of Communication*, 65(6), 1041–1061. https://doi.org/10.1111/jcom.12187
Valentim, V. (2021). Creating critical citizens? Anti-austerity protests and public opinion. *Electoral Studies*, 72 August , 102339. https://doi.org/10.1016/j.electstud.2021.102339
Vicari, S. (2015). The Interpretative Dimension of Transformative Events: Outrage Management and Collective Action Framing After the 2001 Anti-G8 Summit in Genoa. *Social Movement Studies*, 14(5), 596–614. https://doi.org/10.1080/14742837.2014.995076
Wood, L. J., Staggenborg, S., Stalker, G. J., & Kutz-Flamenbaum, R. (2017). Eventful events: Local outcomes of G20 summit protests in Pittsburgh and Toronto. *Social Movement Studies*, 16(5), 595–609. https://doi.org/10.1080/14742837.2017.1319266
Zamponi, L., & Bosi, L. (2016). Which Crisis? European Crisis and National Contexts in Public Discourse. *Politics & Policy*, 44(3), 400–426. https://doi.org/10.1111/polp.12156
Zolberg, A. R. (1972). Moments of Madness. *Politics & Society*, 2(2), 183–207. https://doi.org/10.1177/003232927200200203

15-M Mobilizations and the penalization of counter-hegemonic protest in contemporary Spain

Kerman Calvo ⓘ and Aitor Romeo Echeverría ⓘ

ABSTRACT
This article discusses 15-M and anti-austerity mobilizations in Spain from the perspective of repression and penalization. The literature has paid a great deal of attention to the consequences of this cycle of protest in relation to the quality of democratic participation and governance; it could be argued that the 15-M movement has raised the standards for key aspects of Spanish democracy. In articulating new counter-hegemonic claims, however, 15-M mobilizations have created an opportunity for new forms of repression. Drawing on criminology, socio-legal studies, and mobilization literature, we argue that this cycle of protest has been penalized. This involves a combination of technologies of repression that include invasive policing, securitization, and criminalization. Penalization needs to be seen as a dissent-suppressing mechanism, a negative response by political authorities and private actors that thrives when societies suffer from widespread anxieties about insecurity and crime.

Introduction

15-M and anti-austerity mobilizations are widely credited for providing a breakthrough in public conversations about democracy in Spain and beyond (Flesher Fominaya, 2020). However, much less attention has been paid to the more negative consequences of this cycle of protest. Except for a handful of insightful contributions that speak to legal and criminology audiences in Spain, the international literature on mobilization has largely skipped the discussion of the implications of repression in terms of the quality of democratic life in Spain (for partial exceptions, see, González Sánchez et al., 2019; Flesher Fominaya, 2017). This is surprising, considering the very strong opposition by conservative political parties, most of the traditional media and key state institutions such as the police or the judiciary (García-García & Calvo, 2019; Simsa, 2017; Flesher Fominaya, 2014; AI (Amnesty International), 2015, 2014). In the words of some key activists, 'there was an attempt to criminalize the movement and turn it into something despicable from day one' (Fernández-Savater and Flesher Fominaya, 2017). As early as on 27 May 2011, the (conservative) Catalonian regional administration deployed 450 policemen against 15-M occupiers of Catalonia Square, in Barcelona; 84 people were seriously injured. Repression escalated as the cycle of protest progressed. This includes police violence against demonstrators, massive fining against journalists and decent housing, public sector and environmental activists, or the decisions by several local councils to use public health regulations to close down autonomous community centers (Ávila Cantos et al., 2015; Rossini et al., 2018). Such was the opposition that some activist networks organized a new platform resonantly called 'we are not criminals' (*No Somos Delito*).

Our goals in this article are twofold. First, we provide a more nuanced reading of State-led violence against counter-hegemonic dissent in Spain. We argue that anti-austerity and pro-democracy mobilizations in Spain have been *penalized*. Penalization, a concept developed by criminologist David Garland (1990), accounts for the transformation in the symbolic definitions of punishment in neoliberal societies. Penalization, we claim, is based on the combination of hard and soft forms of repression to define a framework that not only seeks to curtail the organizational capacity of mobilizers, but also to shape societal attitudes in relation to the legitimacy of protest. As we show in this article, penalization operates a multi-level type of intervention that combines police practices, but also operates at the level of public perceptions and the law. Second, we provide an interpretation of this process. We suggest that penalization gives a strong impulse to de-democratization practices in the direction of consolidating formal and informal limitations to the expression of counter-hegemonic forms of dissent. Flesher Fominaya (2017, p. 14) defined counter hegemony as a rupture of the 'consensus around the neoliberal order underpinning state and representative democracy'. The combination of different technologies of repression causes processes of substitution by which activists shy away from questioned forms of mobilization to stick to claims, repertoires and modes of organization with an indisputable seal of correctness. Penalization creates further opportunities for State-led repression against other forms of mobilization. At the same time, penalization responds to pre-existing opportunities and limitations. We understand repression as an unintended consequence of mobilization, one, however, that is mediated by the domestic structure of political opportunities. The 15-M movement unintentionally widened the opportunities for strategies of repression that drew on inbuilt flaws of Spanish democracy in a context of rapidly spreading moral panics about insecurity, disorder, and crime.

After this introduction and a brief methodological note, in the third section we discuss the concept of penalization in the context of contemporary debates about repression. We then substantiate the claim that counter-hegemonic forms of dissent have been penalized in Spain, focusing on three elements: policing (section four), securitization, and penalization (both in section five). In the last section, we discuss the implications of penalization for a larger conversation about the role of contention in shaping the quality of democracy.

Methods

We draw on several sources. In the first place, we have reviewed the literature in Spanish on penal and police reform, criminalization, and criminal justice; this corpus of work provides insightful information, valuable background data and inspiration for our own thinking in relation to penalization. Secondly, we have reviewed an extensive list of NGOS and activists' documentation (mostly in Spanish but also publications in international blogs such as *Open Democracy* or *Freedom House*) in relation to the questions of (a) policing, (b) fines, and (c) criminalization. Some of these are quoted in the article. Particular attention has been paid to publications by activist networks with a legal advocacy orientation (such as *Comisión Legal Sol*). Activists' documents offer relevant data in relation to detentions, violent clashes with the police, and fines. In the third place, we have examined official Government data in relation to demonstrations and punishment (such as the Yearly Book of the Spanish Home Office). These are, however, data of limited quality. Official records, for instance, provide a simplistic description of the nature and size of protest in the country (Romanos & Sádaba, 2022). Also, little of these records ever acknowledge the violent nature of police interventions.

The last two sources are the media and oral testimonies. We have used (and enlarged) a novel database prepared by Juan García-García that collects press items published in four conservative newspapers in Spain (three printed and one digital) in the topics of crowd management, 15-M campaigns, anti-austerity mobilizations and criminalization of protest (see, García-García & Calvo, 2019 for further information about this data). The database covers the years 2011 to 2019 and currently consists of nearly 150 items, although with an uneven temporal distribution (around 75% of these items covered 2011 and 2012 only). Lastly, we have interviewed 10 activists from different locations in Spain, via Zoom and Skype (we include some background information about them in the Appendix). Our initial sample consisted of 30 activists with interesting similarities in terms of age (most of them were 20–29 years of age) and gender (they are all mostly male). All these activists had participated in several forms of anti-austerity mobilization, in issues relating to housing, educational reform and so on. They differed, however, in their disposition to cooperate with this project but more significantly in their ability to provide meaningful and usable accounts of their involvement with protest. After much consideration, we decided to focus on a smaller group of 11 interviewees that met a threefold criterion: (1) having been either fined or forcefully handled by the police, (2) possessing a consolidated trajectory as activists, (3) showing the capacity to elaborate a narrative about their experiences as activists.

Repression and the penalization of protest

The analysis of repression remains fraught with difficulties. As repression is so extraordinarily contingent on case specification, it remains very difficult to theorize about its consequences (Earl, 2011, p. 467). Jämte and Ellefsten's recent work (Jämte & Ellefsen, 2020) confirms the difficulties of building universal arguments in relation to the consequences of soft repression; while some activists succumb to fear and self-censorship, other activists react by radicalizing their approach to contentious mobilization. A similar need for stronger theorization affects the very question about the causes of repression. What are the goals that repression seeks to fulfill? Why do political authorities persist in repression? It is apparent from the specific works on the policing of protest that repression is a crowd management technique, employed the more mobilization adopts certain expressions, and the more law enforcement agencies are rooted in specific traditions and operate upon certain guidelines and organizational cultures (Nordas & Davenport, 2013). But repression, in as much as it touches on fundamental questions about democratic life, *must* be something else. As criminal justice systems expand their reach in most western countries (Bessant & Grasso, 2019), with specific provisions against protest becoming commonplace, a pressing need to engage with the discussion of the causes of repression becomes apparent.

We defend a critical vision of repression as a dissent suppressing mechanism in democracies. Repression affects the organizational and ideational capacities of mobilizers while also delivering powerful messages about the legitimacy of claimants and state responses (Chenoweth et al., 2017). Inspired by Davenport and Loyle's (2012) discussion of the 'puzzle of repressive persistence', we see repression as a strategy with lagged effects, one that aims at a structural redefinition of the shape and outcomes of dissent. Repression is not merely a natural response of States to inside challenges, guided by some forms of inertia whereby the status quo inevitably reacts against demands for substantive reform. Similarly, repression is not only a logical consequence of the very existence of regulations governing the use of public space. Socio-legal scholars attentive to the operations of the law often highlight the disconnection between substance and formality that is inscribed into contemporary legal systems: simply by existing, certain legal categories (such as order, public space, civic life) bring out consequences (repression, for instance) that do not necessarily reflect a concerted decision or program by law enforcers. In contrast, it can be argued that repression has become a fluid script by which elites in democratic systems expel radical actors from the space for democratic deliberation. Repression needs to be examined according to its capacity to curb resistances against long-term political and economic decisions, surely promoting definitions of individual and collective involvement that sets very tight limits on what citizens are supposed to do *as* citizens (Smithey & Kurtz, 2018). Starr et al.'s (2008) work on the consequences of surveillance on social justice organizations 'post-Seattle' provides illuminating insights for an analysis of repression from this perspective. By undermining solidarity, and the capacity of movement organizations to innovate and think creatively, repression intervenes in the intensity of political commitment as well as in the scope of future political work. As the grey areas of unclear behavior from the perspective of legal acceptability expand, activists increasingly retreat towards expressions of dissent with an indisputable seal of legality; this ultimately imposes limits on the issues, tactics and claims that can be brought forward in the political arena.

The complexities in contemporary modes of repression motivates a search for categories that acknowledge traditional technologies of control (policing, mostly), but which also pay close attention to the way legal interventions shape the structure of political opportunities. Public institutions of punishment, originally set up to fight crime, have been activated as a technique for the regulation of social protest. The communicative dimensions of punishment are constantly reinforced; repression is not only seen as an artifact transforming the short-term opportunities for protest; more importantly, it is a channel by which powerful messages are sent by authorities. For instance, authorities can be telling the public that 'order is still in force and that everyone can return to their affairs without worrying about what the protesters shouted' (González Sánchez, 2019). Garland's (1990) idea of '*penality*' draws on these understandings, to describe the complex ways in which policing and legal interventions intersect to alter the underlying definitions of social phenomena. Applied to the handling of mobilization, the idea of penalization allows for a richer understanding of state's responses to dissent, one that transcends simpler accounts of repression either as police brutality or criminalization.

A penalization process includes the policing of protest and demonstrations, but also the set of decisions at the legislative and symbolic levels that undermine the standing of specific constituencies as the bearers of legitimate challenges. Penalization, therefore, is an umbrella concept that can group together different mechanisms of repression that concatenate in complex ways; at a minimum this encompasses policing, securitization and criminalization. Interventions in the law, but also in police practices and the handling of existing administrative and criminal provisions go a long way in shaping collective perceptions about the threats against security associated with contentious action. Pamela Oliver (2008) applied these ideas to the analysis of the US case; this author enlarged the academic conversation about repression, removing the emphasis on the assessment of short-term police-protesters interaction, to pay close consideration to the meaning and long-term consequences of repression. For Oliver, mass incarceration in the United States, a very complex phenomenon that cross cuts pressing questions about race, law-making, class inequalities and social definitions of punishment, must be read as a repressive mechanism against black dissent that works as a pre-emptive technology. Mass imprisonment pre-empts future protest by severely aggrieved populations, also contaminating public perceptions about those groups and their afflictions.

Penalizing counter-hegemony in Spain: The policing of protest

Our interviewees openly defined the evolution post-2011 as one of rapidly intensifying repression: 'repression has become systemic; it is part of the system' (I2). Repression is perceived as a political strategy: 'repression is key to keep everything quiet, still (...) it really wants to prevent people from joining in the fight, to make an example by punishing activists; you know, it is as if they were saying... mind your decisions carefully, because the same can happen to you' (I1). In the case of the anti-austerity cycle in Spain, penalization has combined invasive policing with interventions at the level of public perceptions and the law. Policing is discussed in this section and securitization and criminalization in the next one.

Scholarly work on the cycle of protest anti-austerity in Spain has insisted on the generalized absence of violent forms of protest; this has led to some interpretations of police responses to protesters as similarly nonviolent (see, for instance, Portos, 2017). Violence, however, is strongly underrepresented in Spanish official records on demonstrations (see, Blay, 2013). For instance, according to official data (Ministerio del Interior, 2019), in 2019, only 102 out of 31,918 demonstrations were flagged as involving alterations of public order (traffic cuts in most cases). Contrary to that, activist networks, critical social scientists, human rights NGOs, trade unions and extreme-left political parties identify a punitive turn in the response to anti-austerity campaigners by Spanish authorities that includes violent forms of policing (Bondia García et al., 2015; Comisión Legal Sol, 2015; González Sánchez & Maroto Calatayud, 2018; Oliver & Urda, 2015). According to Comisión Legal Sol (2015, p. 122), there were at least 646 arrests related to protest performances between May 2011 and March 2015. This is widely held to be an underestimation.

Respondents perceive the policing of anti-austerity protests as violent, unpredictable, and overwhelming: 'I hate the feeling of powerlessness, standing before armed people. You know that bad things can happen of course, but you are really overwhelmed by the feeling that you can be fined simply because this guy wants to, particularly after the Gag Law' (I6). They often assess the role of the police as a tool, a political 'weapon': 'the police are an obstacle for political activism, look at what is going on with evictions, the police are really harassing those of us who want to stop them' (I9). Most conversations with activists arrive at several sensitive issues that cast a dark light over key expressions of policing. This includes the problem of defenselessness, both in the sites of violent encounters, but also in relation to the possibility of complaining in cases of alleged police brutality. The so-called 'Sherwood syndrome' is often mentioned. This stands for a police covert tactic by which protesters are provoked by inside agents so that support is raised for harder forms of policing (15MPedia, n.d.). Activists similarly discuss the problems of covert police action and infiltration (see, Rodríguez-Pina, 2012). As recently explained by Schlembach (2018), undercover policing is a recurrent feature of collective protest in Europe to the extent that such policing practices might have had the capacity to shape contentious activism. An activist with extensive experience in austerity and housing-related protest commented more generally on the problem of infiltration:

'Surveillance, monitoring, all bugs us ... people started not talking about stuff in the assemblies in case some people there were undercover police; but we knew that happened in the camp, we knew that a guy who slept over was a policeman because he had been a classmate of one of us; but you cannot really force him out, you cannot force an officer out, what can you do? Funny, whenever we were about to decide to do something, the police came up and asked for our IDs, etc.; it was impossible to trust anybody' (I3).

In what refers to the handling of crowds, policing in Spain strongly conforms with Gillham and Noakes's (2007) model of 'strategic incapacitation'. Three elements of this model need consideration. In the first place, such a model involves a sharpening in the technologies of control and regulation of crowds, combining a permissive orientation towards protest with a tough hand against 'unruly' protesters. In September 2012, a protest action was organized (*Rodea el Congreso*) to bring citizens' indignation to the steps of Parliament (PenP (Plataforma en Pie), 2012). 1,350 riot police were deployed arguably to protect the state from a 'disguised coup d'état'; 35 people were arrested, and 64 people were wounded (including 27 policemen; Fernández de Mosteyrín, 2012, pp. -1142–1144). In May 2013, a national feminist *escrache* was organized in front of the Popular Party's headquarters in several cities against the draft bill to reform abortion legislation. According to a participant, 20 police vans were deployed simply to guard the entrance of the party's headquarters in Madrid (Mato, 2015, p. 89). This was defined by the press as a 'sizeable deployment of police forces' (Enríquez-Nistal, 2013). Throughout 2014, activists clashed with the police in both large and peripheral cities in relation to city planning and local public infrastructures. Burgos (a medium-size city of some 200.000 habitants) was a case in point: residents in the underprivileged *Gamonal* district opposed plans to transform a boulevard for pedestrian use into a parking area. According to press reports, more than 50 people were arrested after several days of street-based violence (EFE, 2017; Europa Press, 2018). Also in 2014, 70 people were arrested in a violent outburst after the police forced the squatters out of the emblematic *Can Vies* social centre in Barcelona (El Periódico, 2014). Conflicts about decent housing have also resulted in violent forms of police intervention, both in sites where activists attempted to stop forced evictions, and when *escraches* were promoted. The activist group '*Red Malla*' talked about more than 70 cases of indictment of decent housing activists in 2018 (Red Malla, 2018).

A strengthening of police capabilities is also a central element in strategic incapacitation. The so-called *Brigada Móvil* of the regional Catalonian police (a specialized unit in charge of protest policing) increased its staff from 275 policemen in 2008 to 496 in 2013 (Camps & García, 2015, p. 56). Despite the impact of the financial crisis on the Spanish national accounts, the 2013 National Budget foresaw an astronomical 1780% increase in anti-riot equipment relative to 2012 (Martín García, 2014, p. 304; González, 2012). This was used not only to expand specialized anti-riot divisions but also to acquire more sophisticated equipment. Heavy spending on equipment increased up to 2015, with the allocation of more than 4 million euros to anti-riot gear. The Spanish national budget for 2021 includes an increase of 65% in police-related spending (Policía Nacional, 2020).

Surveillance is the last element. Surveillance and intimidation are intimately associated: the fear of being monitored discourages further participation. In the words of one of our interviewees:

> 'there are so many weird moments, for instance, when my friends have been fined for participating in demonstrations despite not having participated in that one; or when I was filling my application for my passport and the policeman said: "hey, you are the fellow from *Juventudes Comunistas*' (…) and I asked him how do you know that", because I had not really gone to many demonstrations nor I was a well-known activist, so how on earth did he know that, so obviously an alert must had popped up in his computer' (I2).

Activists talk about so-called 'activist blacklists', covert registries of information of campaigners allegedly used to harass key campaigners. Interviewees relate a wealth of situations in which covert police seem in possession of private information about the personal lives of activists. Although official authorities have often been reluctant to publicly recognize it, activists from the *Casablanca* and *Maravillas* collectives (and other initiatives in Madrid, such as *La Traba*, *La Morada* and *La Casika*), have suffered continuous harassment by local and regional authorities (La Vanguardia, 2012), and heavily monitored groups such as *Distrito14*, *Yesca* or *Bukaneros* are at the heart of controversies about their alleged role of instigators of violent protesting. The placing of CCTV cameras in Madrid illustrates the strong communicative effects of surveillance. In early 2012, representatives from the Ministry of Home Affairs justified surveillance on grounds of a 'likely' increase in disruptive activities and unruly behavior (Fernández, 2012). The municipal police displayed a total of 147 cameras between 2011 and 2014; they became 'an entire mesh of digitized control through which the panoptic gaze is imposed as an element of urban space, under the declared aim to produce safety spaces' (Ruiz Chasco, 2014, p. 302). These cameras, however, were mostly located in the *Lavapiés* district, a well-known breeding ground for popular mobilization in Madrid.

Spanish penal democracy: securitization and criminalization

Repression has also taken the form of interventions at the level of discourses and narratives (securitization) and the law (criminalization). How the police address protest, and more generally how repression is organized bears resemblance to the underpinning values that define the ways authorities see dissent: the more protesters are framed as members of irrational crowds, the higher the odds for responses based on suppression, stigmatization, and marginalization (Atak, 2017). Securitization, a well-known concept in the immigration, terrorism, and international relations literatures stands as a discursive mechanism by which powerful actors frame an issue as a threat (Dunn Cavelty & Jaeger, 2015; Ferree, 2004). In relation to the media, securitization develops in the form of a 'description bias' in the coverage of protest that promotes antagonistic media frames (Boykoff, 2006; Muncie, 2020). Existing research on media representations of 15-M protests reveals how conservative newspapers framed 15-M campaigners as rowdy, troublemakers, shabby, savage, and rabble-rousing people; descriptions linked protesters with animal and barbaric behavior (García-García & Calvo, 2019; Seijas, 2016). According to a conservative commentator, ' ... some crow-like species, a small group of carrion birds ... swarm freely around the Puerta del Sol'. Instances of noncompliance with law were highlighted, including the occupation of public spaces. In the words of another commentator, the *indignados* were 'gangs of slackers and freeloaders lying about on the floor, who yell and harass the city councilors of the PP'.

Seijas (2016) analysis of media representations of the campaign *Hay vidas en juego* by the *Plataforma de Afectados por las Hipotecas* identified a similar set of framing practices by conservative media outlets that led to a description of housing activists as abnormal and (very) dangerous. Public authorities have also engaged with discourse-based practices. For instance, after some 100 students occupied the *Lluis Vives* high school in Valencia in February 2012, the head of police operations in Valencia explained police violence in crude terms: the police ``responds when it is attacked' (Ferrandis, 2012). In relation to the '*Rodea el Congreso*' protest event, the head of security in Madrid argued that the protest looked like a coup d'état (Gracia, 2012). Public prosecutors have recently charged participants in this action with 7 years of imprisonment. As a matter of fact, public Prosecutors (*fiscales*) participated in the demonization of protesters by issuing petitions of pre-trial imprisonment for activists detained by police, by requesting permanent bans on future demonstrations, and more importantly by demanding extraordinarily harsh prison sentences (Camps & García, 2015, p. 62). The 'Alfon case' serves as a good example. Alfon, a 21-year-old man participant in the November 2012 general strike, was put under trial on charges of illegal possession of explosives (after being imprisoned with no trial for 56 days). Upon the request of the prosecution, Alfon was accused of terrorism, facing a jail sentence of 4 years in 2015 (Juanatey Ferreiro, 2012).

Securitization shapes the legitimacy attributed to claims and claimants; more significantly, it eases the way for the adoption of subsequent punitive action. Criminalization is the last element in the penalization of protest that we discuss in this article: it involves a politically inspired intervention in different fields of law with hopes of diminishing the likelihood of protest. Two such legal interventions are relevant here. In the first place, the reform of the criminal code in 2015 by the conservative government of the Popular Party; this introduced harsher sanctions for acts involving disobedience to police officers (González Sánchez & Maroto Calatayud, 2018). Similarly, the reform illegalized some of the most resonant tactics of the 15-M campaigners, such as the 'invasion' of bank branches; it also broadened the definition of terrorism, leading to indictments of artists and singers and to a heightened use of national security arguments to define the response to dissent. In the second place, new security legislation was passed. The government sponsored a new security Bill: namely, the *Ley Orgánica 4/2015, de 30 de marzo, de protección de la seguridad ciudadana* (often known as the 'Gag Law'). This Act imposes limitations in the dissemination of images of police officers and punishes activists who organize protest events in the proximity of core infrastructure. The 'Gag Law' also allows authorities to perform indiscriminate personal identity checks and impose discretionary penalties on some forms of political dissent, including the so-called *escraches*. According to Amnesty International and other human rights organizations, the 'gag law' poses a 'threat to human rights' (AI (Amnesty International), 2014). Our interviewees were also very critical of a piece of legislation that is presented as a legacy of a non-democratic past: 'the gag law stinks of *Franquismo*, you know, it allows control and punishment over people's attitudes; it's not only about controlling massive mobilization but about pursuing specific behaviors and intimidating people' (I1).

Criminalization can target individual expressions of dissent, such as those by artists, key activists, left-wing politicians, or trade unionists. Freemuse, an activist NGO, has observed a sharp increase in 'violations of freedom of artistic expression' in Spain since 2015: 'artists have become increasingly subject to various limitations on their expressions, especially through censorship, detention, and imprisonment' (Freemuse, n.d.). Expressions of contentious feminist activism, participation in digital discussions and lyrics have appeared as targets of this punitive turn. However, criminalization is also adopting a more mass approach, one that navigates through a widening system of administrative fining. The joint reforms of the criminal and security legislations have consolidated a legislative technique by which allegedly minor offenses have become the object of substantial fines. This has removed a great deal of sanctioning from judicial oversight, adding to the imaginary of vulnerability and arbitrariness that is often associated with governmental innovations in the management of societal dissent. The pivotal role of administrative fining in protest-government relations has led to definitions of contemporary repressive policies as 'red tape repression' or *bureau-repression*, (Oliver & Urda, 2015). Fines, which can also be imposed by means of hard readings of existing local civic provisions (Casino Rubio, 2012; Maroto Calatayud, 2013), have been criticized as very effective tools for containing protest. Fines hinder 'solidarity between those who have been fined and other citizens' (Martín García, 2014, p. 305).

Graph 1 reports official data on sanctions related to citizens' safety as imposed by the application of the two Security Acts. It shows a steep increase of sanctioning from 2015. A great deal of these fines are related to 'disrespecting the police'. For instance, from July 2015 to January 2016, the Police filed more than 6.200 penalties under these allegations (Sánchez, 2016). Fines between May 2011 and December 2012 reached a total value of more than 300,000 euros (Oliver & Urda, 2015, pp. 77–78). Official records do not break down data on fines according to type of sanction (the Gag Law also punishes other types of behavior, such as consuming drugs in public); still, between 2015 and 2020 the total number of fines amounted to 563 million. 'Citizen's security' sanctions represent roughly 19% of sanctions.

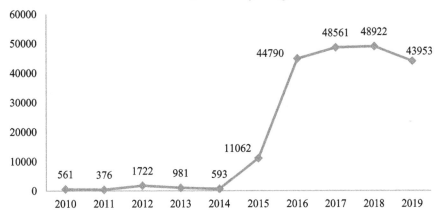

Graph 1 Sanctions, Security Legislation. 2010-2019. Source: *Anuario Estadístico, Ministerio del Interior*.

Discussion: De-democratization and the unintended consequences of protest

Despite the confirmation of the normality of protest in democracies, governments persist in their effort to monitor, channel, regulate and very often attack organized forms of dissent (Davenport & Loyle, 2012). This is particularly evident in the case of forms of protest that question the basic configuration of economic and political relations. Our interviewees criticized political authorities for being particularly hostile against 'anything that sounds radical, Marxist, anti-fascist and young'. Responding to questions about different types of repression, one interviewee argued: 'I think it is obvious, libertarian activism, students and of course anti-fascists ... they are who really suffer from repression' (I8). The scientific literature supports the idea that the forms of mobilization perceived as counter-hegemonic are more likely to be repressed (Boykoff, 2006): States react by expanding the technologies of repression in political strategies with the capacity to reshape the space for contentious activism more generally.

Two features of 15-M and subsequent anti-austerity mobilizations are particularly relevant when it comes to the question of the penalization of counter-hegemony in Spain. In the first place, 15-M campaigns invented age as a meaningful political argument in Spanish politics. However, in questioning the capacity of Spanish democracy to provide intergenerational justice, 15-M mobilizations fueled pre-existing panics in relation to unruly behavior by young people. In the second place, anti-austerity mobilizations displaced the emphasis on issue-politics, to recuperate a supposedly extinct preoccupation with material grievances (Portos, 2021). Grievances not only became determinants of protest; more significantly, they became the cornerstone of a new social conversation about social justice and the limits of Spanish social citizenship.

We argue that penalization and democracy speak to each other in very intimate ways. Penalization contributes to de-democratization; in other words, it contributes to the illiberal assault on existing ideas about citizenship and democratic representation, a process that is analyzed with preoccupations by scholars in many fields, including of course gender equality and sexual rights (Lombardo et al., 2021). Penalization, a concept that we use to provide a more nuanced description to repressive efforts by political authorities and their allies, exposes activists to (sometimes fictitious) trade-offs between ideological coherence and legal compliance that steadily erode the willingness and capacity of mobilizers to face insurmountable risks. Relentless interventions in the fields of discourses and values that insist on protest as a threat, combined by extensive fining and aggressive policing can promote dynamics of self-censorship, excessive precaution, moderation, and institutionalization (Simsa, 2017). In other words, penalization fosters processes of substitution whereby subversive and counter-hegemonic forms of contention are being replaced by forms of protest with an indisputable seal of legality and legitimacy. Our interviewees were unsympathetic with the anxieties of activists working for 'respectable NGOs' who no longer 'dare even to look into the eye of policemen in demonstrations' (I3). At the same time, however, they understood and acknowledged the capacity of institutionally promoted fear to make activists refrain from actions tagged as radical (such as *escraches*, occupations and resistances against evictions). Penalization restricts the repertoire of acceptable forms of protest to actions that comply with administrative regulations, particularly peaceful demonstrations that do not permanently disrupt the normal use of public space. Expressions of dissent in social media have also been affected, particularly in fear of prosecutors that build on the expanded legal definition of terrorism. Not only is this situation widely acknowledged by our interviewees: a wide array of activist communities in Spain are revealing the consequences of contemporary repression in terms of self-censorship, excessive moderation and even demobilization. According to a member of the Madrid-based *Comisión Sol*: 'massive identification requests during demonstrations and protest events, whether or not these result in actual fines, result in the demobilization of normal people because they are scared of being sanctioned' (AI, n.d).

Finally, we situate penalization in a dialectic relationship with the structure of political opportunities. By insisting on associations between dissent and insecurity (or even terrorism), State authorities can curb resistances against effective means of repression. This can explain the willingness of Spanish authorities, for instance, to display violent responses against protesters for Catalonian independence (Balcells et al., 2021; Della Porta et al., 2019). At the same time, repression is also embedded in a pre-existing structure of political opportunities. We agree with Flesher Fominaya (2017) in reading penalization as an unintended consequence of mobilization. Repression and mobilization are often dialectically related, advances in mobilization feed innovation into repression and vice versa. What the literature does not often acknowledge, however, is that the specific configuration of repression is also shaped by the structure of political opportunities. In other words, repressive dynamics are influenced not only by the dynamics of the cycle of protest, but also by pre-existing traditions and case-specific configurations of power. Repressive responses towards anti-austerity mobilizations in Spain build on two key elements that define a distinctive approach to insecurity and criminal justice. In the first place, an ever-expanding scope of punitive legislation, that covers a great number of walks in social life (including protest). The Spanish criminal code stands as one of the most severe in Europe (Brandariz, 2018); longer sentences and a wider number of listed crimes and misdemeanors have led to one the largest per capita prison populations in Europe. The disproportionate size of Spanish police forces is noticeable from a comparative vantage point: while Spain had more than 520 police officers per 100.000 habitants in 2015, Germany had less than 300 and France only 172. These figures are not justified by homicide and theft rates, which are remarkably low in Spain; the 2014 homicide rate was 0.69 per 100.000 habitants in Spain, 1.20 in France and 0.80 in Germany (Eurostat, n.d.). In the second place, a society that fears crime (Zuloaga, 2014). Fearing crime has emerged as an arena of State action where different actors find opportunities and constraints to develop a very wide array of policies, including those related to protest and protesters. Table 1 reports on data on fear of violent crime in Spain and in the United Kingdom. Spaniards are more scared than Britons, despite the glaring differences in crime rates; while there were 35.7 assaults per 100,000 Spaniards in 2013, in England and Wales this figure was 566.5 (Eurostat, n.d.). Whereas there was one intentional homicide per 100,000 habitants in the whole UK, in Spain there was 0.65.

In conclusion, 15-M mobilizations became a significant social, cultural and political phenomenon because they revealed glaring deficiencies in the Spanish democracy, as expressed by corruption, political disaffection, and inequality. They found the way to release large reservoirs of discontent that had been shimmering for quite some time. A new language was invented to provide meaning and organization to many individual experiences with deprivation, frustration, and injustice. In challenging hegemony, however, 15-M mobilizations triggered an equally remarkable response by opponents. In 2011, Spanish democracy already was a penalized democracy, a political system built on an ever-expanding reach of criminal legislation that harbored strong conservative ideas about punishment and insecurity. The more anti-austerity mobilizations questioned core neoliberal principles such as property, deregulation, or corporate autonomy, and the more innovative ideas about direct participation and consensus wiggled their way into the political agenda, the more opponents to mobilization built on the culture of fear and punishment to increase repression. The central role of punishment in shaping societal and political responses to counter-hegemonic protest justifies the presentation of repression as an example of penalization. Different expressions of punishment have been (re)activated to quash the challenge associated with forms of mobilization that questioned the quality of democracy, giving voice to new constituencies that mobilized on new grounds. 15-M mobilizations did not cause repression; these mobilizations, however, opened a window for policies and practices that were inscribed in the core values of Spanish democracy as they have been steadily put in place since the transitions towards democracy. 15-M and anti-austerity mobilizations have contributed to an improvement

Table 1. Fear of crime and Crime rates (per 100.000 ratio of incidents) in Spain and the UK.

	How often do you think that you can become...			
	a victim of a violent crime?		a victim of a theft?	
	Spain	UK	Spain	UK
Never	39%	41%	35%	28%
Sometimes	28%	36%	25%	37%
Often	26%	19%	31%	25%
Always	6%	4%	9%	10%

Source: Jackson and Kuha (2014), for Fear of Crime.

of Spanish democracy in several meaningful ways. At the same time, however, they have opened an opportunity for public and private actors to build on fundamental features of the Spanish approach to criminal justice and security legislation to intensify repression.

Disclosure statement

No potential conflict of interest was reported by the author(s).

ORCID

Kerman Calvo ⓘ http://orcid.org/0000-0001-7603-3077
Aitor Romeo Echeverría ⓘ http://orcid.org/0000-0003-4943-9842

References

15MPedia. (n.d.). *Síndrome de Sherwood.* https://15mpedia.org/wiki/S%C3%ADndrome_de_Sherwood
AI (Amnesty International). (2014). *España: El derecho a protestar, amenazado.* https://www.amnesty.org/download/Documents/8000/eur410012014es.pdf
AI (Amnesty International). (2015). *La Ley de Seguridad Ciudadana, ¡una amenaza para los derechos humanos!* https://www.es.amnesty.org/actua/acciones/espana-ley-seguridad-ciudadana-oct14/
AI (Amnesty International). (n.d.). *Libertad de Expresión en España.* https://www.es.amnesty.org/en-que-estamos/espana/libertad-de-expresion/
Atak, K. (2017). Encouraging coercive control: Militarisation and classical crowd theory in Turkish protest policing. *Policing and Society. An International Journal of Research and Policy, 27*(7), 693–711. https://doi.org/10.1080/10439463.2015.1040796
Ávila Cantos, D., Domínguez Sánchez, A., García García, S., Maroto Calatayud, M., Martín García, O. J., & Oliver Olmo, P. (2015). La burorrepresión de la protesta y de la pobreza. In D. Bondia, F. Daza, & A. Sánchez (Eds.), *Defender a quien defiende* (pp. 141–168). Icaria.
Balcells, L., Dorsey, S., & Tellez, J. F. (2021). Repression and dissent in contemporary Catalonia. *British Journal of Political Science, 51*(4), 1742–1750. https://doi.org/10.1017/S0007123420000307
Bessant, J., & Grasso, M. (2019). La seguridad y el estado democrático liberal. Criminalizando la política de los jóvenes. *Revista Internacional de Sociología, 77*(4), e140. https://doi.org/10.3989/ris.2019.77.4.19.003
Blay, E. (2013). El control policial de las protestas en España. *Indret: Revista para el Análisis del Derecho, 4*, 1–32. https://raco.cat/index.php/InDret/article/view/270197/357773
Bondia García, D., Sánchez Mera, A., & Daza Sierra, F. (2015). *Defender a quien defiende. Leyes mordaza y criminalización de la protesta en el Estado español.* Icaria.
Boykoff, J. (2006). Framing dissent: Mass-media coverage of the global justice movement. *New Political Science, 28*(2), 201–228. https://doi.org/10.1080/07393140600679967

Brandariz, J. A. (2018). An enduring sovereign mode of punishment: Post-dictatorial penal policies in Spain. *Punishment & Society, 20*(3), 308–328. https://doi.org/10.1177/1462474516681293

Camps, C., & García, A. (2015). La gestión neoliberal de la crisis: De la culpabilización a la represión de la protesta. In F. D. Sierra, A. S. Mera, & D. B. García (Eds.), *Defender a quien defiende: Leyes mordaza y criminalización de la protesta en el Estado español* (pp. 45–66). Icaria.

Casino Rubio, M. (2012). Ordenanzas de convivencia, orden público y competencia municipal. *Justicia Administrativa: Revista de Derecho Administrativo, 56*, 7–20. https://dialnet.unirioja.es/servlet/articulo?codigo=3974072

Chenoweth, E., Perkoski, E., & Kang, S. (2017). State repression and nonviolent resistance. *Journal of Conflict Resolution, 61*(9), 1950–1969. https://doi.org/10.1177/0022002717721390

Comisión Legal Sol. (2015). La ciudadanía como enemiga: Balance tras cuatro años de represión de la protesta. In F. D. Sierra, A. S. Mera, & D. B. García (Eds.), *Defender a quien defiende: Leyes mordaza y criminalización de la protesta en el Estado español* (pp. 107–139). Icaria.

Davenport, C., & Loyle, C. (2012). The states must be crazy: Dissent and the puzzle of repressive persistence. *International Journal of Conflict and Violence, 6*(1), 75–95. https://doi.org/10.4119/ijcv-2931

Della Porta, D., O'Connor, F., & Portos, M. (2019). Protest cycles and referendum for independence: Closed opportunities and the path of radicalization in Catalonia. *Revista Internacional de Sociología, 77*(4), e142. https://doi.org/10.3989/ris.2019.77.4.19.005

Dunn Cavelty, M., & Jaeger, M. (2015). (In)visible ghosts in the machine and the power that bind: The relational securitization of anonymous. *International Political Sociology, 9*(2), 176–194. https://doi.org/10.1111/ips.12090

Earl, J. (2011). Political repression: Iron Fists, Velvet Gloves, and Diffuse Control. *Annual Review of Sociology, 37*(1), 261–284. https://doi.org/10.1146/annurev.soc.012809.102609

EFE. (2017, March 6). *Los acusados por las protestas en Gamonal denuncian que las detenciones fueron 'aleatorias'*. Público. https://www.publico.es/politica/acusados-protestas-gamonal-denuncian-detenciones.html

El Periódico. (2014, June 1). *Seis detenidos y 225 identificados en los incidentes del sábado por Can Vies*. El Periódico. https://www.elperiodico.com/es/barcelona/20140601/seis-detenidos-y-225-identificados-en-los-incidentes-del-sabado-por-can-vies-3287773

Enríquez-Nistal, S. (2013, May 17). *Escrache a favor del aborto en la casa de Gallardón*. El Mundo. http://www.elmundo.es/elmundo/2013/05/16/espana/1368728666.html

Europa Press. (2018, February 21). *La Plataforma Pro-Soterramiento impulsa una campaña 'crowdfunding' para hacer frente a las multas puestas a los vecinos*. 20 Minutos. https://www.20minutos.es/noticia/3268329/0/plataforma-pro-soterramiento-impulsa-campana-crowdfunding-para-hacer-frente-multas-puestas-vecinos/

Eurostat. (n.d.). *Archive: Crime Statistics*. https://ec.europa.eu/eurostat/statistics-explained/index.php?title=Archive:Crime_statistics

Fernández, D. (2012, May 3). *Una unidad de élite de la Policía investiga a los líderes del 15-M*. 20 Minutos. https://www.20minutos.es/noticia/1416360/0/policia/investiga/lideres-15-M/

Fernández de Mosteyrín, L. (2012). Rodea el Congreso: Un caso para explorar las bases del Estado Securitario. *Anuario del Conflicto Social, 2*, 1129–1152. https://revistes.ub.edu/index.php/ACS/article/view/6365

Fernández Savater, A., Flesher Fominaya, C., Carvalho, L., Elsadda, H., El-Tamami, W., Horrillo, P., Nanclares, S., & Stavrides, S. (2017). Life after the squares: Reflections on the consequences of the Occupy movements. *Social Movements Studies, 16*(1), 119–151. https://doi.org/10.1080/14742837.2016.1244478

Ferrandis, J. (2012, February 21). *El jefe de policía se refiere a los estudiantes como 'el enemigo'*. El País. https://elpais.com/ccaa/2012/02/20/valencia/1329764951_838007.html

Ferree, M. (2004). Soft Repression: Ridicule, Stigma, and Silencing. In D. J. Myers & D. M. Cress (Eds.), *Research in social movements, conflicts and change: Vol. 25. Authority in contention* (pp. 85–101). Emerald Group Publishing Limited.

Flesher Fominaya, C. (2014). *The State Strikes Back: The Criminalization of 15-M and Social Movements in Spain*. Personal blog: Contentious Politics in an Age of Austerity. https://austerityprotests.wordpress.com/2014/06/05/the-state-strikes-back-the-criminalization-of-15-m-and-social-movements-in-spain/

Flesher Fominaya, C. (2017). European anti-austerity and pro-democracy protests in the wake of the global financial crisis. *Social Movement Studies*, 16(1), 1–20. https://doi.org/10.1080/14742837.2016.1256193

Flesher Fominaya, C. (2020). *Democracy reloaded: Inside Spain's political laboratory from 15-M to podemos*. Oxford University Press.

Freemuse. (n.d.). *Spain*. https://freemuse.org/spain-country-factsheet/

García-García, J., & Calvo, K. (2019). Repressing the masses. Newspapers and the securitisation of youth dissent in Spain. *Revista Internacional de Sociología*, 77(4), e143. https://doi.org/10.3989/ris.2019.77.4.19.006

Garland, D. (1990). *Punishment and modern society: A study in social theory*. The University of Chicago Press.

Gillham, P., & Noakes, J. (2007). 'More than a March in a Circle': Transgressive protests and the limits of negotiated management. *Mobilization. An International Quarterly*, 12(4), 341–357. https://doi.org/10.17813/maiq.12.4.j10822802t7n0t34

González, J. (2012, November 5). *Aumenta un 1.780% el gasto en material antidisturbios y protección*. El Mundo. https://www.elmundo.es/elmundo/2012/10/30/economia/1351613307.html

González Sánchez, I. (2019). La violencia simbólica y la penalización de la protesta. *Revista Internacional de Sociología*, 77(4), e138. https://doi.org/10.3989/ris.2019.77.4.19.001

González Sánchez, I., & Maroto Calatayud, M. (2018). The penalization of protest under neoliberalism: Managing resistance through punishment. *Crime, Law, and Social Change*, 70(4), 443–460. https://doi.org/10.1007/s10611-018-9776

González Sánchez, I., Maroto Calatayud, M., & Brandariz, J. A. (2019). Editors' introduction: Policing the protest cycle of the 2010s. *Social Justice. A Journal of Crime, Conflict and World Order*, 46(2/3), 1–27. http://www.socialjusticejournal.org/wp-content/uploads/2020/07/156_01_Introduction1.pdf

Gracia, A. I. (2012September 25). *La protesta Rodea el Congreso deriva en enfrentamientos y cargas policiales*. El Confidencial. https://www.elconfidencial.com/espana/2012-09-25/la-protesta-rodea-el-congreso-deriva-en-enfrentamientos-y-cargas-policiales_217443/

Jackson, J., & Kuha, J. (2014). Worry about crime in a cross-national context: A model-supported method of measurement using the European social survey. *Survey research methods*, 8(2), 109–125. https://doi.org/10.18148/srm/2014.v8i2.5457

Jämte, J., & Ellefsen, R. (2020). The Consequences of Soft Repression. *Mobilization: An International Quarterly*, 25(3), 383–404. https://doi.org/10.17813/1086-671X-25-3-383

Juanatey Ferreiro, H. (2012, December 12). *FIES: La cárcel dentro de la cárcel*. El Diario. https://www.eldiario.es/politica/alfon-fies_1_5525047.html

La Vanguardia. (2012, September 19). *Interior niega haber investigado a los líderes del 15M y limita su vigilancia a los antisistema*. La Vanguardia. https://www.lavanguardia.com/local/madrid/20120919/54350581475/interior-niega-haber-investigado-a-los-lideres-del-15m-y-limita-su-vigilancia-a-los-antisistema.html

Lombardo, E., Kantola, J., & Rubio Marín, R. (2021). De-Democratization and opposition to gender equality politics in Europe. *Social Politics: International Studies in Gender, State & Society*, 28(3), 521–531. https://doi.org/10.1093/sp/jxab030

Maroto Calatayud, M. (2013). Ciudades de excepción: Seguridad ciudadana y civismo como instrumentos de burorrepresión de la protesta. In P. O. Olmo (Ed.), *Burorrepresión: Sanción administrativa y control social* (pp. 29–64). Editorial Bomarzo.

Martín García, O. J. (2014). Soft repression and the current wave of social mobilisations in Spain. *Social Movements Studies*, 13(2), 303–308. https://doi.org/10.1080/14742837.2013.863147

Mato, M. (2015). Apuntes para pensar el género como elemento constitutivo de la represión. In F. D. Sierra, A. S. Mera, & D. B. García (Eds.), *Defender a quien defiende: Leyes mordaza y criminalización de la protesta en el Estado español* (pp. 67–106). Icaria.

Ministerio del Interior. (2019). *Anuario Estadístico del Ministerio del Interior*. Madrid, Gobierno de España: Ministerio del Interior.

Muncie, E. (2020). 'Peaceful protesters' and 'dangerous criminals': The framing and reframing of anti-fracking activists in the UK. *Social Movement Studies*, 19(4), 464–481. https://doi.org/10.1080/14742837.2019.1708309

Nordas, R., & Davenport, C. (2013). Fight the Youth: Youth bulges and state repression. *American Journal of Political Science*, 57(4), 926–940. https://doi.org/10.1111/ajps.12025

Oliver, P. (2008). Repression and crime control: Why social movement scholars should pay attention to mass incarceration as a form of repression. *Mobilization. An International Quarterly*, 13(1), 1–24. doi:10.17813/maiq.13.1.v264hx580h486641

Oliver, P., & Urda, J. (2015). Bureau-repression: Administrative sanctions and social control in modern Spain. *Oñati Socio-Legal Series*, 5(5), 1309–1328. https://opo.iisj.net/index.php/osls/article/view/418

PenP (Plataforma en Pie). (2012, September 18). *Plataforma ¡En Pie!* https://plataformaenpie.wordpress.com/2012/09/18/documento-base-plataforma-en-pie/

Policía Nacional. (2020, November 4). *La Policía Nacional incrementa su presupuesto de gastos en un 20,81. Ministerio del Interior*. http://www.interior.gob.es/es/web/interior/noticias/detalle/-/journal_content/56_INSTANCE_1YSSI3xiWuPH/10180/12525577/

Portos, M. (2017). Keeping dissent alive under the Great Recession: No-radicalisation and protest in Spain after the eventful 15M/indignados campaign. *Acta Polit*, 54(1), 45–74. https://doi.org/10.1057/s41269-017-0074-9

Portos, M. (2021). *Grievances and Public Protests: Political Mobilisation in Spain in the Age of Austerity*. Palgrave Macmillan.

Red Malla. (2018, February 12). *Más de 70 activistas de la PAH se enfrentan procedimientos penales. Red Malla*. https://redmalla.net/#/denuncia/m%C3%A1s-de-70-activistas-de-la-pah-se-enfrentan-procedimientos-penales

Rodríguez-Pina, G. (2012, September 26). *Policías infiltrados en el 25-S: La Jefatura reconoce que había 'secretas' pero niega que provocasen la violencia. HuffingtonPost*. https://www.huffingtonpost.es/2012/09/26/policias-infiltrados-en-e_n_1915348.html

Romanos, E., & Sádaba, I. (2022). Evolución de la protesta en España (200-2017): Un análisis de sus ciclos y características. *Revista Española de Investigaciones Sociológicas*, 177, 89–110. doi:10.5477/cis/reis.177.89

Rossini, L., Azozomox, & Debelle, G. (2018). Keep your piece of cake, we'll squat the bakery! Autonomy meets repression and institutionalization. In M. A. M. López (Ed.), *The Urban Politics of Squatters' Movements* (pp. 247–269). Palgrave Macmillan. https://doi.org/10.1057/978-1-349-95314-1_12

Ruiz Chasco, S. (2014). Videovigilancia en el centro de Madrid. ¿Hacia el panóptico electrónico? *Teknokultura. Revista De Cultura Digital Y Movimientos Sociales*, 11(2), 301–327. https://revistas.ucm.es/index.php/TEKN/article/view/48243/45139

Sánchez, R. (2016, March 3). *La Policía multa a 30 personas al día por 'faltas de respeto" a los agentes desde que entró en vigor la Ley Mordaza. El Diario*. https://www.eldiario.es/sociedad/sanciones-diarias-policia-ley-mordaza_1_4128315.html

Schlembach, R. (2018). Undercover policing and the spectre of 'domestic extremism': The covert surveillance of environmental activism in Britain. *Social Movement Studies*, 17(5), 491–506. https://doi.org/10.1080/14742837.2018.1480934

Seijas, R. (2016). Criminalización de los movimientos sociales a través del discurso de la prensa liberal y conservadora: El caso de la Plataforma de Afectados por la Hipoteca y los Escraches. *Commons. Revista De Comunicación Y Ciudadanía Digital*, 4(2), 68–92. https://revistas.uca.es/index.php/cayp/article/view/3096

Simsa, R. (2017). Repression of the Spanish protest movement: Mechanisms and consequences. *NonProfit Policy Forum*, 8(3), 1–16. doi:10.1515/npf-2017-0022

Smithey, L. A., & Kurtz, L. R. (2018). Smart" Repression. In L. A. Smithey & L. R. Kurtz (Eds.), *The paradox of repression and nonviolent movements* (pp. 185–214). Syracuse University Press.

Starr, A., Fernández, L. A., Amster, R., Wood, L. J., & Caro, M. (2008). The impacts of state surveillance on political assembly and association: A socio-legal analysis. *Qualitative Sociology*, *31*(3), 251–270. https://doi.org/10.1007/s11133-008-9107-z

Zuloaga, L. (2014). *El espejismo de la seguridad ciudadana: Claves de su presencia en la agenda política*. Los Libros de la Catarata.

Appendix

Background information about interviewees.

	Gender	Age	Activism	Years in activism	Repression suffered
I1	Masc.	23	Student	8	Fined
I2	Masc.	24	Student	10	Fined
I3	Masc.	22	Community (*vecinal*)	7	Fined/Trial
I4	Masc.	26	Student	12	Police Violence
I5	Masc.	26	15-M/ Trade Union	9	Trial
I6	Masc.	27	15-M/Student	12	Trial
I7	Masc.	20	Student/Anarchist	3	Fined/Trial
I8	Masc.	21	Student/Anarchist	5	Fined/Trial
I9	Masc.	29	Community/Housing	14	Fined/Trial
I10	Masc.	30	Union	10	Fined/Trial

The political economy of the Spanish *Indignados*: political opportunities, social conflicts, and democratizing impacts

Eduardo Romanos, Jorge Sola and César Rendueles

ABSTRACT
The 15-M mobilizations shook Spanish society and placed the demand for 'real democracy' at the center of political debate. In order to better understand the scope and impact of the *Indignados'* democratizing endeavors, this article aims to address an issue that has not received much attention: the connection of this protest cycle with the political economy. To this end, both the opportunity structure generated by the economic crisis and the class and generational conflicts shaping the mobilizations are analyzed. The article proposes that the symbolic and short-term success of 15-M in re-politicizing distributive conflicts contrasts with its medium-term inability to materially democratize the political economy. This relative failure can be explained by the confluence of several factors: on the one hand, 15-M's organizational weakness and its disconnection from a somewhat declining labor movement; on the other, the lack of responsiveness of Spain's political institutions to street politics and the powerful structural inertia of economic dynamics created by decades of neoliberalism. The findings of this case study aim to contribute to scholarly debates on the impacts of social movements and their connection to political economy and social classes.

Introduction

The 15-M movement erupted into Spanish life in reaction to the economic and political crisis brought about the Great Recession. Common slogans used by the movement exclaimed: 'we are not merchandise in the hands of politicians and bankers' and 'they call it a democracy, but it's not'. Commonly referred to as *Los Indignados* ['the indignant ones' or 'the outraged'], the protests were motivated by a malfunctioning democracy, political and financial corruption, and cutbacks in public spending. However, while the mobilizations demanded a 'real democracy' that broadened and deepened political participation, within the polyphonic discourse of the 15-M protests, the specific contents of that vision of democracy were never entirely clear.

The exhaustion of the protests in late 2013 and the rise of new political parties led many activists into institutional politics during the transformative local and national elections between 2014 and 2019, which brought an end to bipartisan politics. However, experiences in local government, or the 2020 national coalition between Podemos and PSOE, have been contentious, and various factors have limited 15-M's attempt to re-imagine democracy, in particular from a political-economic standpoint.

Little attention has been given to understanding the evolution and impact of 15-M from the perspective of political economy, social class and capitalism, an area that is receiving growing interest within the broader study of social movements. Hetland and Goodwin (2013), for example, have commented on the 'strange disappearance of capitalism' from this field of research, despite the importance of the political-economic system for social movements. They point out that the dynamics of capitalism and its related ideologies can inhibit or facilitate collective identities and solidarities, but also that class balances (general and intra-movement) heavily shape the goals, strategies, evolution and outcomes of social movements.

Similarly, Zajak maintains that 'we know very little about how social movements transform or replace capitalist institutions' and that it is necessary to reevaluate their role in the capitalism-democracy balance by considering 'if and how social movements may in fact contribute to the (re-)embedding of markets' (Zajak, 2013, pp. 130, 133). The possibility that social inequalities persist and endure within social movements, and how this can 'politicize latent cleavage structures and thus make them the object of manifest social conflict', has also been raised (Zajak & Haunss, 2020, p. 23). In a similar vein, della Porta aims to connect the literature on social movements with the political economy of neoliberal crisis. She also highlights that 'the very logic of accumulation [production-based or by dispossession] impacts the forms of collective mobilization' (Della Porta, 2017, p. 465). Drawing on this idea, Caruso and Cini (2020) have outlined the need for a framework to study the interlinkages of capitalist structural dynamics and the formation of social movements. Conversely, other authors have examined transformation of the political economy by social movements 'from above' and that 'capitalists [and] not just subaltern groups resort to collective action outside of institutional channels of authority and power' (Schneirov & Schneirov, 2016, p. 561; see also, Cox & Nilsen, 2014; Chouhy, 2020).

This research line on capitalism and contentious politics can be connected to ongoing discussions on the political consequences and impacts of social movements. In examining the various debates and disagreements with respect to this, Amenta and colleagues concluded that it is necessary 'to think through the interactions between strategies, organizations, and contexts' (Amenta et al., 2010, p. 287). Giugni and Bosi (2012; see also, Bosi et al., 2019) provide another useful analytic construct through a typology of social movement outcomes that distinguishes between six domains, depending on whether they are political, cultural or biographical vis-à-vis internal or external. For our purposes, two of these outcomes are of particular interest: policy and institutional change (political/external) and change in public opinion and attitudes (cultural/external).

On the basis of these ideas, this article aims to bridge the gap between political economy and social movement studies by examining the development and impact of the 15-M mobilizations on deepening democracy from a political-economic standpoint. To this end, our analysis seeks to answer three interrelated questions: 1) Did the Spanish political-economic model favor or hinder the politicization of certain distributive conflicts and the formation of some collective identities by 15-M, and if so, how? 2) What were the social bases of this mobilization and the role of the working class? and 3) What were the (political and cultural) impacts 15-M had on the democratic re-embedding of markets and social empowerment in the Spanish political economy? In the literature, these questions remain largely unresolved and also speak to more general theoretical considerations, such as: 1) How do capitalist dynamics (and related ideologies) favor or impede the development of protest? 2) How do class balances (and class divisions within movements) influence the development of contentious politics? 3) What are their impacts and the interaction between the strategies, organizations, and contexts that underlie social movements?

Based on a process tracing methodology, this article offers some responses to these questions. Process tracing involves a detailed analysis of a series of events over time, with the specific aim of identifying causal processes that help to explain the development of a particular event, in this case the 15-M protests. In terms of empirical data, the study draws on two types of secondary source material. Firstly, an original analysis of micro data from a survey conducted by the Spanish Centre for Sociological Research (CIS), which involved the recoding of variables. Secondly, the collation of evidence from diverse sources, such as the Spanish Ministry of Labor and Eurostat, amongst others.

The rest of the article is organized in six sections. The first section provides a brief overview of the Spanish political economy before and after the Great Recession. The second section traces the development of the 15-M mobilizations from a political-economic standpoint. The third section considers the elusive role of the labor movement during the cycle of protests. The fourth section analyzes the class and generational conflicts that shaped the social basis of 15-M, and the fifth section assesses the material and symbolic impacts of 15-M in terms of a political-economic democratization. The article finishes with a discussion of the findings and a series of conclusions formulated in response to the questions and considerations posed above.

The Spanish political economy and the Great Recession

The bursting of the financial and real estate bubble during the Great Recession hit Spain particularly hard, ending any previous illusion of an 'economic miracle' (Buendía, 2020). Between 2007 and 2013, Spain suffered the greatest level of job losses in Europe (3.4 million), a huge increase in the public deficit, and a debt crisis similar to that of the rest of the European periphery. However, in order to understand the Spanish political economy and its crisis it is necessary to consider its historical origins.

In the post-war period, the dictatorship of Francisco Franco (1939–1978) diverted Spain from the economic development trajectory of other Western European countries. Following victory in the Spanish Civil War (1936–1939), capitalists and landowners avoided the kind of capital-labor compromise that shaped the 'golden age' of capitalism during the *trente glorieuses*. Franco's dictatorship not only reversed the process of political and economic democratization launched by the II Republic (1931–1936), but also bloodily put down the labor movement (Richards, 1998). The resulting political economy was defined by the subordination of labor (low wages and lack of freedom) and a socially weak, but politically authoritarian state, which propped up a fragile economic structure dominated by rentiers in a clientelist environment.

However, after Franco's death (1975) and the introduction of democracy no radical shift in class-power balances came about. Although the worker's movement reemerged in the 1960s and played a key role in the erosion of the dictatorship (Fishman, 1990), it never acquired sufficient strength to impose a break with the Francoist elites, who managed to ensure a 'pacted transition'. Within the nascent democracy, labor organization was relegated to a subordinate role in favor of maintaining an economic model based on 'low wages, low productivity'. In this respect, the model of democracy that emerged from the transition failed to break with the past. Democratic practice remained mostly unreceptive of demands 'from below' (Fishman, 2019), paving the way for the new bipartisan regime, which remained firmly in place until very recently.

The social-democratic governments of the PSOE (1982–1996) consolidated the political-economic model of transition by implementing an 'embedded neoliberalism' (Ban, 2016; see also, Prasad, 2006, for different forms of neoliberalism); a mix of pro-market economic policy and labor deregulation offset by an uneven development of a welfare state (Recio & Roca, 2001). Unions responded with three general strikes, but their structural weakness (a union density of around 15%) resulted in defeat and the adoption of a more modest and pact-oriented approach. Along with the defeat of the 'no' vote to Spain's entry into NATO, this led to a decline of the social movements that had flourished during the democratic transition, and a collapse in the political aspirations of an entire generation of activists.

The entrance of the conservatives (PP) to government between 1996 and 2004 saw a continuation of the prevailing economic policy. At the same time, the availability of cheap credit created a collective illusion of an economic miracle (Rey-Araújo, 2020). In this period, more jobs were created in Spain than in the rest of Europe and GDP grew by 4%, even though real wages stagnated or were in decline and many young people were still unemployed or in precarious jobs. In reality, the wealth effect was due to the overvaluation of real estate (income from real estate assets tripled during those years) in a country where 85% of the population owned their homes (López & Rodríguez, 2011).

In the meantime, class structure in Spain was transformed by the growth of sociocultural professionals and service workers, the incorporation of women and migrants to the labor market, and the decline of the industrial working class (Garrido & González, 2012). These political processes and structural changes affected social movements and contentious politics. Class ceased to be an axis of political participation and the role of unions was further diminished. Labor deregulation and economic financialization was accompanied by a profound process of cultural change in lifestyles, consumer habits and family relations, bolstering the ideas of progress and modernity that legitimized (and depoliticized) the neoliberal political economy. Market-driven politics seemed to be the price for leaving the authoritarian past behind. Social movement activists were not immune to this dynamic; some of them directed their mobilization efforts outwards, to anti-war movements or international solidarity. In effect, a perceived inability to intervene in the political economy led to its disregard within protest movements.

However, the 2008 recession brought a swift end to any social consensus on neoliberal modernization. The economic crisis in Spain exhibited two distinctive effects. First, it hit Spain and other countries on the European periphery (Portugal, Italy, Ireland and Greece) particularly hard, largely as a result of the rigidities imposed by the Euro

(Lapavitsas, 2012). As can be seen in Figure 1, GDP contraction was much bigger in Spain, public debt tripled in the following years, and unemployment quadrupled – the youth unemployment rate (not shown) reached 57%.

The second feature of the Spanish crisis was increased social inequality. As shown by various indicators in Figure 2, the growth in inequality and poverty was much larger than the rest of the Euro area. According to data from the Luxembourg Income Study, between 2007 and 2013, the three poorest deciles of Spanish society lost about 20% of their income, while the four intermediate deciles lost about 6–7% and the highest income levels hardly suffered any losses at all. These differences contrast with Italy and Greece, where all groups suffered similar losses (Perez & Matsaganis, 2018). In other words, against the widespread perception that the middle-class had paid for the crisis, the working class was in fact hit the hardest. In this respect, the distributive conflict was not only about the '1%', but also the middle and popular classes, who were most affected by unemployment. Contextually, this was highly significant for the 15-M mobilizations, as discussed further on.

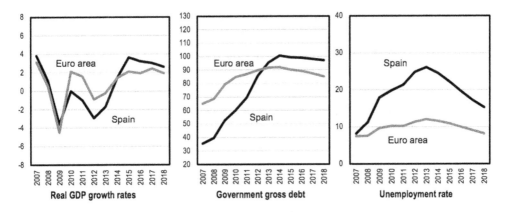

Figure 1. Indicators of the economic crisis. Source: Eurostat.

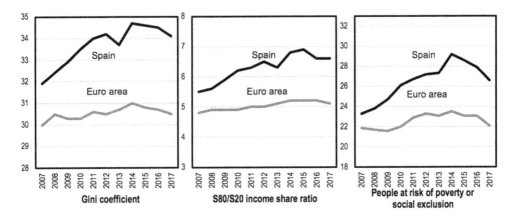

Figure 2. The impact of the crisis on inequality. Source: Eurostat.

The commonalities of the longstanding economic policies of the PSOE and PP and their inability to offer an alternative response to austerity generated significant discontent. This was aggravated by numerous political corruption scandals and the gap between the aging elites and the new generation entering politics. All of this acted to turn the economic crisis into a political crisis, creating the political opportunity structure for the 15-M mobilizations. However, this picture must also be qualified to avoid retrospective bias. While there was growing and diffuse discontent, there was no clear agreement on the latent cleavage structures along which social conflict was to be politicized. On the one hand, the deregulation of the labor market had intensified the precariousness of employment and weakened the labor movement, meaning that unions had lost much of their legitimacy and support to lead a massive mobilization.[1] On the other hand, the grievances produced by the crisis were heterogeneous and had shaken a neoliberalized society with low levels of associationism and fragmented social movements. The social groups hit hardest by the crisis were the least politically active, while the well-educated young people who tended to take part in the protests were organizationally weak. It was not until the demonstration on 15 March 2011, and the eviction of the Puerta del Sol Plaza camp two days later, that a mass mobilization was unexpectedly born.

Street politics against market despotism

15-M mobilized the outrage of an important part of the Spanish population. Slogans such as 'we are not merchandise in the hands of bankers and politicians' echo Polanyi and the idea of a society that defends itself from the markets and the elites. At the same time, the *Indignados'* demand for 'real democracy now' signaled a belief that democratic processes needed to be deepened at all levels of society (Díez García & Laraña, 2017; Feenstra et al., 2017; Flesher Fominaya, 2020). However, it was not completely clear what this idea of democracy really was and what concrete changes it might imply. The polyphonic nature of the discourses within 15-M ranged from moderate to radical reform, depending on whether they were aimed at correcting the shortcomings of the representative system (and renewal of its members) or a democratic radicalization (for an early discussion of 15-M's ambivalences in this respect, see, Moreno Pestaña, 2011).[2] In the political-economic sphere, moderate Keynesian demands against the re-commodification of public services and housing and the excessive power of finance prevailed over those aimed at a radical democratization of finance, firms and workplaces, which ultimately found little purchase.

The protest cycle that started with 15-M began to decline in 2013 (Romanos & Sádaba, 2022; see also, Portos, 2016). For many activists, this heralded a shift from street to institutional politics as new political forces exploited the crisis of legitimization of the traditional bipartisan system (Font & García-Espín, 2020; Rendueles & Sola, 2019; Romanos & Sádaba, 2016; Sola & Rendueles, 2018). In terms of the political-economic dynamics of the anti-austerity protests, it is possible to distinguish three groups of mobilizations that coalesced around: 1) the right to housing; 2) criticism of the financial market, and 3) the defense of the welfare-state and public services. In the following paragraphs we consider each of these individually.

The Spanish real estate crisis led to the eviction of thousands of people who could no longer afford to pay their mortgage. The Platform for People Affected by Mortgages [*Plataforma de Afectados por la Hipoteca* (PAH)] mobilized as a response to this problem.

Launched in 2009, the PAH network operates through a series of territorial nodes and organizations at district, metropolitan and national levels. The period of intense mobilization after May 2011 led to the recruitment of a large number of people into PAH's activities and its organizational structure (Romanos, 2014). Nationally, PAH's actions enjoy ample popular support. Over 1.5 million people endorsed a Popular Legislation Initiative (2011–2013) that called for the regulation of a system of retrospective payments in kind for distressed mortgage holders, the blocking of evictions, and the promotion of social housing.[3] The platform also diversified the number and range of actors involved in the conflict through various scale-shift mechanisms (European Union and regional governments) and elevated the housing issue from the individual (those who 'lived beyond their means') to the collective sphere (defining the economic crisis as a massive fraud). Activists also developed other, more contentious, forms of action: physically blocking evictions, the occupation of apartment buildings, the public harassment and shaming of public figures (Romanos, 2014).

Another big target of the anti-austerity protests were the banks and, in general, financial capitalism. One demand was for a citizens' public debt audit to declare the 'illegitimate' part of debt void. The *Indignados* also organized several campaigns. The *15MpaRato*, for instance, demanded that legal action be taken against Rodrigo Rato – former Minister of the Economy with the PP (1996–2004) and Director of the IMF (2004–2007) – and other leaders of Caja Madrid, one of the largest savings banks, which had to be bailed out. The legal processes that came about because of the campaign resulted in successful convictions and helped to expose the corruption that plagued the country's savings banks. However, despite demands by the movement to 'rescue' these entities and form a socially controlled public bank, they were eventually merged with private entities.

As for the welfare state and public services, the mobilization of the *Indignados* was followed by the so-called *Mareas*. Literally meaning 'tide', but better understood as a 'wave' or 'sea' of protest, workers and users of particular public services (each *Marea* is distinguished by a different color) organized massive marches against privatization and cutbacks, with unions only playing a secondary role. The most significant of these demonstrations were the *Marea Verde* [Green Tide], from the education sector, and the *Marea Blanca* [White Tide], from healthcare. The scale of these mobilizations varied around the country, but following a period of ebb and flow they eventually petered out.

In summary, between 2011 and 2013 a massive cycle of contention erupted, revolving around political-economic conflicts related to housing, finance and the welfare state. Mobilizations were fed by networks of activists with similar repertoires of action (occupation of public space, communication strategies, etc.) that mostly came from the *Indignados* movement. Still, despite their affinity, these mobilizations were unsustainable over time due, among other reasons, to a lack of coordination and an inability to forge a sustained and integrated challenge around a common charter of demands with a strong organizational basis (Rendueles & Sola, 2019). Importantly, this relates to one of the paradoxical characteristics of Spain, made particularly evident in this period of politics: high levels of political and social mobilization and very low levels of associationism (Fishman, 2012; Morales & Geurts, 2007).

The elusive role of organized labor

The emergence of mobilizations such as those mentioned above contrasts with the role of the labor movement during this period, as unions were reluctant to get involved and hence missed an opportunity to accomplish a generational renewal of their base, organization and repertoires of contention (Rodríguez, 2017; Rendueles & Sola, 2018). Throughout the boom years they had adopted a position of 'social peace' and to a large extent the arrival of the *Indignados* caught them by surprise (Fernández-Trujillo, 2021; Wilhelmi, 2021). Although they supported many of the anti-austerity protests – sometimes strongly, at others timidly – they never exercised leadership (Köhler & Calleja Jiménez, 2015; Romanos, 2017). The structure of the labor market was an important hindrance as high levels of unemployment and job precarity weakened their position (Köhler & Calleja Jiménez, 2018). While Spanish labor unions enjoy widespread institutional recognition (collective bargaining covers 80% of workers), they lack a strong rank-and-file (as mentioned above, union density is around 15%) with which to enforce labor agreements (particularly in small companies and the service sector – the core of the Spanish economy).

Between September 2010 and November 2012, labor unions called for three general strikes in response to European austerity policy and two national labor reforms, one by the PSOE and one by the PP. However, the organization of these strikes was not so much strategic as a sort of ritual response to policy reforms that was carried out with little determination. In fact, labor disputes even decreased after the outbreak of the crisis as can be seen in Figure 3, which shows that industrial conflict (days not worked due to strikes) was lower than in previous decades.

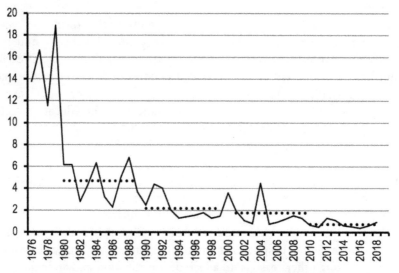

Figure 3. Labor conflict (days not worked in millions) in Spain (1976–2018). Source: Spanish Ministry of Labor. Note: The vertical axis shows the hours not worked in millions. The horizontal lines show the average for each decade. From 1982 to 1985 no data was collected for Catalonia, and from 1986 to 1989 no data was collected for the Basque Country. The general strikes of 1988, 1992, 1994, 2001, 2010 and 2012 are not registered either.

Nevertheless, when we consider union activity in terms of organizational capacity we find a somewhat different picture compared to social movements. Recent protest event analysis (Romanos & Sádaba, 2022; see also, Portos, 2016) shows that no other type of organization had the mobilizing capacity of the unions during the anti-austerity protests. In other words, union mobilization was significantly lower than in the past, but their organizational strength was higher in comparison to other movements. This highlights the relevance of organizational structures for sustained collective action over time. That said, the unions failed to undertake any process of revitalization and had serious difficulties in building alliances with the *Indignados* around a 'social movement unionism' (Köhler & Calleja Jiménez, 2015; for an alternative and more hopeful outlook, see Bailey et al., 2018). Their structures are still anchored in patterns of a bygone era, ill-equipped for a post-Fordist employment market and for the new spheres of social reproduction, such as those that were revealed by the women's strikes of 2018 and 2019 (Campillo, 2019).

Class and generation: the social bases of 15-M

Key to a better understanding of the development and outcomes of 15-M are its social bases. With some exception, the cycle of protest was led by one specific group: young people from the middle-classes who had seen their expectations of social reproduction frustrated.[4] This group have sometimes been presented as 'the precariat', but the label can be misleading since two different groups of precariat, with different resources and partially divergent material interests, can be distinguished: the working class and the middle class.

While the precarious middle-class was made up of young people who lacked stable jobs, they also had abundant cultural and social capital, as well as strong economic backgrounds through their families. To a large extent, these young people were the children of the middle class that expanded greatly in the 1970s-1980s as a result of economic modernization and the development of the welfare state. Hence, even if they suffered some deprivation in the short-term, their opportunities for social mobility were far greater than their working class counterparts. As most of the 15-M activists who later went on to hold leading positions shared this middle-class background,[5] a historical continuity can be traced back to the political hegemony of the middle-classes that dominated political power and the social imaginary after the democratic transition (Rodríguez, 2017).

Generational dynamics have also become an increasingly important political-economic cleavage (Bessant et al., 2017) and is another key to understanding the social bases of the recent cycle of protests in Spain, where its relevance is more pronounced than in other countries, for two reasons. Firstly, the welfare regime is heavily oriented to older generations and secondly, the 'transition generation' (those born around 1950) that came into positions of power (in politics, journalism, culture or academia) at a very early age, had a stranglehold on power for many years, hindering generational renewal.

At an empirical level, the predominance of precarious middle-class youth in 15-M can be observed at two levels: the class basis of protests and collective action frames. As for class, Figure 4 shows three indicators: participation, sympathy and knowledge of the *Indignados*' mobilization by social class.[6] To conduct the social class analysis, we recoded the CIS micro data using Oesch's (2006) classification matrix, which identifies eight social classes based on employment conditions (dominant and subordinate) and work logic (independent, technical, organizational and interpersonal).

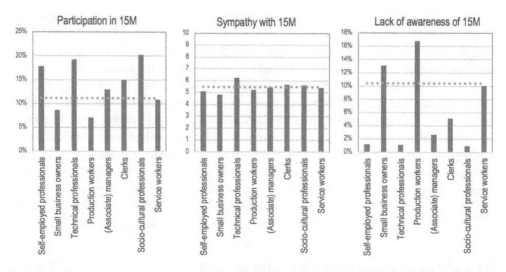

Figure 4. 15-M protests from the perspective of occupational class. Source: CIS Study 2020.

The CIS data shows that approximately 11% of the adult Spanish population participated in some of the demonstrations, encampments, marches or other protests organized by 15-M. However, using the new social class scheme it was possible to identify that the percentage is much higher among middle-class professionals, be they self-employed (18%), technical professionals (19%) or those linked to socio-cultural jobs (20%). Conversely, production workers (11%) are clearly under-represented. The differences are smaller when it comes to the degree of sympathy towards the movement: on a scale of 0 to 10 and with an average of 5.3, the differences oscillate between 4.8 for small-business owners and 6.2 amongst technical professionals. But perhaps it is more revealing to look at the data from the question about whether people had ever heard of 15-M. On average, one in ten people said 'no'; but this percentage is as low as 1–2% in the salaried middle-classes while it grows to 10% among service workers, 13% among small business owners and reaches a high of 17% with production workers. This data coincides with that collected in the Protest Survey project (see, Giugni & Grasso, 2019; Hylmö & Wennerhag, 2015).

Although the class dimension of the *Indignados* has not received much attention, some ethnographic studies corroborate the prominence of these profiles and have analyzed the effects they had on the dynamics of the protests (Moreno Pestaña, 2013; Rázquin, 2017). Despite the protest encampments appearing to be open, horizontal and inclusive, the cultural and social capital of the more active participants in the movement still influenced access and participation,[7] as well as determining the overall dynamics of the mobilization. In general, the prominence of the middle-class tends to coincide with other international studies on the cycle of protests in other countries that occurred around the same time (Della Porta, 2015; Hylmö & Wennerhag, 2015; Tugal, 2015).

Class biases can also be seen in the collective action frames (Gamson, 1992) elaborated by the *Indignados* during the protests. While the discourses of the movement favored inclusivity and an appeal to 'the people from below' or 'the 99%' they also served to conceal internal class divisions (Sola, 2018). One of the most visible groups in the discourse were the university students who, after having learned several languages and completed a master's degree, had to 'go into exile' to look for a job. Criticizing a system that failed to fulfill the meritocratic promise was an effective weapon. But, it was a double-edged sword that presented a situation that affected a minority of young people as a general issue,[8] while relegating the precarious working classes to the background.

However, the young middle-class people that fueled the 15-M movement appear to have had different characteristics and attitudes to the 'postmaterialist' middle-class that composed the social base of the so-called 'new social movements' (Della Porta, 2017). As most of the participants of the movement came from a middle-class in danger of downward social mobility, they mobilized around distributive issues – denouncing banking, defending public services or the right to housing. In doing so, they could have established alliances with the working class, but to a large extent this never happened. The main exception to this is the PAH, which has managed to include people from the popular classes (Ravelli, 2021), as well as immigrants (mostly Latin Americans) who were largely absent from the 15-M mobilizations (Johansson, 2017). However, PAH's success with 'social unionism' has not been replicated with other forms of mutual aid on issues such as food, as attempted – for example, – by the People's Solidarity Network [*Red de Solidaridad Popular*]. Unfortunately, this issue has not received much attention (see, Sola, 2021).

The (limited) democratizing impact of 15-M on the political economy

While 15-M mobilized a large number of people around socio-economic issues related to housing, finance, or public services (and, to a much lesser extent, labor issues), it is not easy to assess its impact on the democratization of the political economy. To consider this question we can draw on the distinction Giugni and Bosi (2012) make between 'material' policy and institutional consequences compared to 'symbolic' changes in public opinion and attitudes. As the protest cycle was followed by an electoral cycle, we can also consider medium term effects and the extent to which any impacts centered on the defense of certain de-commodifying social rights or the democratization of new economic spheres.

Generally speaking, 15-M hardly produced any material political-economic changes, although it contributed to a symbolic reframing of the crisis and its effects by politicizing various economic issues that had remained outside the public agenda or were considered technical issues. Later, participation in electoral politics through Podemos and local platforms made it possible to bring many of these demands to the institutional sphere, and even to implement some of them when these political forces came to power (the city councils in 2015 and the national government in 2020). Nevertheless, they fell far short of the revolutionary slogans of the initial protests.

In terms of symbolic or cultural impact, the re-politicization of the political economy has invigorated the public debate around the causes and solutions to problems such as housing or inequality, presenting them as distributive conflicts amenable to democratic deliberation.[9] A good example is how the introduction of legal mechanisms to expedite evictions became unthinkable in the aftermath of 15-M, which contrasted greatly to the implementation of the same policies by the socialists just four years previously (Otero, 2007). Whether this reframing of the public debate implied a reversal of taken-for-granted discourses is more doubtful. To our knowledge, there are no studies on the medium-term effects of 15-M on public opinion. It could be said that any radical re-imagination of democracy appears to have stopped at the doors of the political economy.

From a material perspective the impact of the movement is considerably less significant. 15-M did not achieve any of its demands in the short term, nor did it manage to stop public spending cutbacks and austerity economics. Certainly, however, it is possible to counter this by arguing that 15-M established certain lines that, in its absence, successive governments would have crossed. That being said, the 2011 reform of article 135 of the Constitution, which introduced a clause that strengthened the legal basis of creditors, was not prevented.

The later entrance of local platforms and Podemos to municipal and national power did not radically change this picture. The so-called 'city councils of change' were hindered by lack of experience, institutional inertia and jurisdictional limits (Blanco et al., 2020). Attempts to re-municipalize services, promote access to housing, and modify urban interventions had ambivalent results, but generally failed to modify political-economic dynamics (Rendueles & Sola, 2019). At national level, the most relevant outcome may be the incorporation of social inequality and poverty into the public agenda, which seems to be an indirect effect of the mobilizations. The socialist government created a 'High Commissioner for the fight against child poverty' in 2018 and, the current coalition government, formed in January 2020, has significantly increased the minimum wage and passed the Guaranteed Minimum Income act (*Ingreso Mínimo Vital*).

Nevertheless, neither street mobilization nor electoral politics has achieved any significant material changes in the economic policy issues that attracted most attention and motivated participation during the anti-austerity protests. The right to housing was undoubtedly the most prominent mobilization and has survived in organizational terms (Flesher Fominaya, 2015), but its effects on the real economy have been scarce (Martinez, 2019). The crash of the Spanish housing bubble was due to the dynamics of global economics, and now real estate financing, in terms of renting, is once again approaching pre-crisis levels. A decade later, some municipalities have reformulated their governance model in relation to housing (Giménez, 2021). However, these local authorities do not have the capacity to legislate on the structural aspects of the problem. That capacity is held by the Parliament, where a new Housing Law is currently being discussed which, being promoted by the coalition government between PSOE and Podemos, does not guarantee the structural measures promoted by the movement (payment in kind, the construction of public housing, limits on rental prices) to re-embed the housing market and limit its most destructive social effects (PAH, 2022).

The undemocratic power of finance was another of the driving forces behind the anti-austerity protests, and the public debt audit figured prominently in the movement's demands. However, public outrage was never really transformed into an articulated public debate that was capable of modifying political agendas. Something similar has happened in relation to national fiscal policies, the energy oligopoly, and Spain's relationship with the European Union. Most likely, one of the main reasons for this is that these are opaque and technically complex problems where, beyond the initial expression of opposition, it is difficult to identify winners and losers and take clear collective action. Nevertheless, it can also be argued that 15-M made a positive contribution to a shift in public opinion around financial capital and the enrichment of banks.[10]

Mobilization in defense of public services also had a modest real effect. On the one hand, the *Mareas* certainly succeeded in slowing down the pace and visibility of privatizations through scale shift mechanisms (Ribera-Almandoz & Clua-Losada, 2021), forcing the conservative governments to pursue less aggressive strategies than they would have wished. But they did not succeed in reversing the segregation of the education system, in particular the diversion of public funds to private education, nor the progressive deterioration of the public health system (see, for example, Amnesty International – Spain, 2020; Padilla Bernáldez, 2019), evident during the COVID crisis.

That said, there is a possible indirect impact of 15-M in the generational renewal of political parties (not only Podemos) and institutional politics. In the ten years since 2011, the main political leaders have changed from the 1950s generation to those that were born around 1980. The present coalition government of Podemos and PSOE has not brought about a radical change to Spanish politics, but it is proposing some initiatives that represent a break with the political framework inherited from the democratic transition. Nevertheless, these changes are more focused on civil rights than economic and social policy. In this sense, 15-M can be interpreted as a process of generational renewal that in other circumstances might have taken place more gradually. Additionally, the fact that the mobilizations did not entail sustained change in class-power balances may help to explain its limited reimagining of democracy in the political-economic realm.

Conclusions

The purpose of this article was to assess the development and impacts of 15-M as a democratizing endeavor – captured in the slogan 'real democracy now!' – from a political-economic standpoint and to connect the analysis to recent debates on social movements. The anti-austerity protests that 15-M was a part of could be seen as a Polanyian 'double movement', a response by 'society' to protect itself against the effects of the neoliberal expansion of the market (Polanyi, 1944). One of the main protest slogans of 15-M ('we are not merchandise in the hands of politicians and bankers') framed the conflict as one between elites and a very broad 'we' that encompassed the whole of society.[11] While we agree with the broad strokes of this picture, our objective was to take a deeper look at the complexity of this 'double movement', the interplay between the driving forces and the gaps between some cultural imaginaries and certain social and material realities.

To do so, we set out three questions at the beginning of the article that are pertinent to contemporary discussions on capitalism, class and social movements: 1) How do capitalist dynamics (and related ideologies) favor or impede the development of protest? 2) How do class balances (and class divisions within movements) influence the development of contentious politics? 3) What are their impacts and what is the interaction between the strategies, organizations, and contexts that underlie social movements? In the particular case of 15-M, the findings of our research offer some answers to these questions.

Firstly, our research shows how the political-economic trajectory of Spain created a particular opportunity structure for such a mobilization. The Spanish model facilitated the politicization of the dispossession of common goods, like housing or public services, by financial capital while hindering the emergence of a union-led response around labor organization, which was weakened by the precarization of the labor market, the disarticulation of the working class, and unions' loss of prestige. This picture is consistent with the general shift from 'production-based' to 'by dispossession' capital accumulation in neoliberalism (Harvey, 2005) and its impact on collective action (Della Porta, 2017), although both models should be understood as ideal types. In line with Harvey's prognosis, mobilization against these processes of neoliberal dispossession has not been made in the name of class, but of society ('the ordinary people', 'the 99%') acting against market despotism.

Secondly, in relation to class divisions, the broad collective identity of 15-M brought together heterogeneous social actors, that allowed the anti-austerity protests to move beyond 'old' and 'new' social movements (Peterson et al., 2015). However, the fact remains that the primary actors in the mobilizations were from the young middle-class. If the balance of class forces within a movement shapes its goals and strategies, this bias has tended to decrease the influence of the social groups most affected by the crisis in the initial wave of anti-austerity protests and in the political parties that emerged from it. This class dimension of the mobilizations, connected to the absence of strong alliances with the unions, has worked to relegate certain social issues, such as unemployment, to the background, making it more difficult to actively mobilize the working classes.

This finding is consistent with Hetland and Goodwin's (2013, p. 91) observation that 'class divisions generated by capitalism may unevenly penetrate and fracture movements' and that 'the balance of class forces *within* movements may powerfully shape [its] goals and strategies'. More generally, the leading role of the middle-class 'precariat' in the protests also raises the question of the ambiguous economic-political role that the middle-class can play under neoliberalism. On the one hand, they may coincide with the working classes in their interest in defending the welfare state, facilitating access to goods such as housing, or fighting against the enrichment of the '1%', but on the other, they may shield segregated education systems (such as in Spain) or remain wary of paying taxes to provide social supports from which they will not directly benefit.

Thirdly, in the relation to the results, while street-based mobilizations contributed to change in the cultural interpretation of the crisis, as framed by political and economic elites, the impacts of this mobilization on the democratization of the political economy have, in reality, been limited. Of course, this is not to say that this is completely unexpected given that the literature shows that most movements seeking radical change only obtain, in the best of cases, partial success. However, it does conflict with the expectations of the movement's own participants -and perhaps also of some observers- who went so far as to speak of a *#spanishrevolution*.

By connecting the questions of capitalist dynamics, social bases of protest, and democratizing impacts, some conjectures on causal links can be proposed. Neoliberal dynamics weakened organized labor and displaced distributive conflict from the sphere of labor to issues of housing, public services and banking. This reduced the likelihood that the protests would be led by unions but, on the other hand, also meant that they were socially more inclusive and, from an organizational perspective, more spontaneous. However, the absence of a stronger relationship with the unions and a failure to attract working class participants appears to have contributed to 15-M's limited impact on the political economy, in particular how weak organizational structures prevented the continuity of large-scale mobilizations.

Of course, it is impossible to know if the counterfactual argument (based on a closer relationship with the labor movement, greater working class participation, and stronger organizational structures) would have achieved more substantial results. However, the outcome of the 1988 general strike, led by the unions, and the 'social turn' that it spurred (increased social spend, including non-contributive pensions, greater unemployment coverage, universal healthcare, and wage increases) suggests that it is a plausible conjecture.

As such, by thinking 'through the interactions between strategies, organizations, and contexts' (Amenta et al., 2010, p. 287) in order to understand the consequences of social movements, one hypothesis is that, in the case of the political economy, impacts largely depend on the capacity of social movements to establish alliances with organised labor. This is a promising hypothesis that seems to offer some direction for more systematic analysis of future cases. Nevertheless, in interpreting this tentative conclusion, it should also be taken into account that two other exogenous factors that may explain the limited impact of 15-M. Firstly, Spanish political institutions and 'democratic practice' is remarkably oblivious to demands and pressure from below (Fishman, 2019). Secondly, after decades of neoliberalism, economic structural dynamics have created an inertia and opacity that severely hinders attempts at politicization and democratic intervention (Sánchez-Cuenca, 2019).

A decade on from the emergence of 15-M, and less conditioned by the affection and empathy engendered in participation, it is possible to take a clearer-headed view of its impact and outcomes for the political economy. The 15-M endeavor to re-imagine democracy had in this field its Achilles heel. However, the more critical position that we have provided in this article should not lead us from one extreme to another. While its material achievements were scarce, its symbolic impact was enormous and, more importantly, it bequeathed a series of ideas, images, and repertoires that may reappear in future mobilizations. In fact, along with other anti-austerity mobilizations, it has inspired the revitalization of the discussion of economic alternatives (Frase, 2016; Malleson, 2014; Wright, 2019) that allows us to be more optimistic for the future.

Notes

1. According to data from the *Centro de Investigaciones Sociológicas* (CIS) the percentage of people who had no confidence in unions grew from 21% in 2008 to 41% in 2010. On a scale of trust from 0 (none) to 10 (a lot), those declaring none went from 15% in 2007 to 42% in 2014.
2. Methodological cautions must be adopted in the interpretation of this discourse given the scarcity of written manifestos, the ambiguity of slogans, and the sampling bias of oral testimonies.
3. According to a survey, 90% of citizens agreed with this measure ('Los desahucios unen a los votantes', *El País*, 17 February 2013).
4. By middle classes we mainly refer to the so-called 'new' middle classes: wage earners that, by virtue of their expertise and/or organizational authority, enjoy more power and income than other workers (Wright, 1985). According to sociological class theory, the differences between the material interests and life chances of the middle class and those of the working class – in terms of economic as well as cultural and social capital (Bourdieu, 2002) – are a source of distributive conflict and shape political mobilization (Oesch, 2006; Wright, 1985).

5. Perhaps the clearest example is the Madrid-based network *Juventud Sin Futuro* (Youth with No Future), which was created from university student associations and played an important role in 15-M and then in Podemos (Montañés & Álvarez-Benavides, 2019).
6. Data from a CIS post-election survey (number 2920) conducted six months after the emergence of the *Indignados* (between November 2011 and January 2012) with a sample of 6,082 interviews.
7. This quote from a young woman of low-income background illustrates these obstacles: 'Then, of course, when I saw Almudena [an activist from Juventud Sin Futuro] doing so many things, I did feel like participating [...] but the truth is that later [...] I didn't know how to really get into that kind of dynamics [...] The truth was that I felt quite insecure, because they were people who knew a lot and I [...] had no idea' (in Gil & Rendueles, 2019, p. 44).
8. Only four out of ten young Spaniards, aged between 25-29, have university studies, and only one out of six has a master's degree or equivalent.
9. Other economic issues, however, have remained outside the public debate: the most striking is that of the Euro, probably explained by Spaniards' high degree of Europeanism.
10. According to data from the CIS, the percentage of people who had no confidence in banks grew from 38% in 2008 to 43% in 2017. See, also, Fundación BBVA (2013).
11. See also, Gerbaudo (2017) or Caruso and Cini (2020) for similar characteristics of anti-austerity protests as a conflict between citizens defending popular sovereignty and oligarchies, or between participative-mobilization and regressive-oligarchic poles.

Disclosure statement

No potential conflict of interest was reported by the author(s).

Funding

This article was supported by the Spanish State Research Agency [grant number PID2019-104078GB-I00/AEI/10.13039/501100011033]

ORCID

Eduardo Romanos http://orcid.org/0000-0002-0200-3470
Jorge Sola http://orcid.org/0000-0002-5144-9575
César Rendueles http://orcid.org/0000-0003-4594-5553

References

Amenta, E., Caren, N., Chiarello, E., & Su, Y. (2010). The political consequences of social movements. *Annual Review of Sociology*, *36*(1), 287–307. https://doi.org/10.1146/annurev-soc-070308-120029

Amnesty International – Spain. (2020). *La década perdida: mapa de austeridad del gasto sanitario en España del 2009 al 2018*. https://doc.es.amnesty.org/ms-opac/recordmedia/1@000032500/object/43241/raw

Bailey, D. J., Clua-Losada, M., Huke, N., & Ribera-Almandoz, O. (2018). *Beyond defeat and austerity: Disrupting (the critical political economy of) neoliberal Europe*. Routledge.

Ban, C. (2016). *Ruling ideas: How global neoliberalism goes local*. Oxford University Press.

Bessant, J., Farthing, R., & Watts, R. (2017). *The precarious generation: A political economy of young people*. Routledge.

Blanco, I., Salazar, Y., & Bianchi, I. (2020). Urban governance and political change under a radical left government: The case of Barcelona. *Journal of Urban Affairs*, *42*(1), 18–38. https://doi.org/10.1080/07352166.2018.1559648

Bosi, L., Giugni, M., & Uba, K. (Eds.). (2019). *The consequences of social movements*. Cambridge University Press.

Bourdieu, P. (2002). The Forms of Capital. In N. W. Biggart (Ed.), *Readings in economic sociology*. Wiley-Blackwell (pp. 280–291). https://doi.org/10.1002/9780470755679.ch15

Buendía, L. (2020). A perfect storm in a sunny economy: A political economy approach to the crisis in Spain. *Socio-Economic Review*, *18*(2), 419–438. https://doi.org/10.1093/ser/mwy021

Campillo, I. (2019). 'If we stop, the world stops': The 2018 feminist strike in Spain. *Social Movement Studies*, *18*(2), 252–258. https://doi.org/10.1080/14742837.2018.1556092

Caruso, L., & Cini, L. (2020). Rethinking the link between structure and collective action. Capitalism, politics, and the theory of social movements. *Critical Sociology*, *46*(7–8), 1005–1023. https://doi.org/10.1177/0896920520911434

Chouhy, G. (2020). Rethinking neoliberalism, rethinking social movements. *Social Movement Studies*, *19*(4), 426–446. https://doi.org/10.1080/14742837.2019.1697663

Cox, L., & Nilsen, A. G. (2014). *We make our own history: Marxism and social movements in the twilight of neoliberalism*. Pluto Press.

Della Porta, D. (2015). *Social movements in times of austerity: Bringing capitalism back into protest analysis*. Polity.

Della Porta, D. (2017). Political economy and social movement studies: The class basis of anti-austerity protests. *Anthropological Theory*, *17*(4), 453–473. https://doi.org/10.1177/1463499617735258

Díez García, R., & Laraña, E. (2017). *Democracia, dignidad y movimientos sociales: El surgimiento de la cultura cívica y la irrupción de los indignados en la vida pública*. CIS.

Feenstra, R. A., Tormey, S., Casero Ripollés, A., & Keane, J. (2017). *Refiguring democracy: The Spanish political laboratory*. Routledge.

Fernández-Trujillo, F. (2021). La conflictividad laboral y el 15M. Diez años de renovación del sindicalismo. In E. G. Betancor & A. Razquin (Eds.), *Diez años construyendo ciudadanía en movimiento(s). El 15M y otras luchas hermanas* (pp. 105–116). Bellaterra.

Fishman, R. M. (1990). *Working class organization and the return to democracy in Spain*. Cornell University Press.

Fishman, R. M. (2012). On the significance of public protest in Spanish democracy. In J. Jordana, V. Navarro, F. Pallarés, & F. Requejo (Eds.), *Democràcia, Politica i Societat; Homenatge a Rosa Virós* (pp. 351–366). Universitat Pompeu Fabra and Avenc.

Fishman, R. M. (2019). *Democratic practice: Origins of the Iberian divide in political inclusion*. Oxford University Press.

Flesher Fominaya, C. (2015). Redefining the crisis/redefining democracy: Mobilising for the right to housing in Spain's PAH movement. *South European Society and Politics, 20*(4), 465–485. https://doi.org/10.1080/13608746.2015.1058216

Flesher Fominaya, C. (2020). *Democracy reloaded: Inside Spain's political laboratory from 15-M to Podemos*. Oxford University Press.

Font, J., & García-Espín, P. (2020). From Indignad@s to Mayors? Participatory Dilemmas in Spanish Municipal Movements. In C. F. Fominaya & R. Feenstra (Eds.), *Routledge handbook of contemporary European social movements: Protest in turbulent times* (pp. 387–401). Routledge.

Frase, P. (2016). *Four futures: Visions of the world after capitalism*. Verso.

Fundación BBVA. (2013). *Valores políticos-económicos y la crisis económica*. https://www.fbbva.es/wp-content/uploads/2017/05/dat/Presentacionvalueswordwidel.pdf

Gamson, W. A. (1992). *Talking Politics*. Cambridge University Press.

Garrido, L., & González, J. J. (2012). Mercado de trabajo, ocupación y clases sociales. In J. J. González & M. Requena (Eds.), *Tres décadas de cambio social en España* (pp. 89–134). Alianza Editorial.

Gerbaudo, P. (2017). *The mask and the flag: Populism, citizenism and global protest*. Hurst & Co Publishers Ltd.

Gil, H., & Rendueles, C. (2019). Entre el victimismo meritocrático y la resignación. Dos percepciones antagónicas de la precariedad juvenil en España. *Cuaderno de Relaciones Laborales, 37*(1), 31–48. https://doi.org/10.5209/CRLA.63818

Giménez, F. (2021). Impactos culturales, políticos e institucionales de la lucha social por la vivienda. In P. Ibarra, S. M. I Puig, & A. S. Mittelman (Eds.), *Impactos. ¿Qué consiguen los movimientos sociales?* (pp. 181–190). Bellaterra.

Giugni, M., & Bosi, L. (2012). The impact of protest movements on the establishment: Dimensions, models, approaches. In K. Fahlenbrach, M. Klimke, J. Scharloth, & L. Wong (Eds.), *The 'Establishment' responds: Power, politics and protest since 1945* (pp. 17–28). Palgrave Macmillan.

Giugni, M., & Grasso, M. T. (2019). *Street citizens: Protest politics and social movement activism in the age of globalization*. Cambridge University Press.

Harvey, D. (2005). *The new imperialism*. Oxford University Press.

Hetland, G., & Goodwin, J. (2013). The strange disappearance of capitalism from social movement studies. In C. Barker (Ed.), *Marxism and social movements* (pp. 83–102). Brill.

Hylmö, A., & Wennerhag, M. (2015). Does class matter in anti-austerity protests? Social class, attitudes towards inequality, and political trust in European demonstrations in a time of economic crisis. In M. Giugni & M. T. Grasso (Eds.), *Austerity and protest: Popular contention in times of economic crisis* (pp. 83–109). Routledge.

Johansson, S. (2017). *The Involuntary Racist. A Study on White Racism Evasiveness amongst Social Movements Activists in Madrid, Spain* [Master's Thesis], Linköping University.

Köhler, H.-D., & Calleja Jiménez, J. P. (2015). "They don't represent us!" Opportunities for a social movement unionism strategy in Spain. *Relations Industrielles/Industrial Relations, 70*(2), 240–261. http://dx.doi.org/10.7202/1031485ar

Köhler, H.-D., & Calleja Jiménez, J. P. (2018). Spain: A peripheral economy and a vulnerable trade union movement. In S. Lehndorff, H. Dribbusch, & T. Schulten (Eds.), *Rough waters: European trade unions in a time of crises* (pp. 65–85). ETUI.

Lapavitsas, C. (2012). *Crisis in the Eurozone*. Verso.

López, I., & Rodríguez, E. (2011). The Spanish model. *New Left Review, 69*, 5–28. https://newleftreview.org/issues/ii69/articles/isidro-lopez-emmanuel-rodriguez-the-spanish-model

Malleson, T. (2014). *After occupy: Economic democracy for the 21st century*. Oxford University Press.

Martinez, M. A. (2019). Bitter wins or a long-distance race? Social and political outcomes of the Spanish housing movement. *Housing Studies, 34*(10), 1588–1611. https://doi.org/10.1080/02673037.2018.1447094

Montañés, A., & Álvarez-Benavides, A. (2019). Juventud sin Futuro' y el giro institucional post 15M de los movimientos sociales. In R. D. García & G. B. Nuez (Eds.), *Movimientos sociales, acción colectiva y cambio social en perspectiva* (pp. 117–129). Fundación Betiko.

Morales, L., & Geurts, P. (2007). Associational involvement. In J. W. V. Deth, J. R. Montero, & A. Westholm (Eds.), *Citizenship and involvement in European democracies: A comparative analysis* (pp. 135–157). Routledge.

Moreno Pestaña, J. L. (2011). Le mouvement du 15-M: Social et 'libéral', générationnel et 'assembléiste'. *Savoir-Agir, 17*, 113–118. https://doi.org/10.3917/sava.017.0113

Moreno Pestaña, J. L. (2013). Democracia, movimientos sociales y participación popular: Lógicas democráticas y lógicas de distinción en las asambleas del 15M. In J. Escalera & A. Coca (Eds.), *Movimientos sociales, participación y ciudadanía en Andalucía* (pp. 263–301). Aconcagua Libros.

Oesch, D. (2006). *Redrawing the class map: Stratification and institutions in Britain, Germany, Sweden and Switzerland*. Palgrave Macmillan.

Otero, L. (2007, September 29). *El Gobierno creará diez nuevos juzgados para agilizar los desahucios por impago de alquiler*. El País. https://elpais.com/diario/2007/09/29/economia/1191016813_850215.html

Padilla Bernáldez, J. (2019). *¿A quién vamos a dejar morir? Sanidad pública, crisis y la importancia de lo político*. Capitán Swing.

PAH (Plataforma de Afectados por la Hipoteca). (2022, February 2). *Se aprueba la Ley de Vivienda del Gobierno en el Consejo de Ministros*. Plataforma de Afectados por la Hipoteca. https://afectadosporlahipoteca.com/2022/02/02/se-aprueba-la-ley-de-vivienda-del-gobierno-en-el-consejo-de-ministros/

Perez, S. A., & Matsaganis, M. (2018). The political economy of austerity in Southern Europe. *New Political Economy, 23*(2), 192–207. https://doi.org/10.1080/13563467.2017.1370445

Peterson, A., Wahlström, M., & Wennerhag, M. (2015). European anti-austerity protests – Beyond "old" and "new" social movements? *Acta Sociologica, 58*(4), 293–310. https://doi.org/10.1177/0001699315605622

Polanyi, K. (1944). *The Great Transformation*. Farrar & Rinehart.

Portos, M. (2016). Taking to the streets in the shadow of austerity: A chronology of the cycle of protests in Spain, 2007-2015. *Partecipazione e Conflitto, 9*(1), 181–210. https://doi.org/10.1285/i20356609v9i1p181

Prasad, M. (2006). *The politics of free markets: The rise of neoliberal economic policies in Britain, France, Germany, and the United States*. University of Chicago Press.

Ravelli, Q. (2021). Debt struggles: How financial markets gave birth to a working-class movement. *Socio-Economic Review, 19*(2), 441–468. https://doi.org/10.1093/ser/mwz033

Rázquin, A. (2017). *Didáctica ciudadana: La vida política en las plazas. Etnografía del movimiento 15M*. editorial Universidad de Granada.

Recio, A., & Roca, J. (2001). The Spanish socialists in power: Thirteen years of economic policy. In A. Glyn (Ed.), *Social democracy in neoliberal times: The left and economic policy since 1980* (pp. 173–199). Oxford University Press.

Rendueles, C., & Sola, J. (2019). *Strategic crossroads: The situation of the left in Spain*. Rosa Luxemburg Stiftung.

Rey-Araújo, P. M. (2020). The Contradictory Evolution of "Mediterranean" Neoliberalism in Spain, 1995–2008. *Review of Radical Political Economics, 52*(2), 287–311. https://doi.org/10.1177/0486613419882122

Ribera-Almandoz, O., & Clua-Losada, M. (2021). Health movements in the age of austerity: Rescaling resistance in Spain and the United Kingdom. *Critical Public Health, 31*(2), 182–192. https://doi.org/10.1080/09581596.2020.1856333

Richards, M. (1998). *A time of silence: Civil war and the culture of repression in Franco's Spain, 1936-1945*. Cambridge University Press.

Rodríguez, E. (2017). *La política en el ocaso de la clase media. El ciclo 15M-Podemos*. Traficantes de Sueños.

Romanos, E. (2014). Evictions, petitions and *escraches*: Contentious housing in austerity Spain. *Social Movement Studies, 13*(2), 296–302. https://doi.org/10.1080/14742837.2013.830567

Romanos, E. (2017). Late neoliberalism and its Indignados: Contention in austerity Spain. In D. Della Porta, M. Andretta, T. Fernandes, F. O'Connor, E. Romanos, & M. Vogiatzoglou (Eds.), *Late neoliberalism and its discontents in the economic crisis: Comparing social movements in the European periphery* (pp. 131–167). Palgrave McMillan.

Romanos, E., & Sádaba, I. (2016). From the street to institutions through the App: Digitally enabled political outcomes of the Spanish Indignados movement. *Revista Internacional de Sociología, 74*(4), e048. http://dx.doi.org/10.3989/ris.2016.74.4.048

Romanos, E., & Sádaba, I. (2022). The evolution of contention in Spain (2000-2017): An analysis of protest cycles. *Revista Española de Investigaciones Sociológicas, 177*, 89–110. http://dx.doi.org/10.5477/cis/reis.177.89

Sánchez-Cuenca, I. (2019). *La izquierda: Fin de (un) ciclo*. Los Libros de la Catarata.

Schneirov, M., & Schneirov, R. (2016). Capitalism as a social movement: The corporate and neoliberal reconstructions of the American political economy in the twentieth century. *Social Movement Studies, 15*(6), 561–576. https://doi.org/10.1080/14742837.2016.1215242

Sola, J. (2018). La invisibilización de la clase trabajadora. In A. Tarín & J. M. R. Otero (Eds.), *La clase trabajadora. ¿Sujeto de cambio en el siglo XXI?* (pp. 103–122). Siglo XXI.

Sola, J. (2021). La reconstrucción de la solidaridad en un contexto neoliberal: Doble movimiento y apoyo mutuo tras el 15M (y más allá). *Encrucijadas. Revista Crítica de Ciencias Sociales, 21*(3), v2103. https://recyt.fecyt.es/index.php/encrucijadas/article/view/81063

Sola, J., & Rendueles, C. (2018). Podemos, the upheaval of the Spanish politics and the challenge of populism. *Journal of Contemporary European Studies, 26*(1), 99–116. https://doi.org/10.1080/14782804.2017.1304899

Tugal, C. (2015). Elusive revolt: The contradictory rise of middle-class politics. *Thesis Eleven, 130*(1), 74–95. https://doi.org/10.1177/0725513615602183

Wilhelmi, G. (2021). *Sobrevivir a la derrota. Historia del sindicalismo en España, 1975-2004*. Akal.

Wright, E. O. (1985). *Classes*. Verso.

Wright, E. O. (2019). *How to be an anticapitalist in the twenty-first century*. Verso.

Zajak, S. (2013). A political economic view of social movements: New perspectives and open questions. *Moving the Social, 50*, 121–142. https://doi.org/10.13154/mts.50.2013.121-142

Zajak, S., & Haunss, S. (2020). Social stratification and social movements: An introduction. In S. Zajak & S. Haunss (Eds.), *Social stratification and social movements: Theoretical and empirical perspectives on an ambivalent relationship* (pp. 1–7). Routledge.

Index

Note: Figures are indicated by *italics*. Tables are indicated by **bold**.

acampadas 2, 12, *13*, 19, 23, 26, 59, 81, 138
Accornero, G. 51
activism 3, 40, 41, 43–4, 48–50, 58, 71, 83, 89, 98, 105, 107, 115–16, 122, 124–5
activist blacklists 160
activist careers 39–40
activists 2, 8, 12, 13, 18, 20, 25, 39, 44, 46, 48, 49–51, 58, 65, 67, 71, 78, 81, 88, 89, 107
Adell, R. 38
Alfon case 161
Amster, R. 157
anarchist consciousness 45
anti-austerity mobilizations 154, 156, 163–5, 165, 185
anti-austerity protests 79, 137–8, 148, 158, 174, 176, 177, 178–9, 182, 183–4
anxiety 4, 105
Arruzza, C. 58

Barad, K. 96
Becker, H. S. 40
benefactors 44
Berezin, M. 136, 145
Betancor, G. 38
Bhattacharya, T. 58
Bicycle Logistics 101
biographical illusion 42
biographical trajectories 44
Brigada Móvil 160
buen vivir 67
Butler, J. 47, 105, 109

capital-centrism 67
capitalism 43
career concept 40
care-tizenship 106
caring democracy 3; catastrophic times, mutual aid in 96, 106–7; community woven together by 101–6; democratic experimentation 98–100; neighborhood support networks 107–9; pandemic, digital ethnography in 97; working groups participation *103*
caring geographies 106
Caro, M. 157

Carrasco, Cristina 71
Catalonian police 160
city councils of change 182
class and generation 179–181
collective commitment 47
collective memories 139
communicative dimensions 157
community counselling 101
comprehensive approach 42, 51
Consejero, Fabiola Mota 3
counter-hegemonic protest penalization: counter-hegemony 158–160; de-democratization 163–6; methods 155–6; penalization 156–8; repression 156–8; securitization 160–2, *163*; unintended consequences 163–6
criminalization 4, 155, 156, 158, 162
Critical Economics Conferences 67
cross-checking 42
cultural change 26, 174
culture of transition 43

Davenport, C. 157
degrees of involvement 41
democratic laboratory 9, 11–14, 26
democratic turn 9, 23–5, 95
description bias 161
direct democracy 122, 129
disintermediation 107
dispossession 184
diversity 24–25, 41, 63, 66, 68, 100, 140

ecosystem 2–4, 19, 96, 106, 115–116, 118, 122, 125–127
Esposito, R. 100
ethical revolution 114
excessive precaution 164

Facebook 38, 98
feminism 22–3, 58–60, 63–7, 72, 102, 126
Feminism Committees (FC-15 M) 59, 62
feminist coven 65
feminist economics (FE): conferences, political pillar of 66–8; dialogues and

convergences 61–3; methodology 60–1; 15-M Feminism Commissions 63–6; proposals submitted and attendees 70; Spanish timeline 66–8; thematic areas and structure of **69**; women's and grassroots 58
Feminist Economics Conference, 2013 69
feminist movement 68
feminization 59
Fernández, L. A. 157
Fersch, B. 38
Fillieule, O. 40
five semi-structured individual and group interviews 60
Fominaya, Flesher 155
Food Emergencies 101
Fourth wave 58
Francoist dictatorship 38
Fraser, N. 58
Freedom Summer 40

Gag Law 159, 162
Galcerán, M. 64
GAM *See* Mutual Aid Groups
Garland, D. 155
gender-based violence 50
gender issues 67
Gibson-Graham, J. K. 67
Great Recession 173–6
green tide 48

hapticality 108–109
heterogeneous movement 3, 50
horizontal and vertical conceptions 50
Housing Rights 101, 106, 124

ideological and sociodemographic characteristics 41
Indignados 102; activist careers, social movement through 39–40; class and generation 179–181; democratizing impact of 181–3; Great Recession 173–6; institutional spaces 49–51; longitudinal field studies 41–3; market despotism, street politics against 176–7; militant microspheres 49–51; mobilization 47–9; organized labor 178; politics 47–9; real democracy 171; social reality, changes in representations of 43–6
informants data **121**
inner revolution 45
innovation experiments 26
institutionalization 164
intensity of recollections 141
International Association for Feminist Economics (IAFFE) Conference 2012 67

Janoschka, Michael 3
Jornadas de Economía Crítica 66
Juventud sin futuro (JSF) 41

life before capital 63
lifelong activist 47

Local Commerce Support 101
longitudinal approach 42
Loyle, C. 157

macro-sociological analyses 43
Madrid, 15M movement in: activist careers, social movement through 39–40; institutional spaces 49–51; longitudinal field studies 41–3; militant microspheres 49–51; mobilization 47–9; politics 47–9; social reality, changes in representations of 43–6
marginalization 161
market despotism, street politics against 176–7
mass: imprisonment 158; incarceration 158; mobilization 4
media blocking 43
memories in movements 136
methodological triangulation 60
micromachismos 49
microsociological analyses 40, 50
militant research processes 58
mobilization 47, 183; memoires 149
movements-parties 100
Mutual Aid Groups 3, 94–8, 100–110

neighbours 44
#NiUnaMenos 58

Oliver, Pamela 158
organized labor 178

participation and democratic innovation 100
participatory democracy 129
penalization 155, 156–8, 157, 158; counter-hegemony 158–160; criminalization 160–2, *163*; de-democratization 163–6; methods 163–6; protest policing 158–160; repression 156–8; securitization 160–2, *163*; unintended consequences 163–6
Pensioners' mobilisations (PM) 140
Periódico del 15 M 47
Perugorría, I. 38
Pignarre, P. 95
Podemos Party 51
police reform 155
political and professional spaces 48
political change 26
political economic democratization 4
political economy, Spain: class and generation 179–181; democratizing impact of 181–3; Great Recession 173–6; market despotism, street politics against 176–7; organized labor 178; real democracy 171
political socializations 39, 43, 45
politics as caring 63
Porta, Della 138
Prado Galán, L. 38
precarity 105
Prieto, D. 38
PSOE 108

public service orientation 129
Puig de la Bellacasa, M. 95

radical democracy, educommunicative legacy for: educational agency 128-9; educommunication paradigm 117-18; knowledge production 116-17; learning processes 116-17; media ecology approach 118; methods 118-122; new media ecosystem 125-7; pre-existing, strengthening of 124-5; public service orientation 128-9; social movements 116-17; subscribers and users, community of 127-8; synergies and mutual support 127
Rancière, J. 100
Razquin, A. 38
real democracy 26, 137, 171
redistribution 59
red tape repression 162
regeneration 100
re-imagining democracy: Spain's 15-M movement 1-4
repression 4, 157, 158
repressive persistence, puzzle of 157
revolutionary organization 49

Sawicki, F. 42
Schlembach, R. 159
securitization 4, 158, 161
self-censorship 156, 164
self-esteem 47
self-referentiality 100
self-reflexivity 60
Sherwood syndrome 159
Siméant, J. 42
Skype 156
Smaoui, S. 38
socialism: change 59; movements 39, 43, 68, 117; peace 178; representations 44; trajectory 43
socio-material practices 3, 96
Spain, counter-hegemonic protest in: de-democratization 163-6; methods 155-6; penalization 156-8; penalizing counter-hegemony 158-160; repression 156-8; securitization 160-2, 163; unintended consequences 163-6
Spain's 15-M movement: *acampadas* 2; citizen participation 14-16; civil society organizations 17-19; democracy 11-14; democracy, public opinion on 16-17; democratic laboratories 9, 11; democratization 7; electoral landscape, transforming 17-19; hybridity 9; indignados 1; institutions, democratic innovation in 21-3; mobilizing memory 2; movement-produced knowledge 2; new social movements 7; occupied squares 8; occupy movements 6; party forms 19-21; political parties 1; pre-scriptions 7; pro-democracy movements 1;

radical democracy 10; real democracy 8, 11; social capital 14-16; social movements 7; tracing and measuring social movement 1
Spanish political laboratory 38
Spanish protest culture, recollections and sediments in: active political subject 146-8; analysis 139-141; data 139-141; efficacy 143-4; heuristic, mobilising memories as 139; methods 139-141; 15-M legacies in 137-9; mobilising memories *142*, 142-3; organisational and protest learning 144-5; political consciousness 145-6
Starr, A. 157
State-led violence 155
Stengers, I. 95
stigmatization 161
strategic incapacitation model 159
street mobilization 26, 182, 184
street politics 79, 80-2, 100, 176-7
suppression 161
surveillance 160
survival strategies 64
symbolic-cultural approach 116

Tejerina, B. 38
Telegram 101, 107
threat to human rights 162
transferable innovations 3
transformative social action 47
Tronto, J. 96
troublemakers 44
Tuppersex 48

urban democracy through social movements: anti-austerity social movements 79-80; citizen propositions 84-8; democratic transformation, critical consideration of 88-90; electoral programme to 82-3; institutional politics, street politics to 80-2; local consultations 84-8; research methods and data 78; transferable democratic innovations 83-4

vibration process 138
Vicari, S. 136
#VivasNosQueremos 58
volunteers 107
vulnerability 3, 95-6, 98, 102, 105

#WeStrike 58
WhatsApp 101, 107
white tide 48
Women's Day March 65
Women's Day Off 58
Wood, L. J. 157

Xela 101

Zoom 156

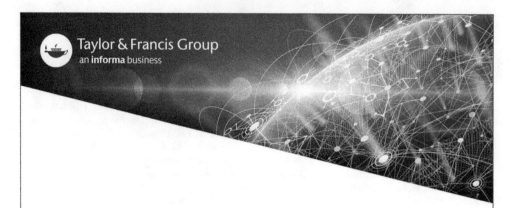

Printed in the USA
CPSIA information can be obtained
at www.ICGtesting.com
LVHW080735200324
774517LV00074B/689

9 781032 590110